# GENOCIDE

## OF THE MIND

# Also by MariJo Moore

*The Diamond Doorknob*

*Spirit Voices of Bones*

*Red Woman With Backward Eyes and Other Stories*

*Crow Quotes*

*Tree Quotes*

*Desert Quotes*

*The First Fire*

*The Cherokee Little People*

*The Ice Man*

*Feeding the Ancient Fires: A Collection of Writings by North Carolina Indians (Ed.)*

# GENOCIDE
## OF THE MIND

NEW NATIVE AMERICAN WRITING

Edited by MariJo Moore

Foreword by Vine Deloria, Jr

NATION BOOKS
NEW YORK

Published by Nation Books

A Member of the Perseus Books Group

Nation Books is a co-publishing venture of the Nation Institute
and the Perseus Books Group

This publication is made possible in part with public funds from
the New York State Council on the Arts, a state agency.

Books published by Basic Books are available at special discounts for bulk
purchases in the United States by corporations, institutions, and other
organizations. For more information, please contact the Special Markets
Department at the Perseus Books Group, 2300 Chestnut Street, Suite 200,
Philadelphia, PA 19103, or call (800) 810-4145, x5000, or
e-mail special.markets@perseusbooks.com.

Library of Congress Cataloging-in-Publication Data is available.

Book design by Paul Paddock

ISBN-13: 978-1-56025-511-6

ISBN-10: 1-56025-511-0

10  9  8  7  6

For our elders—

past, present, and future . . .

# Acknowledgments

The essay " 'Indians,' Solipsisms, and Archetypal Holocausts" was published in *Off the Reservation: Reflections on Boundary-Busting, Border Crossing, Loose Canons,* Boston: Beacon Press, 1998. ©Paula Gunn Allen. Used by permission of the author.

The poems "The Steelworker," "Reading Poems in Public," "The Comet," "Inheritance," and "Going Home" were published in *Carving Hawk: New and Selected Poems,* Buffalo, N.Y.: White Pine Press, 2002. © Maurice Kenny. Used by permission of the author.

The essay "Everyone Needs Someone" was published in *Red Ink* magazine, Tucson, Ari.: University of Arizona Press, 2001. © MariJo Moore. Used by permission of the author.

The essay "Yellow Woman and a Beauty of the Spirit" was published in *Yellow Woman and a Beauty of the Spirit: Essays on Native American Life Today,* New York: Simon & Schuster, 1996. ©Leslie Marmon Silko. Used by permission of the author.

The poem "A Brief Guide to American History Teachers" was published in *Returning the Gift,* Vol. 29 in *Sun Tracks,* an American Indian Literary Series, Tucson, Ari.: University of Arizona Press, 1994. © Carter Revard. Used by permission of the author.

# CONTENTS

## One
### KEEPING THE HOME FIRES BURNING IN URBAN CIRCLES

## Two
### YOUNG AMERICAN INDIANS: THE NEED TO RECLAIM IDENTITY

## Three
## NATIVE LANGUAGES : WHERE WILL THEY GO FROM HERE?

# FOREWORD

## Vine Deloria, Jr.

ndians have been coming to town since there were towns. Indeed, scattered across the continent were villages of respectable size in pre-Columbian times, and even then one could distinguish between "city" and "country" folk. The villages were, however, the center of ceremonial activities, and visits to them were greatly anticipated by people who lived away from the large settlements in small clusters of three and four houses. Some villages were made as a representation of the larger cosmos, sometimes dividing the streets to present forces of light and darkness, other times to reflect sky and earth or the historical heritage of two aboriginal groups that had combined as one people. The feeling of urbanity therefore produced a positive sense of belonging and helped the people to focus their lives on something greater than themselves.

Today cities represent economic activity, the chance to enter the great race and achieve prosperity—at least prosperity of the moment. Skyscrapers do reach for the heavens, as many architects have noted, but they are placed helter-skelter on the ground with no apparent design and an inability to reflect the glory of the greater cosmic scheme. Taken as a whole, cities reveal the confusion of spirit that is the hallmark of modern industrial man. The city centers often reflect the values of society, and the presence of financial districts pretty much describes what our vision of the world and ourselves is. Today we flee these places and recapitulate them in the suburbs in massive shopping centers with automatic teller machines that connect us to the city's heartbeat. It is all so sterile.

At first Indians were attracted to the white man's cities. There they could barter for manufactured goods and enjoy some of the luxuries of the industrial life. The cities seemed like endless horns of plenty that could never be emptied. In Massachusetts the Indians were enticed to organize themselves into towns similar to those of their white neighbors and, adopting Christianity, which seemed to be the religion of the city, became organized into "praying towns." In New Mexico when the Spanish arrived there were over one hundred thirty towns, or pueblos, scattered all over the Rio Grande valley, and as the Spanish influence increased, all but nineteen pueblos maintained their traditional ways. The remainder disappeared or became predominantly Spanish towns. Some Indian villages were simply consumed by the approaching white man, and who can now find Indian village sites that lie beneath Chicago, Cincinnati, Minneapolis, Milwaukee, or a bevy of other cities.

With the policies of the past century Indians have seen a constant migration of people beyond the traditional homelands to the cities of America. Whether seeking employment or education, the Indians have become a constant source of immigrants and, like other groups, have had to begin at the bottom of the economic pyramid and work their way toward economic stability. Other groups reproduced, as best they could, the conditions of their home country, so that for a while during the last century, large cities had Chinatowns and Little Italys, Polish, Irish, German, and Scandinavian districts.

There they could have churches and other social institutions that continued to use their native language and celebrate their religious holidays, sometimes founding schools and colleges that would reflect their own heritage.

American Indians, on the other hand, came from small tribes that could not possibly produce enough people to form neighborhoods where customs, rituals, and languages could be preserved. Instead, people from different tribes melded together and created a new social identification of "Indian." Intermarriage between tribes, whose members met either in government schools or after arriving in a city, reinforced this identity so that intertribal organizations took the place of the mother country of other groups. Although the name served to identity the people as belonging to a separate and distinct race, it failed to heal the ache in their hearts at not having immediate friends and relatives with them. Thus came the fierce determination of people living in the cities to remain a separate group.

People began to improvise in the sense that while they went to dances and powwows that were not held strictly in accordance with the old teachings and customs, they felt that customs should give way to precedence over the expediency of arresting their identity while living in a foreign setting. With the improvement in the economic fortunes of Indians living in the cities and with better highways available to them, they began traveling back to their home reservations to attend tribal ceremonies and dances even while supporting the activities in the urban areas that they felt were also authentically Indian.

It is difficult, if not impossible most of the time, to tell which people were born on the reservation and which were born in the cities. People move back and forth with ease depending on the economic opportunities available to them on the reservations. The development of local industries, including gaming casinos, has helped to create a sense of tribalism that transcends the institutional restrictions imposed by the urban areas. Reservation people are as likely to visit the city for celebrations as are urbanized Indians to go home for various events. The Indian communities are achieving a stability that projects an improved life ahead for the people and their children. Adaptation, not accommodation, has become a reality.

# INTRODUCTION

## MariJo Moore

*"The preservation of the collective memory by a group, even a small one, is a true tablet of salvation for the entire community. It is by means of such tablets that traditions and cultures cross the seas of time."*

—Octavio Paz

An essay is a meditation on a topic that can be either dear or disheartening to one. In some instances, the subject matter can be both. The compositions in this collection cannot be termed as bureaucratic despotisms, scholarly articulations, or coercion to a seemingly uncaring society. They are creations from the heart, ideas whose time has come, memories invaded by daily existence. Each essay beats with a plurality of meaning: spiritual, intellectual, and emotional, as the poetic contributions provide the necessary rhythm to which kindred perspectives flow.

There have been many genocidal attempts, without and within, to destroy and/or misrepresent the histories, futures, languages, and traditional thoughts of Native peoples. But traditions, unlike doctrines, can persist and evolve at the same time. This anthology is a response to modern-day Native people becoming more and more disgruntled with spurious representations. Each writer has built a bridge between what has been "presented wrongly" and what needs to be "expressed accurately." Bridges best described as a prepositional decree: *by* instead of *about*. These bridges support revelations in opposition to repudiations and personal testimonies challenging thematic stereotypes.

Although some American Indian writers have made it into the so-called literary mainstream, most live on the periphery of the defining "western world of literature." Some names may be easily recognized, others not. Regardless, each offering should be read with astute diligence and equal attention. These contributions will no doubt purport this anthology into a nonsanctioned role in the literary realm. Several Nations from the United States and Canada are embodied in this collection. Even so, no individual writer attempts to speak for his or her entire Nation, only from personal experiences dealing with non-Indians as well as Indians. Sadly, for whatever reasons, some of our worst enemies are on occasion our own people.

The wisdom gathered here cannot by any means be considered anechoic. These expressions will continue to reverberate extensively because we choose to stand on our bridges to tell the world who we are, how we think, and how we live in modernity yet incorporate ancestral knowledge. This anthology is a testament to American Indian consciousness continuing to circulate, regardless of past or present genocidal attempts, whether cerebral, endemic, systematic, or otherwise.

# One

## KEEPING THE HOME FIRES BURNING
## IN URBAN CIRCLES

*The parts of Indian cultures that have been lost, and those we are con-*
*stantly losing, are equally as valuable as the land that was taken. Those*
*of us who choose to live in two worlds are doing what we can to keep the*
*fires of our ancestral knowledge burning. Though a difficult task, we will*
*not let these fires be extinguished. We often look to traditional teachings*
*in order to make sense of a world that is seemingly going off center.*
*Today, American Indian blood courses through the veins of many races,*
*many cultures, and in many unknown places, yet we remind ourselves to*
*remember who we are, where we come from, and rely heavily on spiri-*
*tual advice to guide us on our paths. We hold fast to what we know, try*
*to teach our children to respect and understand ancestral values, only to*
*constantly realize that so much of what it means to be American Indian*
*has been lost or misrepresented, and we are often misunderstood. Still we*
*go forward, adding newfound embers now and then to the olden fires*
*that have existed since time immemorial. Determined to honor those*
*who have gone before, realizing the trivializations they endured, we*
*ardently face the daily trials required to live in two worlds: the traditional*
*and the modern.*

# To Carry the Fire Home

### Kathryn Lucci-Cooper

Sometimes at night when I cannot push aside my thoughts and find my way to sleep, I revisit my grandmother Gladys's house. I walk through each of the rooms to recount the placement of her furniture, the crocheted doilies on the back of the couch, the rocking chair, the keepsakes in her tiny glass cabinet. I see her standing at the kitchen sink, washing dishes and singing, "Jesus Loves Me." It is the song that she would sing to us each morning as she pulled away our warm quilts and fed us bowls of rice with honey and melted butter. My grandmother was a devout member of the Church of God. My grandmother was Cherokee.

It is during these walks among the ancestral spirits of my family that I try to make sense of my mixed heritage. This gathering of women, who sang gospel hymns and listened to the lulling sounds of mountain music, were also the women who sought college educations for their daughters. They did this with the same determination that allowed them to breathe forth a living from the apple trees and cornstalks growing in the midst of southern Appalachia's coalfields. These aunties and grandmothers were also the keepers of my Cherokee heritage.

The women in my family were stubborn, high-minded oral historians. They kept each of us within the circle even as they sang hymns and listened intently to sermons by breathless preachers pounding fists upon Christian pulpits. They attended these Sunday gatherings wearing hand-covered smiles, homemade dresses, and fashionable hats. And at the close of each service they would walk the mountain paths to homes where sacred fires were kept burning, ceremonial boogers danced, and Cherokee Little People performed mischievous deeds among backyard strawberry patches. Growing up as a child, it was a reasonable coalescing of Christian principle woven within the warp and weft of Cherokee storytelling and handed down as a basket of mountain tradition. We never knew anything was different about us. We thought all people were pretty much the same, just a mixture of cultural identities.

It was not until I left this circle of sacred fires that I would realize just how personally defining those mountain paths would become for me. In 1972 I boarded a bus bound for the university and became an urban Indian. Like so many others, I would never again be laced to the cradleboard of traditional innocence or wrapped in the green quilt claiming of those hollows. Instead, I found myself competing in a world of people who could not understand the language of my thoughts. A people controlled by material wealth and enslaved by issues of time. I was compelled to conform or fail. It was my first real failure.

Becoming an urban Indian woman meant movement from a traditional circle of elder women who easily defined themselves, into a new circle of women who seemed not to have a definitive place within their community. It also meant a diminishment of self so as to become indistinct from those who were participating in this modern academic environment.

*So What Would Be the Reality of This Cultural Bargain for Me?*

There were two life-altering realizations that became painfully evident those early years away at college. The first one was that I was not tall. My folks had always told me how very tall I was. The women of my family were all only about four feet eleven. My sisters, all three of them, hovered within the same range of stature. I, on the other hand, was a full five feet two inches in height. I was not aware of my less than impressive size until I found myself walking on campus surrounded by women who averaged five feet five inches. I was not tall!

The second rescission occurred in an anthropological methods course. I was taken from class by a favorite professor who introduced me to a Lakota, Greek Orthodox priest. He was a confident man who had been involved in the recent takeover of Wounded Knee in South Dakota. My mentor had merely wanted me to meet what he thought would be a fellow Indian. What happened was the first of what would be many instances in my life where I would be made painfully aware of the conflict between reservation-born and nonreservation Indians. This priest's only response to our introduction was a flat dismissal: "I mean, really, is everyone around here a Cherokee?"

I didn't know how to react to this first blow to my cultural identity. I had come from a home where a person's spoken word was not lightly challenged, an Indian home, where respect for all people was gifted to the young by those who were older and understood the circular nature of this gift. Yet, there I stood, in that long second-floor hallway, surrounded by classrooms and feeling very small for my full five feet two inches of height. I wasn't aware a reservation could define you. I had been taught tradition . . . ancestry . . . elders determined tribal identity.

"Just say a little prayer for him, and go on" was my grandmother's response some weeks later when I recounted for her the details of this valued suffering. It was as though there were no real question before her. I remember the dark, sweet-smelling mixture of apple butter cooking on the open fire seemed to command more of her attention than my storytelling. How could she just wave away this incident without any emotion?

My mother was also of little help. After all, she had married my father, a Sicilian, and had thrown herself into his culture. She would only occasionally shift direction when situations surrounding her immediate family made any escape impossible. She could pass for Sicilian and often did among my father's circle of friends. She had her own reasons for doing so. She had her own story.

I feel sure that being Cherokee in the 1920s and '30s was not easy for my mother. She faced not only the difficulties of being thought of as poor in a working-class community, but it was also a coal mining region populated, for the most part, by immigrants. A community who identified themselves proudly as a people who were "first generation this country," while ironically my mother's people saw themselves as First Nations people. My mother fought prejudice from all sides. She found herself needing to make a trade. She chose my father's way.

I did not want to find myself negotiating a similar trade within my own life. I embraced the teachings of my grandmothers. I was determined not to make an either/or choice. Despite my obvious confusion, I was, however, expected to complete college.

I never did. Four years later, and twelve credit hours short of my degree in anthropology/labor studies, my husband and I gave birth to our first son and I became a full-time mom.

*What Was My Community?*

Moving with my husband to the city, first San Diego and then Atlanta, would bring with it a dramatic shift from the life I had been taught to live and the actualization of everyday life in yet another new urban community. There was no night sky . . . no way to acknowledge the ancestral fires. There were no evening songs from the insects . . . no cicada to announce the coming of the green corn. There was no fresh soil . . . no water beetle to bring forth the soft mud. There were no flowing rivers . . . no water to go to. There was in fact no real "place" for me to connect.

I threw myself into political activism. My father, a coal miner, was a fierce labor supporter. Growing up, our household was filled with the stories of violent labor struggles and heroes who often lost their lives while striving to provide safer working conditions in the local coalfields. These stories and the grassroots labor movement among the migrant workers of the United Farm Workers union gave me a sense of home while living in California. Not just by way of the labor struggle itself but also by being close to individuals who seemed as out of place in their present circumstances as I did in mine. Political activism became my new religion—first, among the Socialists of my college campus, then among the Communists, and finally among the anarcho-syndicalists. My prayer offerings became picket signs; political chants and slogans were my prayer songs. My two oldest sons began elementary school before they were allowed even to know the taste of grapes.

### But Where Had I Placed (or Misplaced) My Remembering?

My mother would often tell me, "I've put all my strawberries in your basket." I look back now upon this declaration from a renewed cultural perspective. It is an awareness made distinct through the claiming power of traditional story. Over the years, traditional storytelling has served as secret witness to my ancestral identity.

Those of us who are Indian understand that it is the telling of stories, our very breath, that brings forth tribal identity and defines purpose. Our oral tradition, which is both ceremonially sacred and ritualized through the use of language, is also living thought. The elder women of my family nourished themselves through the telling and retelling of stories. Their stories brought them merciful shelter through the spoken transformation of time and place.

The question of how to adapt to the present dominant culture while maintaining tribal values is a five-hundred-year-old conflict among First Nations peoples. When my mother said that she had put all of her strawberries into my basket, she was in effect referring to this conflict.

In the traditional Cherokee story of the origin of strawberries, an angry wife leaves her husband and home after a quarrel. The Sun, having pity for what has happened, decides to place offerings of many different fruits along the path before her. It is not until she is presented with a patch of strawberries that she stops to eat. Once nourished by these small offerings of reconciliation, the memories of home were brought back to her. As she sat among the strawberries, her face turned to the west, these memories were called forth. This "call" to home grew stronger with the passage of time. Soon she felt compelled to begin her journey back. The story ends when her grieving husband meets her kindly along the path of her return.

Like the angry wife of this story, my mother encouraged me to search for an understanding of what other worlds had to offer. But in doing so she was also reminding me to give honor to that basket of reconciliation and to always carry it with me as a means of finding my way home. She knew the longer I waited with my face turned to the west, the stronger the remembering would become for me as well. However, I was not always met "kindly" upon the path of my return.

The struggle to resolve the "quarrels" of urban demands and institutionalized education brought forth and preserved the gifts of our tradition. The women in my family overcame these urban demands through the telling and retelling of stories. These stories were not just our oral history. They were, rather, a way of establishing a connectedness between the universe and ourselves. My ancestors may have been forced to move from the mountains of western North Carolina a century earlier, but within their baskets of meager belongings my grandmothers carried with them the traditional fruit of their reconciliation. It was the fruitful offerings of their stories.

### Who Are My Elders?

The grandmothers within my family held on to what they knew to be a sacred calling. My mother answered this call as best she could while tending to the needs of her children. She had responded to her cultural challenges in her own individual way, as did the women who had come before her. Each of them was forced to reconcile the rapid changes of their modern lives while preserving the sacred stories that defined where they had been. All of these brave women shielded the truth of our family behind those hand-covered smiles, and oftentimes tucked up under those fashionable hats, and always just beneath those spoken "amens" at the Church of God.

My great-grandmother Bertha suffered from tuberculosis. It was a disease that plagued several members of our family. Grandma was bedridden throughout most of my childhood. The local county Department of Health warned my parents to keep us away from her or they would be forced to confine her to a state hospital, a sanatorium. This threat sent my mother and Grandmother

Gladys into a fearful panic. Any time our family attracted the attention of someone from a state agency, we were fearful. But no matter how severe the scolding, my sisters and I would nevertheless sneak into Grandma's bedroom, where we would sit for hours, listening to the telling and retelling of our creation stories.

It was by way of my great-grandmother's telling that I would learn the paths of escape that our ancestors took along the New River from western North Carolina through Virginia during the 1838 Removal. It was there that we learned of our Overhill Cherokee cousins who aided our escape by warning us of the troubled coming of this displacement. And it was there, beside the bed of this frail woman, that we would first learn our story of the Fire. The Fire became for us girls the way we would forever define home.

My great-grandmother gave to us our place in the world. We were not separate from the mountains or the New River. The valley itself was sacred. The Fire that passed from hand to hand was our way of staying connected to this sacred place. Each generation within our family had carried the Fire with them. The burning embers were placed within a small black pot, carefully tended, and brought to each home as they traveled during those many years of movement. We learned that our family was forced to move through the mountains year after year until they were allowed to settle almost a century later in the deep valleys along the New River in southern West Virginia. It was the Fire that kept us connected to the start of this journey, moving with us from western North Carolina and flowing northward as the New River does, in a direction peculiar to the flow of other rivers. This Fire is our living relative; just as the River and this Story are our living relatives.

These relations—the Mountains, the Rivers, the Fire, the Stories— are the center of our identity. They are also my community. The women of my family were aware of their importance. They cared for them throughout their lives. They understood the movement for our family was not yet over. They also understood the importance of defining the true community of our kinship.

Moving to North Carolina ten years ago felt like the apogee of my own circling migration. In fact, it was the very antithesis of this thought. The move for me would be a final return home. In 1999 my sisters and I with all our children in tow revisited the paths of our family's forced migration. This journey took us through the mountain hollows of western North Carolina, along the New River, the Gauley River, and finally into the Kanawaha River valley. We gathered stones from the waters of these three great rivers as we breathed new life into the traditions of our family and spilled forth our stories to yet another generation. My grandparents may have been pushed out of the land that gave birth to them, but they never lost sight of the water or the fire that brought life to them.

My grandmother and great-grandmother died within a year of each other. I was living away from home, and even now their deaths don't seem real to me. I never moved back to the mountains. Faced with the realities of today's economics, I have continued to live within an urban environment. This compromise allows my husband and me to provide for our four sons. Although the challenges that my children and I face today are seemingly more complex than those our ancestors faced, they are in fact not so very different after all. It is the same reconciliation of traditional self-identity. It is the same call to remembrance. It is the same need to ensure that the future generations are given the gifts so carefully guarded by those who came before us. It is the same care that must be given to those burning embers that will in the future be passed from breath to hand and ignite the Fire that will then be carried home.

# BLOOD FLOWING IN TWO WORLDS

## Mary Black Bonnet

I live in two worlds.

I was born an American Indian but removed from my birth mother when I was eighteen months old and placed in a non-Native home, where I was raised within an entirely different culture. I don't remember my childhood before the adoption, but there were signs that I was feeling out of place. I was slow at learning to walk and talk, and for a while my adoptive parents thought I was mentally impaired or had fetal alcohol syndrome. I didn't. I know now, as an adult, that I was suffering from severe adjustment issues. Gone were all the relatives' faces I had known, gone were all the people who had carried me around, cuddled with me, put up, however annoyed, with my crying. Gone were the faces of my two sisters and three brothers, though my second oldest sister would come to live with me later. I can say with most certainty, I was miserable. I didn't want to be in that new place, however "better" people thought it would be. My adoptive mother has told me repeatedly that the first time she took me into her arms I punched her in the face. I always think to myself, "That is because I must have known the horrible abuse I'd soon be forced to suffer and was getting my licks in early."

So, I grew up in that life that was "so much better" than the poverty I came from, the "savageness" I had been saved from. But

I was miserable, I felt out of place, like I didn't belong. Surrounded by nice material things and people who went to well-paying nine-to-five jobs, I attended the best schools. But I was merely going through the motions of living. I felt like something was missing but didn't know what. It wasn't something I could describe or see or taste. It was something I felt, an emptiness that came from the pit of my stomach. Perhaps it was because my adoptive father was horrifically physically, emotionally, and sexually abusive to me, and my mother's presence seemed nonexistent. Maybe it was because my adoptive father continually told me I didn't matter, so I felt insignificant in my own universe. I wasn't sure what it was, but it was a feeling that would stay with me for all of my child-hood, through my teenage years, and well into adulthood.

I often dreamed of a better place. A fantasy place where there were no human beings other than me and numerous animals. To me that was a perfect life. Nature and animals. I didn't need con-tact with human beings, only my creature friends.

As I grew older, thanks to being able to see the actual adoption papers when I was doing a school project, I found the answers to the questions that had riddled my childhood: Who was my birth mother? Where was I born? This was a small treasure I held quietly inside my heart. As horrible as it sounds, it was as if I were a pris-oner just waiting for the moment to break out, be free, escape. So, I did. When I turned twenty-four, I took off on a two-week trip to Rosebud, South Dakota.

It was a hot, dusty August day at the Rosebud Fair and powwow when the dust blew me into Auntie's life. I told the powwow announcer what I was doing there. He made an announcement asking anyone to please come up and give me any information they had regarding my family. I waited anxiously, watching the faces of the women sit-ting under the arbor. Where was my mother? Was she thrilled to know I was back; had she even come to this powwow? I continued to watch the women, seeing if any jumped up and came running toward the podium. When a male voice caught my attention, I turned to face a tall, lanky man who introduced himself as my uncle. I was extremely disappointed though I didn't say so. I wanted my birth mom and was hoping it would be she who showed up to greet me.

The man talked of my siblings and how they were spread all over. I asked him where my mother was, and he told me she had died in 1991. I became upset and ran away. I was sitting in my tent, crying and cursing, saying I wanted to leave, nothing else mattered, that all I wanted was my birth mother, and now that she wasn't here anymore, I didn't want to be either. My friend who had come with me and was always the voice of reason, told me, "Well, let's just calm down a minute. You have an uncle, and he said you have family in the area, so don't you want to find out about them?" I was mad at her for being so rational, but at the same time I realized I'd better go find that man or I might lose contact with my birth family.

I told him I was ashamed about running away, and he said, "No, I'm sorry. I should have handled that better." We went to a quiet part of the grounds and talked more. We walked over to where my aunt was sitting, and he introduced us. I met my cousins, with whom I made small talk for a while before we went our separate ways. I was tired and sad, and ended up crying myself to sleep, amazed at how happy and sad I could be at the same time.

In the days that followed, Auntie took me around the reservation and showed me where my mother was buried. We had to go from cemetery to cemetery because they were not exactly sure of the burial place. Eventually, we were in this little village called Mosher, where Auntie stopped by a relative's house to use the phone to call the woman who kept the records for the cemeteries.

The man who lived there was my cousin, and he remembered me as a baby when my mom lived right across the road. It felt good to have someone validate my existence. I had been carrying this fear inside that all this was going to disappear, that I really wasn't who I thought I was and didn't come from where I thought. Auntie told me she had been told my mom was buried in Okreek—the same town Auntie and Uncle lived in. We went to the cemetery and Auntie pointed out the burial site, as it was an unmarked grave. There were many unmarked graves because people could not afford the cost of headstones, which is why a cemetery keeper needed to be a historian of sorts. Many of my relations were buried there, and my auntie explained who they were. I spent some time sitting beside my mother's grave and talking to her. I told her about how I had come all the way back to the reservation from Indiana and wanted so much to see her, but as she knew by then, I was in good hands with Auntie and Uncle.

Nights were spent in Auntie's house, as she told me stories of growing up, of the culture and history of our people, ceremonial dos and don'ts. During the hot days, we sat in her kitchen as she told me of herbs used for medicines and the sacredness of this, as well as other important teachings. The two weeks I spent there went by much too fast, and before I knew it, it was time for me to go. I didn't want to leave; Auntie and Uncle told me I was welcome to stay with them. But I had unfinished business in Indiana before I could come back to live on the reservation. I told her I'd make a commitment to come back in a year. This was in August 2000, and by May 2001 I'd returned to my auntie's humble home to stay.

I loved sitting and talking with Auntie: She fascinated me. Living almost as a recluse, she had a morning routine of sitting in her self-assigned chair by the window and watching the birds as she drank her coffee. Or sometimes on Saturday mornings she'd sit in bed and watch that weird painter guy on TV—the one who painted "friendly trees." I'd climb in bed with her and we'd watch it together.

My auntie has taught me so much. Since meeting her, she's always been there for me and supported my writing. She tells me how proud she is of me, and how far I could go. Whenever I write something, or one of my writings is published, she always wants to read it. She's taught me so many things about life and keeping myself grounded, humble, and distanced from all the crap that goes on in a small community. And she has shown me how to deal with all the fake people in the world.

When I first started attending the tribal college, other students were really mean. They stole my backpack, threatened me, and said I thought I was better than they were because of my clothes. I was extremely upset and told Auntie. She said to me, "They are disturbed because you got to get away from all the poverty and have had the opportunities that many of them never had." The next day I got dressed for school, wearing some old overalls. When I walked from my bedroom and Auntie saw me, she said, "Don't you dare change the way you dress for them, I won't allow it. Because if you change the way you dress, eventually you'll change other things, and pretty soon you won't be you anymore. You wear what you want and don't worry about what they say, my girl." She then explained how she had moved away to California for a while but had eventually come back to the reservation. While away, she had worked in the public schools and worn outfits that were appropriate for her position. So when she returned to the reservation, she continued to dress the same way, nice clothes and all. But people gave her so much crap that she began to dress down. She didn't want me to give in as she had. I went and changed my clothes, feeling better.

I wanted to be Auntie. To have her wisdom, her stories, the way she handled herself, and her strong, confident spirit. The way she'd gladly speak to people even if she didn't like them. Auntie has a strength that resonates from her; she says things straight up, tells you exactly what she thinks, and doesn't sugar-coat her words, which I found unnerving at first.

I loved living in South Dakota. I felt a hum that ran from the pit of my stomach down through my body, out of my feet, and into the ground. Wherever I looked, there were people who looked like me, with dark skin, dark eyes, and dark hair. There were powwows to attend and people to meet. I had connected into that part of myself I'd lost so many years before. I was home.

While in my herpetology class, I met a wonderful young man named Rich who had grown up on the reservation. We were the only two in the class, but I liked it that way because we talked to each other, and Rich was the kind of person I liked being around. He talked about philosophical things, deep issues, and what he thought makes people tick and why. The class ran for the month of June, and by the end we were good friends.

During this time I had rented a trailer, which was in horrific disarray. I had big plans to fix it up and was really excited because prior to this I hadn't picked up a wrench, much less rebuilt a trailer. Rich, on the other hand, was skeptical, but as I took him through the trailer he caught my excitement. He helped me re-lay floors, caulk holes in walls, fix plumbing, and do all the other things needed to make the place habitable. By the middle of July we were finished and our relationship had changed as well. We had become best friends and fallen in love. What was so wonderful about how we fell in love is that when we were rebuilding that trailer, we were building and securing the foundation of our friendship as well as our relationship.

In July 2002 Rich and I were married. People said it was the most beautiful wedding they had ever attended. We hardly had any money because I had spent the previous year as Miss Indian Day and had a giveaway the week before. The church wasn't decorated extravagantly, only some flower arrangements here and there thanks to my adoptive mother. I didn't care what it looked like; all that mattered was that I was going to be in a wedding dress, walking down the aisle, and becoming connected in a deeper way to the man I loved with all my heart. Rich and I are not churchgoers—we follow the Lakota spirituality—but the pastor of the church allowed us to bring an aspect of our culture into the wedding ceremony. Rich's dad performed the Lakota prayer and blessed us. We had written our own vows and used some parts of traditional ones. It was beautiful.

Now Rich and I are attending the University of South Dakota. As we wake up every day and grow closer to graduating, we know we are going to have to continue the fight we have fought since arriving in Vermillion. The fight for ourselves as Lakota people, the fight to keep ourselves balanced on the Good Red Road, to live the way we know we should be living. The fight to make sure we don't give up the teachings Rich was raised with and the ocean of knowledge I've swallowed to catch up. We are frustrated at having to live in a place where we must put up with bullshit from shallow people, empty souls, and professors who think just because they have a degree, they are better than us. When in reality, the things I've gone through in my life have already prepared me for whatever could come my way. My life experiences make me think everything out, analyze everything, and make sure I always know what the other person is going to do before he or she makes a move. I knowingly put up with the shit long enough to get the hell out of here.

I know who I am, where I come from, and how hard I fought to get here. No amount of non-Native perspective or white-run schools will allow me to forget that struggle, that journey, or that victory. As my auntie told me once long ago, I was born an Indian, I will die an Indian, and no one can take that from me. When things get tough, I try to remember this, because nothing is truer.

Since I first went back to my birth family, Auntie has been there for me no matter what. As time has evolved I hear her voice in my speech, her wisdom in my words, and often think of her advice when making a decision. Now that I live in Vermillion, which is two hundred sixty miles away from her, it gets hard sometimes. I miss her motherliness, her small, cozy abode. Getting up early in the morning, seeing her in her spot by the window, cigarette in hand, coffee cup close by as she watches birds flock to her garden. But when I tell her I want to come home, go back to our tribal college, she tells me that I will be better off with an education from USD. She explains that while it is hard to be gone from the place I love and my birth family, it is only for a short time. She tells me I must walk in two worlds in order to survive. That my Lakota blood can flow in two worlds as long as I keep the teachings and values of my people in my heart and take knowledge from the white man's world and schools. She tells me I am wise enough to know the difference between the bullshit they can give and the great wisdom that comes with being at a larger university. She has to give me this pep talk every few semesters when I feel deeply buried in schoolwork and so distant from my tribe and my people.

Auntie has helped me become a wiser, more grounded woman. I love her more than I could ever express, and I only hope she knows what a gift she's given me, and how grateful I am. I love her deeply for teaching me how to allow my blood to flow in two worlds to order to survive.

# HOME : URBAN AND RESERVATION

## Barbara Helen Hill

In the grand scheme of things, it might not matter to most people where a person lives or even from where he or she comes. But to a person of Native American Indian, North American Indian, Haudenosaunee, or any other "Indian heritage," it does matter, and matters very much. Our people, as most people, come from a Nation, Clan, or tribal background. Our Nations—Haudenosaunee, Creek, Cherokee, Sioux, Okanagan, Ojibway, Navajo, Zuni, Blackfoot, Blood, and all the other hundreds of Nations that no longer exist—were at one time living and faring well on lands as far and as vast as the eye could behold. We had forests as thick as hair on a head and water as pure and clear as one could imagine. Then the visitors came.

The visitors came to take the riches from this land and brought with them their ideas of "civilization." Apparently our people did not fit in with the visitors' idea of civilization because we were then relegated to tracts of land called reservations. We were put on government subsistence and placed in schools where we were beaten if we spoke our native tongue. Colonel Pratt summed up the idea of civilizing the Indian and educating the savage when he developed the first school for Indians. His statement "We will kill the Indian and save the man" summed up the government's plan for our people: annihilation, assimilation, and decimation. If that wasn't bad enough, they then thought of another plan.

In 1924, when the Canadian government was sending in troops of Mounties to "get rid" of the traditional government and replace it with the elective system, the United States government was putting in place the Relocation Act. Indians were given the "opportunity" to move to cities for a "better life." After the government took their land and put them on reservations, it then took their livelihood of hunting and fishing and harvesting. Placing the Native people on land that would not grow a blade of grass, never mind crops, was just another way to assimilate, annihilate, and decimate. The promises of jobs, good money, and new places to live was a lie. In reality the government hoped that if the Indians moved into the cities and "disappeared" into the mainstream society, governmental obligation would end. What the Indians found were poorly paying jobs, if there were any jobs; ghettos to live in with heartbreak, loneliness, confusion; and homesickness that lead to alcoholism, death, and dishonor, not necessarily in that order.

Our paths were set. We've been pointed in this direction since the first boarding school was established and the first plan was put in place to "educate the savage." Our footsteps fall in those who have gone before. Very few succeeded in the thirties and forties. Some had big plans to leave the reservation to become successful in the big city, and if they failed, they didn't just fail themselves but their whole family, Clan, and Nation.

This is not even close to being analogous to those who came through Ellis Island. When they came from other countries, they brought with them their culture, their traditions, their languages, and their foods to family or friends who helped them out. Our people were stripped of all that before they first moved to the cities. Or they were shamed into leaving who they were at home—

a place of which they were to become ashamed. This was taught to them, beaten into them. It was a heritage passed down.

I am Mohawk from the Six Nations of the Grand River Territory in southern Ontario. When I moved to Buffalo, New York, in the late sixties, the residue from the pain suffered from Indians living there years before was still in all corners of the big dream. Some of the men had found jobs as ironworkers, steel painters, carpenters, et cetera. The women either stayed at home with the kids or found jobs as day workers, waitresses, or barmaids. I got a job doing day work and then as a barmaid. I looked for other work, but I was afraid, lonely, confused, and intimidated, and although I didn't know it at the time, I was ashamed. I gravitated to the people who were from my community and frequented the bars and restaurants where they hung out. I became friends with their friends and moved where they moved. When I later moved to Rochester, New York, to be with relatives and friends, I ended up doing the same thing. I went where they were, where it was familiar, and where the other Indians lived. It was like moving from one reservation to another.

In the city, alcohol can become your lifelong friend because it is what you see, what others do, and what you learn to do. It is what is handed down, like brown eyes and dark skin or, in my case, blue eyes and golden skin. I ventured out to other parts of the city, but they didn't feel familiar. It was like leaving the reservation school to go to high school in a nearby town. It doesn't feel familiar, is strange, and doesn't fit right. In other parts of the city there were always Chinese, Polish, or Scandinavian people who had languages, cultures, and traditions foreign to my people. We Indians would always turn around and go back to our own little ghettos because that is where it was safe and familiar. We didn't move away for very long if we moved at all. It was too painful, for it was like leaving home again.

During the nineties I moved back to Buffalo, but it hadn't changed much for Indians. The Indian ghetto had moved across the river, and the people were now more isolated. The old bars and restaurants were now parking lots or office buildings. The areas that had once been Italian and Indian were now Puerto Rican and other Spanish nationalities. Some Indians who chose to stay in the area were so far removed from their heritage that they spoke Spanish, and quite fluently.

The Indians living in different parts of the city or that moved across the river had started something different from when I lived there so many years ago. They had socials where potlucks were a special menu of corn soup, fry bread, meat, and vegetables, along with a lot of pies. These socials were not just for urban Indians but for reservation Indians, who were invited as well. The urban Indians still felt isolated and shunned by most reservation Indians. But the "singers" would come from the reservation and help with these socials. There weren't a lot of people in the cities who could sing the social ceremonial songs, and so singers had to be hired.

The urban Indians are now a product of marriages between reservation Indians and the people they felt safe with. The Indians who were forced to move and succeeded most often did not return to the reservation. Some married their own kind, but more often than not married into the "white" nation. Those who didn't succeed either became alcoholics, or died, or both. Out of these arose the generations of urban Indians in the ghettos who carry on the pain and the shame that was given to their families when they left the reservations. Living in the city during the late nineties, I saw many young mixed-breeds—as they were called—trying desperately to find out who they were and what it means to be Indian. They wanted the language, the culture, and the traditions.

There is a mixture of love and hate between the urban and

reservation people. There is no trust or support, and those who want to go back to the reservation from where their ancestors came have a very hard time. The plan of the government is working well. The reservation Indians have an animosity toward the urban Indians and are viewed by some as not even being Indian. The reservation Indians believe that if you are not raised on the reservation with your traditions and culture, you are not really Indian. The urban Indians then feel anger at reservation Indians and feel that they are being stingy. It can be very complicated at times.

Quite often the urban Indians, because of being away for so long, take on the ways of the other cultures and abandon their own. The next generation becomes further removed and then this new generation comes along, wanting to go "home." This is a catch-22 for most. No one knows for certain what a family has gone through. No one knows why his or her great-grandfather or great-grandmother left the reservation. Was it because of the Relocation Act of 1924? Or was it because someone told them that it was "better out there?" No one talks about it anymore. It is as if someone silently says "This is how it is" and moves on.

Within the Indian community, as in any other part of the city, there is gossip. Gossip is a form of anger and jealousy. If we are talking about someone else, then we don't have to acknowledge our own pain or hear anyone talking about us. And so it goes on. The reservation Indians talk about each other and the urban Indians, and the urban Indians talk about each other and the reservation Indians. Only now it is the indoctrinated reservation Indians holding back the information and the teachings from the "wanna-be Indians" living in the cities. The children of the former removed Indians want to learn. They then are shamed and put down by the older "stingy" Indians living on the reservation. It goes on and on and on.

While living in the city, I found that I wanted the best of both worlds. I wanted to be in the city to attend plays and concerts and do some shopping. But I also wanted to be in the country to have the quiet. To solve that problem I would go to the country when I had time off from school or work. I would try to do the social things in the city during the week. I was still able to go home for the ceremonies and to visit family. But there are many who are not so lucky because they have no home to go back to. When their families didn't move back to the reservation but intermarried within other cultures, they lost their connection. It is more difficult for these young people to reconnect. Clans follow the matrilineal line. In our home communities if you do not have a Clan to go home to, you are not considered an Indian. That presents a problem in itself because here in Canada the government has set up a line with patrilineal descendants. Legally you are Indian in the eyes of the law if your father is Indian but not in the traditional way if you mother isn't. We now have a lot of Indians with a card saying they are Indians but with the traditional people denying them anything. They are not considered Indians because their don't have a Clan, thus they are denied traditional information.

Those young people having an Indian father and a non-Indian mother are treated badly by the so-called "traditionals" when they attempt to go to ceremonies. The traditional people in some communities are very judgmental and stingy with knowledge. It is my opinion that those people are not actually traditional, in the sense that they do not practice what they preach. There are many Indian teachings about kindness, acceptance, tolerance, et cetera, but these people don't seem to remember or practice them. It seems the keepers of traditional knowledge are most often government helpers in that they shun and shame a person for being who they are and continue to keep the young people at bay if they are not born and raised on reservations. The government taught that to the people back when they first put them in boarding schools.

And so it goes. The Indian people on reservations continue to be leery of the urban Indians. In Canada the government brought about the Indian Act in the 1700s and 1800s. My father told me that at one time you needed to get permission to leave the reservation. During the Depression some men chose to move off the reserves to work to feed their families. They had to enfranchise or sell their rights. That meant that they no longer could be called Indian. When they wanted to return, they couldn't, because in the eyes of the government they were no longer Indian, and neither were their children or grandchildren. That added to the animosity between reservation and urban Indians. Those who moved away were looked upon with suspicion and anger or jealousy for having taken that step.

Part of the agreement between the Indians and the government in making the treaties was the promise of education and health care in exchange for the lands taken. That agreement, or treaty was for all Indians forever. In Canada those treaties were between the Indians and the Crown of England, or the federal government. For the past number of years the federal government has been passing down responsibility to the provincial government.

In 1986 the Indian Act added Bill C31. This meant that those children of the enfranchised Indians could now become Indian. See the confusion? More animosity. The government put this law into effect saying that it would not interfere with the funding for the reservation Indian. We cannot be sure of that, because at the same time the funding began to be cut to the reservations, and that has added fuel to the fire. The government has been depleting those funds and trying to stop its responsibility to the Indians. It has continued the animosity between reservation and urban

Indians by not providing the dollars to the urban Indians and making it impossible for people to have the health care and the education that was promised to them.

When I decided to move back to the reservation, I had a home to go to. I'm one of the fortunate ones. Just as alcohol played a part in my life in the city, sobriety played a part in my returning home. Some are not so lucky. When they try to "go home," they have to build a home from scratch. They are building relationships with family, friends, Clan, community, and Nation, and usually they have to build the physical building as well. If sobriety isn't a priority in their lives, they have a harder time.

Life, they say, is what you make it. For me, it is also where you make it. I enjoy living in the city if I can be where there are trees, flowers, and birds. In the country on the reservation I have all that and more. There is nothing like going to sleep listening to the songs of the insects, the animals, and the birds, and waking up to them as well. Yes, it does matter to me where I live. I need to have that connection to nature, and I have it here. Would I move to the city again? I would move wherever the Creator wants me to be so that I can do whatever it is that I am supposed to be doing for the Creator. *Nyah weh.* Thank you.

# INDIAN IN A STRANGE LAND

## Wiley Steve Thornton

I grew up in Osage County, Oklahoma, a place of grass, rolling hills, and distance. It's a place of blackjack oaks, cedar trees, and little creeks that run across the land like the veins on the back of my hand. Just open land with nothing on it but green grass stretching for as far as the eye can see, and green hills with red-tailed hawks circling above. Back home they say you can move away, but those Osage hills will always call you back. The hills are mottled with limestone along the ridges, and the cedar trees look like they have been there since the beginning of time. During the cold, sunny days of winter, the hawks sit puffed up on fences and telephone poles, watching for something to hunt. The Osage call these hawks "the peerless ones."

At night, when the sun goes down, the sky is thick with stars that seem to go on forever. I used to lie on my back and study all those stars. If I looked at them long enough, I would see that every problem I had meant nothing compared to the universe. The old people said we came from the stars and that we were all *Tzi-Sho* (Sky People). They say we were once noble, clean, and pure. When we first came to Grandmother Earth, "the Sacred One," we named the plants, animals, and trees. We were the *Wa-sha-she* (the Name Givers), and we came down like an eagle landing on the top of the red oak trees. To be under that sky with the clouds, wind, and

Grandfather Sun looking down on me makes me glad that God made me an Osage. Aieeeeh!

The Osages moved to their Oklahoma reservation in 1872. This was the last reservation for our people. Our original homeland was in Missouri, and that's where our villages were. We also controlled western Kansas, northeastern Oklahoma, and northern Arkansas. Before we moved to Oklahoma in 1872, we had a reservation in southern Kansas. Originally, there were five bands of Osages: the Big Hill People, the Thorny Valley People, the Heart Stays People, the Down Below People also known as the Little Osages, and the Upland Forest People. My great-grandparents on my maternal grandmother's side came from the Upland Forest People. But when they all moved to Oklahoma, they split into two bands because of the death of *Gra-Mo'n* (Arrow Going Home). The two camps became the Claremore and Black Dog bands.

Chief Black Dog, who was over seven feet tall, was one of our great chiefs along with Man Not Afraid of the Pawnees and *Paw-hus-ka* (White Hair). These men were our great warrior leaders during the 1800s. Black Dog II, son of Black Dog, was the chief when our people came to Oklahoma to our last reservation. He died at the age of sixty-two in 1910. My grandmother was born in an Osage lodge in Black Dog II's camp in 1900.

I never thought I would leave my homeland. I didn't even think about leaving. In fact, I wish I were there right now. But here I am in New York City, struggling with the differences! I miss seeing Indians, just regular Indians. Indians I can talk with about who snagged whom, how the dance was last weekend, who's working for the tribe, and who's mad at the tribe. People at home talk about the old days, how they used to do things around there, or the things our elders passed down to us. Indigenous peoples all over the earth talk the same way. They always start out "The old people said do it this way or that way." It's like a guidebook on how we are to do things, how we are to conduct ourselves.

One time I was at a dance and this young man was speaking for his sister because she was head lady dancer. He was in his early twenties, and he was telling everyone how her ancestors had once been chiefs and headmen of the tribe. He talked like Indians are supposed to talk, going back to the beginning and working to the present. I asked my grandma why he spoke like an old man. She said he had been raised in the old way, which meant that his grandparents had raised him.

When I was a boy, I went with my mom and dad to one of the dinners that we had on Sundays after peyote meetings. Dinner was ready by noon, but everyone was still in the meeting at twelve forty-five. So, the cooks sent one of the men helping with the cook fires to see when all the people were coming. He went to the meetinghouse, then came back and said, "Put everything back on the fire, they just now started talking about Columbus!"

As an adult, I lived out in the country in my grandma and grandpa's house. I always enjoyed living there because I had so many good memories of visiting my grandparents when I was young. I really looked up to my grandparents. It seemed as long as they were alive, everything was all right in the world. They were traditional Indians, and the love I have for them has not diminished over the years. My grandparents knew how to do things in the Indian way. They, as well as their entire generation of Indian people, were born at the turn of the century. They are all gone now.

However, living in my grandparents' house had some downsides to it. The house wasn't insulated. It was extremely cold in the winter and equally as hot in the summer. The well ran dry, so the Osage Agency put in a cistern for me. Before this I had to go to town to get drinking water and water for cooking. To haul water in my junky pickup, I'd sneak into town like a married Indian guy sneaking out of the house to go to a 49 (an all-night dance celebration). I'd hook up a water tank to the truck, drive to the fire station, and have the firemen fill it up twice every two weeks. I was always worried about getting a ticket because the truck had a bad muffler and the signal lights didn't always work. The truck was black but faded, rusted up, and so dirty I was afraid to wash it because the dirt was the only thing holding the body together. It was fast though, with a 350 Chevy engine, and whenever I punched it, it would run like a bunch of Indians picking up their commodities at the government agency.

The house needed a new roof, so when it rained, water leaked into the living room. There was a fireplace and a propane heater, but most of the time it was cold because I was always broke and had no money for propane. And in the hot summer months the air conditioner would always trip the circuit breaker. Along with a leaky roof, a dry well, and cold winter nights, my grandparents' house also had visits from a ghost car.

The car began coming to the house while my grandparents lived there. They would hear a car drive up, sometimes even see the lights and hear somebody walking onto the porch. But when they looked outside, there was no car or driver. I think it might have been the spirit of someone who died while driving drunk and continued to wander the road. The old people say when someone dies drunk, that person doesn't get to move on to the Spirit Land. The car visited while I lived there, and I guess it is still going by our house to this day.

It always seemed to me that my grandparents' house was waiting for something. Maybe it was waiting for my grandparents to come home. When they were alive they knew how to make things happen. They had a lot of personal power: strong spiritual power. That is the only way I know how to describe the way they lived. I liked living there. It was so quiet and peaceful. The house was surrounded by hills with a small creek in the back that wove its way through the woods like a king snake. I had a connection to the earth and sky while living there. I liked sitting on the front porch and watching the clouds drift through the light turquoise sky of Oklahoma. I'm Deer Clan, and sometimes late at night when I went to the bathroom, my deer relatives would be there, feasting on the grass in my backyard.

Being in Oklahoma seems to be all behind me now. I really didn't want to leave because my mom, brothers, sisters, and all of my buddies were there. That wasn't always a good thing though. I was getting tired of borrowing money just to pay my bills and always being broke. Realizing it was time to book out, I thought I would go to New York for a year and make a little money. At the end of June 1993, I started my journey, reminding myself of what Will Rogers said about all those "Okies" going to California during the Depression. By going to New York I would "raise the IQ of both states." I had doubts about going, but I loaded up my clothes, my favorite Indian blanket, one of my eagle feathers for protection, and took off.

As I was leaving Osage country, I war-whooped, heading east with the promise that I would someday be back. Heading up I-40 on the way through Missouri, I stopped at the Sonic in Joplin and told myself, "I can just turn around right now and be back home in three hours if I want to." But I kept on going to New York. It took me three days to get there and was low-budget all the way. Coming through New Jersey, I had to deal with lots of traffic. Everybody was always trying to pass by and cut me off. As I got closer and closer to New York, the land kept getting more and more crowded. I couldn't understand why so many people lived so close together.

When I finally arrived in New York City, I was amazed at how different things were from back home. I rented a two-bedroom apartment that was really small compared to the house in which I had been living. I had to ride the bus and the subway, where I was always crowded in like a sardine in a can. Everybody seems always to be in a hurry in New York. Why, I don't know. Oftentimes this would remind me of the army—hurrying up just to wait. When I walked on the city streets, I felt like an ant in a maze. The city always made me feel so small. Back home in the country, under the open sky with the hills and prairie surrounding me, I felt just the right size. I blame the Lenni Lenape for all of this. They should never have sold this island to the Dutch.

After about two weeks in the city, I found a job at the National Museum of the American Indian. It is a strange place to work. There are sacred objects, ceremonial objects, human remains, and medicine bundles—representations from many tribes. It was odd how non-Indians cared and knew so much about Native American objects. They seemed to feel more for the objects in their care, however, than for the actual Native people. They certainly didn't understand that some of these things were still alive with a spirit in each one.

Since moving to the city, I have met many different kinds of Indians. There are Indians who are political, Indians who want to be artists, Indian actors trying to become famous, and Indians who were adopted as kids and raised by non-Indian people. There are also Indians who don't want to be Indian anymore. I could never understand these people. I guess maybe they had such a hard time growing up in alcoholic homes, it was just easier to live in the white world and to forget about their past. There are also Indians who want to be "gurus" for the white people. It seems most of these Indians are northern people who attend Sun Dances and sweats. A lot of these folks are just passing through New York though. They always have a group of non-Indians and a big-breasted blond woman with them. I am happy to be an Indian. I didn't come here to be anybody else. When I arrived, I just wanted a job and to be able to pay my bills.

I hope New York hasn't changed me for the worse. When I go back home, some people treat me differently and some whom I thought were my friends avoid me. They think I'm trying to be a white man because I moved to the city. But most of my friends still treat me with respect, and a lot of people think it is a good thing that I moved east and got a job, especially my elders. I think this is because since I moved, I have stopped drinking. Now I attend peyote meetings and dance in our ceremonies.

My mom died in 1997. It was really hard for me to deal with her passing; she was my best friend in some ways. I stopped drinking alcohol in 1998. I grew tired of the way alcohol made me act and think. Physically, drinking was harder on me than it used to be, and it never made any of my problems better. Alcoholism is one of the worst addictions of Indian people all across this country, causing the death of so many. Entire families in my tribe have been wiped out by alcohol. I lost many of my friends and relatives to alcohol-related deaths. I decided I wasn't going to let alcohol kill me, so I stopped drinking.

I miss going to Oklahoma powwows, hand games, and dances. The powwows here in the city just don't compare. I miss talking with my friends back home and having lots of laughs. I miss seeing my relatives and just visiting with people. My apartment is the smallest space in which I have ever had to live. It is hard to be in this box with a lot of other boxes around it. The noise really gets to me, and sometimes I have to get out of the city for a few hours. My uncle Ed tells me that even though I am in New York, the same sun shines on me here as it does on those back home, that "Grandfather Sun" is always up there shining down on me.

Whenever I travel back to Oklahoma, whether it is for a few weeks or just for a few days, I struggle with my return to the city. As soon as I get back to New York, I feel as though a part of me is left behind in those Osage hills. It's like I'm in two places at the same time. This is how I feel most Native Americans exist in urban America today. We have to live in two worlds. In the Native American world, our relatives surround us. We are related to everything. We walk upon our Grandmother Earth, the "Sacred One" and we address the sun as "Grandfather." We live where we bless ourselves every day. Where everything we do has a meaning. We listen to our elders and sing the old songs. Our ceremonies take place throughout the year. Everything we do begins with a prayer to the Creator. We are always on Indian time and there is plenty of joking and good Indian food to eat.

But we also have to exist in the non-Native world. A place where we have to dress in a certain way, go by clock time, and always are serious at work. A place where money is all that counts along with how much we earn and how we earn it. Money is extremely important here in the city. New York is where some of the richest people in the world live. It is also a place where some of the poorest people are homeless. People appear to always be in a hurry. Everyone seems to be a stranger. They pray once a week while in church and they pretend to have no relatives. If Native Americans ran this country, I feel sure things would be different. Seeing all of this makes me feel sorry for non-Native people. I walk a fine line and keep one foot in each world. That is how it is for me.

Osage people say that we are all pitiful before the Creator. They also say we must be humble. In the city, I often meet people who love Indians and Indian things. There are sure a lot of people who want to be Indian. There are some people who claim they have Indian blood. Some of these people think Native Americans have all the answers. This is not true. We have our problems too. However, most of us do know who we are and where we come from, which is a good thing.

# Everyone Needs Someone

## MariJo Moore

*My granddaddy was Cherokee*
*with eyes and hair black as tar*
*and shiny as a crow's back.*
*My Irish grandmother said*
*I looked like him.*
*I hoped so because I liked him.*

Memories of my paternal Cherokee granddaddy float into my writings. I see his faint outline in a ragged gray suit and worn fedora as he stands on a street corner in front of my grandmother's tiny shotgun house in Halls, Tennessee. He is drunk and smiling. I am five years old, and he tells me not to trust white people. "They'll take everything you've got and then give you something else so they can take that away too," he says. Although I was taught never to look into his eyes or speak back, I can hear the screaming in my heart, "But my mama is white!"

I am seven years old, sitting at a small Formica kitchen table in Aunt Fredonia's house. My daddy, dark and handsome, beer glazing his eyes, sits next to me. Granddaddy is there also. I have said something disturbing, because Daddy pats my hand, shakes his head no, and Granddaddy goes outside to throw up. Several years ago, Daddy filled in the rest of this memory by saying

Granddaddy was fond of eating opossum. He would catch one, put it in a little wire cage, and "grain it." By feeding the opossum corn for several weeks, Granddaddy made sure the meat would be free of anything that might taint it. On this particular night of my memory, there was an opossum Granddaddy had cooked sitting on the table. According to Daddy, I thought it was a dog and said so.

Granddaddy knew about animals, about the earth, and the traditional ways of planting. He told me how Selu, the Corn Mother, brought this wonderful food to our ancestors. When I look out my writing-room window in the summer and see the seven stalks of corn growing from the kernels I have planted, I remember how Granddaddy planted his corn. He would put seven kernels in a hill and beans alongside. The beans would twine around the cornstalks and replace what the corn took from the soil. I remember seeing his dark, calloused hands pulling the tender green ears from their stalks. He would pile the ears on the back porch of his old house, shuck a few to boil in an outside pot, and give the rest to others.

Granddaddy and Grandmother were quite a pair. He was a thin Indian man whose dark-pitted eyes looked like a tunnel a train had just passed through. She was a tiny red-haired Irishwoman whose ocean-blue eyes reflected frustration filtered though six pregnancies. Unable to be together peacefully, they lived in different houses for more than twenty years, never bothering to divorce. After every harvest, Granddaddy would come to her back door, knock quietly, and gift her with bushels of corn. She would accept the corn, tell him not to come in the house if he had been drinking, and then prepare to bake a skillet of corn bread for him. While she ground some of the corn into meal, he sat under a giant oak tree in her backyard, rolling cigarettes and singing softly.

I suppose corn was their way of showing forgiveness to each

other. A way of creating good memories to pacify the bad. In the Selu story Granddaddy liked to tell, the woman provided corn for her family, and her husband, Kanati, supplied meat. In the traditional Cherokee wedding ceremony, the man gives the woman a ham of venison, and she in return gives an ear of corn. The roles were a bit reversed for my grandparents, since he grew the corn and she hunted for a way to make money to provide for six children.

I can remember one of Granddaddy's neighbors hanging a dead crow on a stick in his garden to threaten other crows and scare them away from his corn. Granddaddy never did anything like this. Oh, the crows definitely came to enjoy his corn, but he always left some near the garden for them. Most of the crows would eat this corn and not bother the ears on the stalks. Occasionally, a few young ones would help themselves to the growing corn, so he eventually did put up a scarecrow. The crows were not fooled, but Granddaddy had fun telling how the scarecrow would walk around the field at night, looking for the spirit of Selu. He liked changing his stories to fit the imagination of his audience. I suppose I am also guilty of this at times but consider it the unmistakable mark of a true storyteller. Not lying, just embellishing. People expect this of creative minds.

Late in the summer I listen as Selu's spirit walks the mountains around my home. When golden tassels turn brown on the mature ears of my seven stalks, I gather the corn, then shuck and roast it. I remember Granddaddy's singing, and I always shed a tear or two, wishing he were here to enjoy my little harvest.

> I liked the way his voice sounded
> like soft running water over smooth pebbles
> whenever he would tell me to ignore
> the poor black children living down the road

*whenever they would laugh, point at us and demand,*
*"Talk some Mexican!"*

Granddaddy stood five feet four inches and was slight of stature. "Paper-sack brown" was how my family described his coloring. Shiny, crow-black hair and eyes, he called himself a "full-blooded Cherokee." Many times people mistook him for one of the Mexicans who came to the rich bottomlands of western Tennessee every fall to pick cotton. He never bothered to correct them.

When I was growing up in the fifties, it wasn't as acceptable to be American Indian as it is now. There was no *Dances With Wolves* over which non-Indians romanticized. No rebellious young people totally distraught over the Vietnam War, looking for answers to society's ills through spiritual teachings. No one looking to become a medicine healer, shaman, or pipe carrier overnight. And very few who wanted to claim Indianness in order to escape the accusation of the raping of the environment. Indians were looked down on even more so than today. I still carry a bit of the pain of having Indian blood, although I have learned it is not only my pain I am carrying but also Granddaddy's and those who have gone before.

Through my writings and travels, I have met many people who claim Indian ancestry for various reasons. Some are sincere in saying they are proud to have Indian blood. There are also those looking for something they never received as a child: a belonging. They have become disillusioned with their religions, families, or lives and want a mystical connection to prove they can fit in somewhere. Others are interested because of the misconception that all Indians can attend college free and get hoards of money from the government. Some who claim Cherokee ancestry want to get enrolled because Qualla Boundary in Cherokee, North Carolina, has a casino from which per capita checks go to enrolled tribal members.

Many people want an Indian name, thinking this will somehow grant them authenticity and acceptability. They go to great lengths to find a medicine man or woman or, more preferably, a shaman to give them an Indian name. Name giving in Indian culture is serious business, and each tribe has a traditional manner in which this is done. Some Indians feel comfortable sharing their true Indian names and others do not. Many factors are considered before one is given a name. I am not referring to English names or nicknames, but one's true Indian name. Traditionally, families give the oldest woman on the mother's side— and in special circumstances by the granddaddy—Cherokee names. Names are always given in Cherokee and only when the one doing the naming decides, not at birth along with an English name. Some children are named for a personal trait or characteristic, or after relatives who have passed on.

When I am asked "What is your Indian name?" sometimes I answer "Buy My Books" to ease the tension. But just as often, people feel obliged to share their "Indian names" with me. Soaring Elk, Turquoise Butterfly, and Long Arrow are just a few. These people are non-Indians who are taking a part of Indian culture without understanding the whole. Some of these names, I believe, actually come from books written on the subject "how to be Indian" or from movies depicting Indians as either pagan savages or mystical children of the land.

One of my elder aunts has shared her dismay with me several times concerning non-Indians who grab an Indian name. She said one is not Indian because one has an Indian-sounding name, wears Indian jewelry, performs a sweat, or observes a special ceremony such as the Sun Dance. Her opinion is one is either born with Indian blood or one is not. I was. I never knew Granddaddy's Indian name, and I didn't ask.

> *"Sometimes,"*
> *he would tell me,*
> *touching my crying eyes with a copper-colored hand,*
> *"it's better not to claim you're Indian*
> *in these parts of Tennessee.*
> *Everyone needs someone to look down on.*
> *Everyone."*

I am sure at one time Granddaddy was extremely proud of his Indianness, but because others constantly put him down, this changed. People often make fun of what they don't understand. Granddaddy preferred to pray down by the Obion and Forked Deer rivers or in the woods. I think these were the only two places he felt safe and at peace with the world. Because he did not attend a Christian church, he was ridiculed and, more often, ignored. I know this hurt him terribly. Indifference is so much worse than hate.

As I think of the shame and humiliation he endured because of his beliefs, I wonder why people of one religion feel it is necessary to put down another. As a child, I remember being taken to two different churches. In the Baptist church I heard how God loved only the Baptists, and in the Church of Christ I heard how only people from that denomination were going to heaven. No wonder in my confusion I cried to spend time with Granddaddy down by the river.

No doubt people will always have disagreements concerning religion. I have read that the basic philosophy of religion is supposed to be centered on the search for answers to the mysteries and purpose of life. But I wonder, is religion really a designer of morals and definer of justice and the chief arbiter of one's conduct? If so, can a particular religion bring peace on earth? Can it bring a significant change in society concerning peacefulness?

Looking back over the past two thousand years, filled with continual warfare, bloodshed, and exploitation, I realize that when faiths were contained within their own cultural boundaries, most people were not concerned with the beliefs of others. But when Christianity hit this continent, it hit hard and with a bang that still reverberates throughout Indian country.

Today, after four centuries of "religious imperialism," many tribal ceremonies have disappeared. Some people, like Granddaddy, held on to traditional beliefs regardless of the persecution. However, being looked down on as well as misunderstood eventually sickened his soul.

> But Granddaddy died long before I learned
> the truths behind stockade forts made of greed
> thousands of tears trailing in the snow
> unwanted lands reserved
> the ridiculous act of termination
> and the never-ending stings of discrimination.
> Long before he finished telling me the stories
> of how our family had to hide out in the caves
> of western North Carolina.
> Long before the Cherokee blood in my veins
> began to truly overflow the Irish.

When Granddaddy passed to spirit, I was still quite young. My parents were divorced, and my dad, who never wanted to talk about being Indian, moved out west. For a long time I wandered through my life searching for a way to belong to two worlds. Because I was extremely proud of my Indianness, I began to search for knowledge about my Indian ancestry and coaxed some information from family elders. This helped to flesh out the skeleton stories Granddaddy had told me.

The family left North Carolina and headed west during the Removal of 1838 known as the infamous Trail of Tears. While some were being taken to stockades to be held as animals, other family members hid out in the mountains and were never heard from again, probably dying of starvation and exposure. The family members who didn't die on the long walk settled in Indian Territory, which is now Oklahoma. Later, some of the family moved to eastern Texas. Why, no one knows or remembers. So much of Cherokee history, including that of my family, has been fragmented, whitewashed, or forgotten.

I do know that Granddaddy's daddy was born about 1848. He and his fiancée came to western Tennessee from Texas around 1877. Other family members soon followed. That was as far as they got on their journey to return to the homeland. They all settled in Halls, Tennessee, Lauderdale County, which is where Granddaddy was born in 1884. He remained in the area until his death in 1964.

Another story I was able to uncover concerns my maternal Cherokee/Dutch great-grandmother and Granddaddy being cousins. Her mother and his mother were sisters. Granddaddy's daddy shot my maternal great-grandmother's daddy in the leg because of a dispute over a card game. When gangrene later set in, he died. Her mother had died a year or two before, and so my maternal great-grandmother was left on her own to raise several younger siblings. She was thirteen at the time.

In some cases, it is very hard to trace ancestry of Cherokees.

Numerous families who left the homeland before the Removal, and those who hid out, either escaped or were "adopted" into non-Indian families and are not easily traced. Several were afraid to claim tribal affiliation due to fear of the government. Many of the records of my family were either destroyed or just not kept. I do know Granddaddy didn't want an enrollment number. He said the government had taken everything else, and they damn sure weren't going to take his name and give a number in its place.

*And when he died*
*his eyes no longer shone, his hair was dirty, matted,*
*and the smooth stones in his voice were muddied gravel.*
*Granddaddy died drunk and alone*
*speaking his language to the stars.*

In his later years Granddaddy was known as the "Indian man with the diamond doorknob." He lived in a one-room, tar-paper shack with a glass knob on the front door. At certain times of the day the sun would hit this doorknob just so, and it would shine like a diamond.

Granddaddy was also known for his homemade potato beer. He would take a five-gallon butter churn and add the following ingredients: six sliced raw potatoes, water, a five-pound sack of sugar, Blue Ribbon malt that came in a can from the grocery store, and three or four yeast cakes. His final ingredient was a fresh banana that he said gave the mixture a "little bit sweetening." He would stretch a thin piece of cheesecloth over the top of the churn and let the beer "brew" for at least two weeks. He would then strain the beer through the cloth into old quart beer bottles he had "boiled to clean" in a tin washtub. He would cap the bottles with a hand capper and sell the potato beer to whoever might be "thirsty for it."

Some people called Granddaddy crazy. He drank heavily and was known to be quite a carouser in his time. But his craziness has manifested itself in my spirit as the madness of creativity, and for this I am grateful. The words he spoke to the stars are the words that sparkle in my writings, and the blood he passed on to me is the blood of survival.

Conceivably, Granddaddy was right about everyone needing someone to look down on to feel better about the odds life presents. If so, then are we all possibly the same inside, regardless of race, skin color, or social status? Is the idea of needing someone to look down on a Jungian theory? Perhaps. I'm almost certain Granddaddy never heard of Carl Jung, but he sure knew how to read the hearts of others. Maybe we all should look into our own hearts and see if we are indeed looking down on others, and if we are, ask ourselves why. Isn't it time we concentrate on the similarities we share instead of the differences? To realize we are all part of the whole? This just might be the answer to stopping some of the hate in the world.

Yes, I am a dreamer. Some of us are born to be. Without dreams I could not be a writer. The poem that is woven into this writing woke me one morning, begging to be written down, after Granddaddy had visited me in a dream.

My deepest belief is in spiritual interconnectedness—that everything has a voice and speaks to those who will listen. I continue to listen to the spirit-of-place: to the winds as they blow over blue-ridged mountains, to the voices of birds and animals, to the sound of unburned fires lying in ancient trees. And I continue to write, trying as Granddaddy suggested, leading others to the truth concerning American Indians. I know he is pleased. My dreams tell me so.

# Unci (Grandmother)

## Ben Geboe

I'm going to tell you a story that is very strange and dear to me. My beloved Sioux *unci* (grandmother) passed away recently and left a wide space in my heart. But there is more than that to the actual story.

I flew back to the Yankton Sioux Reservation for Unci's funeral, which was beautiful. The family had laid her out in the living room, and that's the best way to do it. It was so much better than putting her in a church or funeral home. It was like an old-fashioned passing, with Indian singing and old Indian-language Bible hymns.

My grandmother and I had a very special relationship. It was very deep, and most likely the real reason I have become a Native American cultural preservationist. I'll have to tell you how we met: It was quite the work of Wankan Tankan—the Great Mysterious One.

When I was fifteen, my family and I left the Rosebud Sioux Reservation in South Dakota and moved to Utah, where my dad got a job as a supervisor at an Indian boarding school. I was very homesick for the reservation, and it was painful to be in Utah with the Mormons and their terrible racism. They hated the Indian kids at school and would always tell me about it because I looked so white.

I took a job after school and on weekends at a fruit stand on the highway out of town. I worked for a frosty Japanese woman who had been interned in a camp during World War II and stayed in Utah after the war was over. She hated whites, and I could see why, so we kind of got along. One day I was working and a car pulled up with a big Indian man driving. There was an Indian woman sitting next to him, and an Indian woman in the backseat. As he walked into the fruit stand, my boss said, "Well, go sell him some fruit. He's an Indian and so are you."

So I went over and said hello. He told me that he was on the way to California. I knew he was Sioux because of his quillwork belt buckle and big beaded watchband. So I said, *"Anpetu waste"* (a good day greeting). He laughed and asked if I was going to the Indian school in town. I told him no, my dad was working there, so I had to go to the public school. I said that I had grown up on Rosebud and that I missed being around Indians. He was on his way to his daughter's wedding in California with his wife and her best friend. His wife had severe diabetes and problems with getting around, so her friend had come along to help out.

The man bought some grapes and walked away but returned a few minutes later and asked if he could use the bathroom. I told him I was so glad he stopped by because I really missed being home on the reservation, and how he reminded me of this because he talked Indian. I picked out some fruit for the trip, a gift to honor him and his family. He smiled, thanked me, and told me to take the gift out to the women in the car. When I handed the woman in the front seat the fruit, I said, *"Anpetu waste,* these are for your trip. I met your husband in the fruit stand and I wanted to give these to you for your trip." I told her that I was part Indian and was homesick for Rosebud. She said, *"Pilamiya,"* (Thank you).

The Indian woman in the backseat leaned forward and asked,

"Child, what is your name?" I answered, "Ben Geobe." She clasped her hands around her mouth, gave a small yell, and asked, "Is your father Gordon Leigh Geobe?"

"Yes, he is!" I said in total surprise. She then looked straight at me and said, *"Takoja mitawa.* You are my grandson!" I began floating in the air, holding her hands tightly for a few minutes. It was so strange the way this was happening, and we were both in shock. When the man came back to the car, we retold everything; it felt as if we were reciting a miracle. Continuing to feel the connection, we exchanged numbers and addresses and they agreed to stop by on their way back from the wedding in California. We parted telling each other to have a good journey and travel well, as there is no word for good-bye in Lakota. When I walked back into the fruit stand, my boss seemed to be dying of curiosity. After telling her what was going on, I called my mom at home and she called Dad. When I got off work, we sat around the kitchen table, talking about what had happened. I told my story again every time one of my siblings came in. My dad related to me the sad tale of abuse and alcoholism that had kept him and his mother apart. The woman I had met today had given him up when he was five years old. She had hoped his father could raise him better than she could because he had a job as an Indian cop at the time and her family was dirt poor.

But my dad's dad was a terrible drunk and womanizer. His legacy of abuse stopped with my dad, thankfully. My dad was beaten, but he never beat us; yelled at, but he never yelled at us. He always had problems with severe depression but never showed any meanness. While growing up, he was taken care of by his Indian stepmother, Sybil Picotte, most of the time. She is the one we always knew as Unci when we were growing up.

So the story became clear. To me it seemed that my dad would never forgive his mother, so I told him I loved him and I would not be in contact with her if he so desired. He told me straightaway that the Creator put us together and I should have a relationship with her. After all, she was my relation too.

When she came back through Utah, my dad saw his mother for the first time since he was a five-year-old boy. Although obviously angry with her, he was very civil. It felt very strange, but we took pictures and began writing letters. Her name was Lorene Shields, and her maiden name was Red Lightning. She sent me newspaper clippings of her other children and grandchildren.

The first time I returned home to visit Unci, I was surprised that everything was the same: The family was still split into two halves—Indian and white. My father's family is all Indian. Some of his roots come from the northern tribes of Oklahoma; however, most of his people are from the Dakota bands of the Great Sioux Nation. He has repeatedly told me that Indians have always been here. We are from this land. No matter how many Bering Strait theories come forth, this is our land and it will always be our land. Our forefathers were once mighty warriors who crafted a living by chasing the millions of buffalo that ran free on the plains. Now most of our people spend their time living quietly on the reservations.

Indian people can be honest to a fault, so much so that they hurt each other with truth. You always know where you stand with Indians, even when it's not so nice. But is that any better than white people who create nice talk and flattery yet avoid the truth? One can suffer by being bathed in a barge of lies and half-truths, or suffer just as easily by being confronted with the truth full force.

My mother's family is all white. Her people came down from the north coasts of Norway. These individuals are and always have been hardworking and very odd. They are sincere to a fault, love to feud, and are ardent believers in Christ. They are also very light-handed with each other. The family ended up in South Dakota by following an ad for land: a promise of a free homestead to settle on rolling hills of endless prairie. Of course this was Indian land, which is the subject least broached at family reunions. They are lovely people, and Auntie Winnie makes great green Jell-O salad with fruit cocktail.

My uncle from my mother's side of the family picked me up at the airport on that first visit to see Unci. We ate a quick meal quietly and were soon speeding across a lonely stretch of road. The small prairie hills gave way to great expanses of grassland dotted with occasional tree-lined ravines. The green and brown grasses gently blanketed every hill and slope for miles. My white uncle glanced at me and asked why I was going to the Yankton Sioux Reservation. I told him I wanted to visit Unci for a few days and then I would stay with him afterward in Martin. He looked at me with a troubled face, not saying a thing, but I sensed his puzzlement. I reminded him that I was from the reservation. He looked disturbed at this. I knew he thought I didn't belong there, I could feel it, yet I didn't explain or ask why. This is the way things are back home for me—a place with different worlds on the same stretch of land, two different families, two different histories, and many unanswered questions.

Looking back, I think the thing that pissed off my uncle the most was that he didn't know where to go once we got to the reservation. The white towns all have streets with names that run parallel to a dusty main road lined with old buildings. There is always some brick bank, a bar, and maybe a lone grocery store. Cruising around always helps to find the right house number on the right street. The rez roads don't have neat little signs directing you where to go. There are a few churches and missionary schools but no towns. Most of the housing is found on scattered tribal sites far from anything organized around a main street. The post office and tribal school are all in the same building as the tribal hall. My uncle had to pull up to another car, then go into the gas station and ask where the house was located. He was told, "Take this right, then, when you pass a small field, go the other way and there is an old farmstead; go that way, then you will see the blue house, that's it." Indians never post signs around the land because they don't have many visitors, and I've heard the joke that it would only aid those government agents when they come looking for Indians. Everyone deserves a head start!

Both sides of my family, living within fifty miles of each other, have met only once, which was at my parents' wedding. My mom kept a lot of old black-and-white photos of her wedding day. Dressed in the attire of 1964, the entire wedding party looked sharp and very organized. I don't think my folks knew what they were doing, except that they loved each other profoundly. One group photo tells a tale of two races merged into one family by a lovely young couple. For a moment this family seems to be united in spirit, captured in time. But that is only a photograph; they belong worlds away from each other. I belong there somewhere between the two races, who are anxious and angry at each other because they don't know anything about each other.

After my visit with Unci on the rez, my Sioux aunt offered to drive me to my white uncle's place. We piled into her van and headed out. Slowly the brown hills and tired gray road engulfed us in silence. We passed by small communities, a few gas stations, and a lot of grazing livestock. When we arrived in Martin, I directed her to the narrow street where my uncle lived. He came up and she looked at me nervously. I laughed at the thought that she was scared of leaving me here in this all-white town. We exchanged a few words about the next time I was to visit the rez, and then I headed into my uncle's house, into the other of my two worlds.

My Indian reservation home will remain a place of beauty and deep culture no matter how far away I go. I chose to live off the reservation in order to attend college. I came to New York six years ago, after attending Haskell Indian Junior College in Lawrence, Kansas. All the students were planning their futures. Everyone else seemed to know what to do. Everyone knew how to act around people. Everyone was cool. For me, leaving college and moving to New York was the beginning of a period of disorientation and anxiety that had me convinced I was seriously ill. In fact, I thought I was dying. I had no physical signs or symptoms, but I felt myself fade away from the familiar into a world I did not know. Being in New York City is like moving to the United Nations—you don't know anything about how diverse people are when you get here, and you learn by slow exposure. All I could think to do was to keep moving. I don't need to go into any details; besides, it was really the feeling, the emotion, that was an integral part of what was going on. Yet at the same time there was nothing going on. I was young and drinking a lot, but now I don't drink at all.

It is difficult to describe what I have been through, something that has been the basis for fantastical folklore and myth. How do I talk about my experiences without confronting something that a boy scout could have dreamed up, without driving people away with nasty rhetoric? Again, the dilemma of the urban Native person shines through, as it is truly complicated and an almost unknown dichotomy. How do you live in a time when most people believe you are dead—from a people of the past—and you feel you have been made allergic to your true roots? You do, you just do.

Unci is buried in the tribal burial ground on the reservation with most of the old-timers. The site is on a lovely high hill overlooking the Missouri River to the south and the Great Plains to the north. A few years ago, the tribe bought four buffalo. Now there are thirty, all of which are grazing adjacent to the burial ground. When the Smithsonian National Museum of the American Indian in Washington, D.C., cleaned its closets eight years ago, several Yankton body parts taken as war trophies were found. These were repatriated and buried on scaffolds on the same hill with Unci and other elders.

That is my little story, but I know it is not the only one out there. The world is a lovely place and connections can be made. I am grateful for making the connection to my *unci*, for having the opportunity to get to know her before she died. I will continue to be grateful for my time with her as I struggle to live in between two worlds.

# From Brooklyn to the Reservation:
## Five Poems

**Maurice Kenny**

**The Steelworker**

For Peter

*In the hot Brooklyn night we stood*
*at a bar drinking beer, and he said,*

> *"Riding the sky on steel girders*
> *solid under my feet, wind balances;*
> *beer tastes good after work*
> *in these neighborhood bars on Nevins St.,*
> *but with all the big wages*
> *there is nothing to pray to*
> *here in the Brooklyn ghetto*
> *where my kids don't know*
> *if they're Black or Puerto Rican;*
> *too many bars on Nevins St., too many beers*
> *make me dizzy; I forget to sing*
> *and will slip one noon*
> *from those high steel girders."*

*And he took hold the shadowed hands*
*of Wolf and Bear and Turtle.*

## Reading Poems in Public

I stand on a stage and read poems,
poems of boys broken on the road;
the audience tosses questions.

I tell of old chiefs swindled of their daughters,
young braves robbed of painted shields,
Medicine Man hitting the bottle;
I chant old songs in their language
of the Spirit in wind and water . . .
they ask if Indians shave.

I recite old stories,
calendar epics of victory battles,
and cavalry dawn massacres on wintered plains,
villages where war ponies are tethered to snow . . .
and they want to know
how many Indians commit suicide.

I read into the microphone,
I read into the camera,
I read into the printed page,
I read into the ear . . .
and they say what a pretty ring you wear.
The tape winds, the camera reels,
the newspaper spins
and the headlines read:
Ruffian, the race horse, dies in surgery.

At the end of the reading they thank me;
go for hamburgers at McDonald's

*and pick up a six-pack to suck as they watch the death*
*of Geronimo on the late show.*

*I stand on a stage and read poems,*
*and read poems, and read . . .*

## The Comet
Seattle, Washington

> *In the bar*
> *a Mohawk sings, a drum*
> *beats song into beer*
> *bottles, coffee mugs, ears.*
> *Coins tinkle into a hat.*
> *While*
> *in the men's room*
> *atop the urinal*
> *standing before erotic*
>
> *scribbles and slogans*
> *over the rain of piss*
> *a vase of iris and spring*
> *pussy willows*
> *embarrasses the pisser*
> *with surprise and joy.*
>
> *Macho*
> *holding himself*
> *with poems drumming*
> *in the bowl*
> *cannot compromise*
> *with beauty.*

*Song enters*
*iris tickles spine as he turns*
*zips up for the next beer; rain*
*outside hides Mt. Rainier*
*but feeds sky and earth.*

*Confused by beauty*
*in such odd places*
*he drops his coin*
*amongst the tinkles in the hat.*

## Inheritance

*Your pleasure was running*
*to be on the go, downtown*
*to try on hats where you got lice once*
*and brought them home to us.*
*When you learned to drive*
*his Chevy you drove us to Canada.*
*They wouldn't let you cross the bridge*
*President Roosevelt built for us*
*because you weren't a citizen*
*of these United States.*

*Your running taught me how to run.*
*I keep Greyhound rich.*
*However, I learned*
*from your embarrassment never*
*to try on hats or cross bridges*
*into lands where I am not wanted.*

## Going Home

*The book lay unread in my lap*
*snow gathered at the window*
*from Brooklyn it was a long ride*
*the Greyhound followed the plow*
*from Syracuse to Watertown*
*to country cheese and maples*
*tired rivers and closed paper mills*
*home to gossipy aunts . . .*
*their dandelions and pregnant cats . . .*
*home to cedars and fields of boulders*
*cold graves under willow and pine*
*home from Brooklyn to the reservation*
*that was not home*
*to songs I could not sing*
*to dances I could not dance*
*from Brooklyn bars and ghetto rats*
*to steaming horses stomping frozen earth*
*barns and privies lost in blizzards*
*home to a Nation, Mohawk*
*to faces I did not know*
*and hands which did not recognize me*
*to names and doors*
*my father shut.*

# Two

## YOUNG AMERICAN INDIANS:
## THE NEED TO RECLAIM IDENTITY

*Today's Indian youth are often faced with the temptation of defining them-
selves in relation to stereotypes and misjudgments. Culturally relevant
opportunities to express themselves can play a definite part in allowing
youth to avoid these temptations. Many reservations are now incorporating
culturally based programs into their curriculums to ensure their youth have
opportunities to carry on the languages, traditions, and values of their
people. But what of those of American Indian ancestry who do not live on
reservations? Who either were not born into a tribal situation, or have left,
for one reason or another. Do they have the tribal identities and opportunities to learn of their heritage? Televisions bring the hype of commercials
designed to deflate the spirit and inflate the ego into many households, providing a constant challenge of blending the old with the new. Many youth
are torn between the need of extended family and values based on material gain for the self. Many get caught in the spirit-stealing seduction of
drugs and alcohol.*

*Some have managed to survive this dichotomy, holding on to tradi-
tional teachings as they live in nontraditional settings. Some have given
up entirely and decided to denounce their "Indianness." Some are still
caught in the middle, striving to survive with their integrity intact. All
know what it means to exist between two worlds, trying to belong to both.*

# THE GENOCIDE OF A GENERATION'S IDENTITY

## Gabriel Horn

One of the defining moments that set me on the path of my Indian life occurred nearly forty years ago, when I was a teenager. Not unlike many teenagers today, I had been living in self-exile from a fragmented and uprooted past. My two uncles owned a home just north of the city of Tampa, near the place where the Second Seminole War had begun when Osceola rescued his people as they were boarding ships docked in Tampa Bay. Government soldiers and bounty hunters were busy selecting from the group the darkest men and women for the reward they would receive from slave owners for runaway slaves. From his place of hiding, Osceola observed that some of these people were those the Seminoles had adopted and those Osceola regarded as Seminoles. Osceola led the attack that would free them all and begin another war against genocide that has never formally ended. His courage then affirms the spirit of what it means to be Indian now.

Irony and coincidence do not just accidentally come to pass in the Wheel of Life, and my living in this place with my two traditional Indian uncles at this important and impressionable time for me was simply the way it happens when we live within the sacred Wheel. These two Indian uncles heeded their responsibility to the future of our People. They helped to raise their young nephew, involving themselves deeply in my welfare. They encouraged my academics but also focused on my Indian education. In many ways, they saved me, too, from the white man's civilized world because they loved me, and I was the future.

They taught me about the Great Mystery, the essential concept of Native American belief. Over time I would learn the significance of understanding this indefinable and incomprehensible totality that always was and always will be, and that without this understanding there exists no way to truly comprehend what it means to be an Indian. I would learn from my traditional uncles, and later from my experiences as a teacher of the People, that this concept of the Great Mystery remains the essence of *Gichie Manido*, *Wakan Tanka*, *Sakoiatisan*, and *Wah-kon-tah*. As a man and a student of history, I would also learn that cultural genocide begins when one people robs the religious views of another people through indoctrination and fear, and how the practitioners of Christianity made every effort imaginable to impose their anthropomorphic God on Indian children, stealing our future of the most precious and vital view of life and of the world and of the universe.

But my two uncles would do even more than teach me about the Great Mystery and save me from cultural genocide. They would especially care for the part of my Indian identity that I was about to be taught did not come in parts and percents of blood or from a tribal enrollment number and government legislation. They would introduce me to my Native heart.

By the time I had reached my middle teens, I had become uncomfortably accustomed to people I hardly knew, or even knew at all, asking me personal questions about my racial and cultural identity. From teachers to counselors to my peers, even to complete strangers, I seemed to attract such curiosity. Today these kinds of interrogations affect so many urban Indians of racially mixed ancestry, and they do not always come from curious and misguided white and black people. The personal assaults on our identities now even come from our own people. Whether these questions are asked with a kind intention or a cruel one does not make them any less of an intrusion. Now, of course, I can call upon any number of quick responses to fit the situation and help control such rudeness and lack of cultural etiquette on the part of the inquisitors.

Back then, however, when I was still so young, I could respond to the dominant society in which I lived only based on ways I could understand, ways that would be most acceptable, ways that did not incorporate a traditional perspective, a perspective that Osceola must have known well. I mean, what could I know? What could any urban Indian kid know, cut off from his or her past, living in the white man's world? Just about the time when my uncles embraced me, so much of my knowledge about who I was fell under the influence of how that white man's world portrayed Native People.

Are you a real Indian? How much Indian are you? What kind of Indian are you? You can't be full Indian. These questions and statements dogged me then, and they dog me now. Only forty years ago they snapped and nipped away at a boy's identity even as he headed for the path of heart. Like so many young Indians then and today, I was only a kid trying to find a niche in the world and escape the government and self-inflicted cultural genocide that one day in the not too distant future may show the Indian on paper as not existing at all.

As I struggled not to accept the discomfort that always accompanied these questions, my mind's eye often involuntarily flashed on the infamous local Indian caricature. He was a popular and stupid-looking image of a bucktoothed Indian whose smile and goofy red-painted face appeared all over the city and epitomized the concept of cultural genocide. The comical creature was often pictured bashing in his own head with an anvil, an advertiser's catchy display for the compounding interest rate of the rich and well-established Seminole Bank of Tampa. His exaggerated and stereotypical features stand strikingly similar to the present day Cleveland Indians baseball mascot, Chief Wahoo. In the same dark spirit of cultural genocide, this abomination was named Savvy Seminole. In the superficial reasoning of racism perpetuated by the Cleveland Indians baseball team and its fans, the Seminole Bank's executives would one day explain to me in front of TV cameras and news media that the depiction of Savvy Seminole never was intended to be racist, quite the contrary. For example, they had explained that the name Savvy means business smart. Affirming their nonracist intentions, they said that it was not the same kind of Savvy as in Savage Sam, Florida State University's mascot.

As I look back at my life now, I am certain that other degrading images and names of Native People, like Redskins, had already filtered through my mind and self-image when I was so small I could not yet walk, but then, that is an effect of cultural genocide. However, it was Savvy Seminole who really made me knowingly ashamed, aware, and angry at the philosophy and the people that created and accepted him.

Often, Savvy Seminole would mock me from area billboards on my way to school. He would peer down at me with those distorted eyes bulging over that big-nosed, hideous face while I sat for a traffic light at a busy intersection in the passenger seat of my uncle's old car, checking the side-view mirror for the shape and size of my own nose.

Just a few years ago I remember showing my youngest son a photo I had taken of him, one I thought particularly handsome. I remember hearing him say from his bedroom how big his nose looked in the picture. I remember how his words squeezed my heart so tight, I thought it would burst. I remember how the hatred for those images and the people who knowingly perpetuated them burned stronger in me than ever.

Savvy Seminole was how civilized white and black people living in America thought of Indians then, and still in many ways choose to think of Indians now. The rationalization of cultural genocide is simple. Americans need to have these images and names in order to deny their history, for a history wrought with genocide and a democracy riddled with evil must be denied or the foundation of the United States would crumble. American images such as Chief Wahoo and Savvy Seminole enable the oppressors more easily to accept the stealing of a people's continent and inflicting genocide upon its Native inhabitants. When I think back to forty and fifty years ago, those images and names pained me in ways I cannot even know now. What I do know is that I became aware that this was how I feared the white man's world would always see me even though at the same time what I still longed to be more than anything else was an Indian like my elder uncles.

And so, through my own journey as a teenager, seemingly always shadowed by a city, perhaps I can shed some light on the shadows of that world, returning to those days that helped to shape my Indianness, even as I was being torn apart.

Savvy Seminole tormented me every time I went through the city. Indians still see him now in some form on ESPN or on *Monday Night Football* or in a baseball context or comically referred to on sitcoms. At that time in my teenage years, Savvy's face was just another Indian face plastered all over town, but he did not resemble my uncles. He did not resemble me any more than Savage Sam or Chief Wahoo or any other Indian mascot resembles my beautiful daughter or my handsome sons. They do not resemble my wife. Such racially and culturally demeaning images cannot reflect what I have seen in the physical features of any young or elderly Native American living today within the artificial boundaries of urban and rural America. Such racism degrades not only the victim but also those not intelligent enough to recognize and respect the beauty in other people or even other forms of life.

Humiliation of the Indian elevates the white man's and black man's status in America and their own distorted sense of identity. Humiliation, though, can eventually turn to rage, and that rage would fuel my warrior spirit until one day I would lead a protest in the city against the Seminole Bank for perpetuating racist stereotypes of American Indians. I would carry out an attack against the bank and its president and board of directors, those responsible for Savvy Seminole's existence, and I would finally kill that symbol once and for all.

And yet it was during the negotiations when I realized that this was, in fact, how the white man looked at me, or how he did not look at me whenever he spoke. I had seen that look on the faces of my teachers. I have seen it since on the faces of prospective employers. I have seen that look on the faces of fat-cat politicians. Then I noticed how the white man looked at Indians when the Jewish president of the bank would not look at me. Even as I confronted him, he declared to the reporters that he was a victim of prejudice himself. I'm a Jew, he said. Certainly I am sensitive to these issues of prejudice. I noticed that neither he nor any of the bank's executives would speak to me but chose, rather, to direct their statements to others who had participated in the protest who were not Indians: the student government representative from the local university, a professor, a minister, and those of the media writing the stories.

It was the first time I recall hating myself and hating them. It would become a hatred that would fester like a disease in my mind and body and would be the major factor in my attempted suicide at the age of twenty-three. Perhaps, in a similar way, at the very least, this kind of degradation remains a contributing cause for the countless other young Indian suicides because it has to do with self-image. Though my own attempted suicide would fail, the rage of my youth would persist into my latter years, and as a man it would threaten to take my life, burning holes in my stomach and devouring the organ, which filtered my bitterness.

While standing on the patio of my uncles' house one day, a new kid in the area stopped by with a Cherokee girl from school whom I liked. I had learned she was Cherokee during the two times we talked outside of school. I understood that through conversing with people, we get to know each other without asking personal questions but, rather, allowing one another to share what we choose to share. I guess the boy with her had heard that I was Indian and wanted to put me in an uncomfortable position in front of this pretty girl, thereby elevating his own status, which always seems to be the way it is when people put other people down or try to make other people feel displaced and inferior.

"How much Indian are you?" he asked. It was a question designed to demean. It was a question that I would discover as a writer and teacher haunted the minds and hearts of too many young Indians all across America. I remember dealing with this assault on our identities in American Indian movement survival schools. Young Indians of all ages, colors, and tribes would come to the AIM schools and learn that being Indian did not simply mean the color of one's eyes and hair or hue of skin. I also remember dealing with identity police as the cultural arts director of the Minneapolis American Indian Center. I remember the beautiful Indian children I would visit as a writer in urban schools on the Northwest Coast. I can smile now at the diversity of their looks, and how they each replied in their circles how much Indian they were, and how I helped us laugh at such a ridiculous idea.

How much Indian are you? I have heard it from white people and black people. I have heard the question from the mouths of bureaucratic and government-defined Indians protecting the casino cash. It was and is a question that comes from a civilized world and philosophy that has us surrounded and sometimes feeling overwhelmed.

As that boy tried to take me off guard, I glanced at the girl I liked and looked down at my sandals. The sandy earth always seemed to comfort me. It felt good standing there in the backyard of my uncles' house on the skin of Mother Earth, even if I did not yet know the words Mother Earth.

Ever since I began struggling for a place in the civilized world, I had sought the approval of that world. Still, I wanted to be fair to the Indian world that had loved me. I knew that I had ancestry in my blood that was not Indian, but I also knew that I loved my uncles and had their Indian blood in me. At this point in my young life the degradation of not knowing exactly what percent Indian blood would racially and culturally define me, and having to fight back such ugly images as Savvy Seminole, I responded the way I thought most clever. "I'm half," I said, my brown eyes squinting defiantly at my young enemy. I truly believed that my response would satisfy all considerations. Having been so proud I thought it up, I answered again, "I'm half."

He did not seem prepared for that reply, so he sneered. The pretty girl seemed intrigued. One of my uncles, though, had heard the brief discussion that took place that afternoon right outside the window, and when I stepped into his study that evening, he called me to the table, where he was reading and sipping black coffee.

"Gabriel," he asked, gesturing with his free hand, "which half of you is Indian? Which half isn't? Is it your upper half or your lower half? Your back half or your front? Well?" he said, seeming to grow somewhat impatient. "Which one is it?"

For a brief moment I actually pondered the answer and considered the possibilities. Then, suddenly, I felt silly, and I am certain my expression reflected this, because those penetrating sky-blue eyes of his smiled. I shrugged and I told him that I could not answer his question. Then his lips tightened into seriousness, and he asked me to shut my eyes. I did as he wished and stood there in the darkness.

"What does your heart tell you, Gabriel? What does your heart tell you, Indian or white?"

My automatic reply sprang without haste and burst into the spoken word. "Indian," I said, opening my eyes.

He sat back in his chair. "Gabriel," he said, "then that is what you are. Our People do not come in percent of blood. Our People do not come in parts. You can't be part this, part that. You either are Indian or you are not Indian at all."

And so I was forever set on the path of heart.

I wonder sometimes, though, how many times this heart can broken. I know so many young Indian women who have given birth while still teenagers. I know that they give their children birth names like Donald and Raymond and Robert and Rebecca rather than Native names that could help guide the children in the Circle of Life. Of course, giving a child an Indian name would require responsibility and selflessness on the part of the parents. I know Indian males still in their teens who have three and four children with as many young girls. Just as giving birth does not define a mother, neither does seeding life define a father, so another generation of Indians whose greatest treasure was always the children becomes further fragmented and removed from its heritage.

Attending urban powwows, or even returning to the reservation for powwows, cannot fulfill these urban Indians when their own people pause to honor an American flag circling the arena while a dancer in the uniform of the oppressor holds it, dancing. Neither can the Indian gangs find fulfillment hanging around outside the circle selling dope, or just hanging around looking for something they cannot define.

And what can be even more threatening to our future is that too often, greedy tribal governments, not wanting to open tribal roles to share tribal responsibility, do not recognize many of these children, who are often born in urban hospitals, as Indians. Neither does the federal government, leading me to think that our own people have joined that government and now take part in this kind of paper genocide. But what is an Indian anyway? Simply having Indian blood computed on a tribal ID card does not define an Indian. Of this I can be certain. Then perhaps, with children being born in urban areas to Indian teenagers with little understanding of motherhood and fatherhood, and with paper genocide continuing among tribal officials, we have assumed the role of our oppressor and carry out genocide against ourselves.

Perhaps the real in-my-face awareness of our genocide occurred not too long ago when my uneducated and unemployed teenage nephew pulled over to say hello to me. He was driving his new Cadillac. He had showed the car to me once before. It had a TV set mounted to the dash along with a CD changer hooked up to a stereo with speakers occupying the entire rear of the car. Eminem rap rattled the car's grille as the dark power window slid farther down, revealing a kid I loved but who was too confused himself even to know who he was. I could see a designer logo across his T-shirt, while on his head he sported a Cleveland Indians baseball cap.

My heart squeezed and my breath seemed momentarily suspended. Perhaps in some way he was I and I was my uncle. He was the future now, and this time I was the link to the past. I guess every age has its situations. Every age has its challenges. I shook my head slowly as my lips tightened. Then I forced a smile. *"Ah-neen,"* I said, greeting him in the language of his ancestors.

I know that genocide remains the most perverse human act. It eradicates entire peoples. It annihilates whole cultures. It rips beauty, wisdom, and understanding from the world and robs a people of its identity.

Thus, when it comes to the act of genocide, I also know there can be no alternative to finding ways to fight for life. As long as there are those among us who believe in the old ways of seeing and being, there can be no surrender to genocide. Ever!

# WE, THE PEOPLE: YOUNG AMERICAN INDIANS RECLAIMING THEIR IDENTITY

Lee Francis

For the People, whether urban- or reservation-born, it's really about story. The ancients among the People understood that all of creation—seen and unseen—tells story. In the long-ago time, from birth to earth, the People learned about their harmonious place in the order of all creation by listening to and telling story. Their identity was inextricably interwoven in the stories they were told. For Native People, story was and continues to be essential to an individual's identity construction and development.

Most young urban American Indians live in a world very different from the long-ago past. They face many challenges. Drug use, alcohol abuse, and violence are a regular part of their lives. Living with a single parent is not unusual either. After school they come home to an empty place because their parent is working. At school their classmates mock them if they say they are American Indian. They rarely fit in because they know they are somehow different from the others. Their identity as an American Indian becomes blurred. They do not know the history of Native American Indian people. They do not know the stories.

No one tells them that a couple of centuries ago, our non-Native relatives came across the great waters to the land of the People. As more and more immigrated from their original homelands, the People told stories to their non-Native relations. They told stories about all of creation. About being connected. Related. They told stories about walking in harmony and balance and what the consequences are when that doesn't occur. Stories were told about protecting and caring for the earth long before there was an Environmental Protection Agency. In the stories, the People revealed their identities to their non-Native relations.

As the People died by the millions from massacres and the disease brought by their non-Native relations, fewer and fewer stories were told. The task of telling story fell to the few remaining elders. The stories changed. The elders told story about smallpox and greed. They told story about rape and murder. About the massacres of Native men, women, and children. They also told story about generosity, caring, and community. The elders among the People told story after story. Yet, the influence of their non-Native relations was evident as the creation and migration stories began to subtly change. They began to include the beliefs, values, and attitudes of their Christian non-Native relations. For example, honoring and celebrating the importance of women in Native societies was discouraged. And the stories began to emphasize men having control over women. Men never controlled women prior to the arrival of our non-Native relations. Each had their own important tasks to ensure that their community was completely functional.

Then came the boarding school experiment. Indigenous children were abducted and taken thousands of miles from their home place. The purpose of the boarding school was to indoctrinate or brainwash the children. Telling story in their own languages was forbidden. Those who disobeyed were held in solitary confinement in small prisonlike cells for weeks or even months. In the boarding schools they were told different stories. These stories were about selfishness, getting ahead, isolation, and "rugged individualism." Some returned to the reservation. Even so, the stories emphasizing the values, attitudes, and beliefs of the People told in community settings since the beginning of time were slowly lost.

Later, many of the People were forcibly relocated or migrated to towns and cities. The majority of stories urban Native youth heard and learned were those told on the stage, and later on radio shows and in movies. Today stories are seen on television, videos, and DVDs. No longer are the stories about community. Instead, urban Native youth hear and see stories that focus on me instead of we. Little wonder, then, about the dysfunction among Native youth both on and off the reservation in today's world.

To reclaim their identity, American Indian urban youth need to learn the stories of the People. They need to learn, remember, and tell the ancient origin and migration stories, the stories that focus on Native values, attitudes, and beliefs. And they need to tell new stories about growing up and living urban lives. These new stories need to incorporate the wisdom of the People about the land and relatedness to all of creation. To tell new urban stories requires learning about the People who first inhabited the land in the urban area where they now live. Once these stories are learned, it is important to tell stories about those People. They need to tell stories of their accomplishments and tragedies. What they believed and experienced. Link those stories with those of the People from whom urban Native youth are descended. In this Internet age there is no excuse for not knowing. It is in the stories, old and new, where urban Native youth will be able to reclaim their Native identity. They will be able to know their harmonious place in the order of all creation.

My personal experiences reflect the truth of what I am saying. One story is told by my son. A second story is by an urban Native person in a class I teach at a university.

My son was born in Fairfax, Virginia. He is an urban. Since

infancy, my spouse and I told our son story. We told story about all of creation, seen and unseen. We told him about the People. We told him story about the People of Fairfax, Virginia. He learned about the civil war and the pogroms committed against the People. We told him stories that incorporated the values, attitudes, and beliefs of the People. We told stories about hummingbird and coyote and the tree people and the cloud beings.

Now our son is an adult. For all his years growing up, I was sincerely convinced that he didn't hear a word we said. How wrong I was. Over the past several months he has told his mother and me story after story after story. Telling us about his life, he interweaves the values, attitudes, and beliefs of the People, which have been told for thousands of years.

Our son tells story about his accomplishments, his dreams, and his tragedies. Again and again he includes the land and the People in his story. "It's about being connected," he announced to me one day. I looked at him, waiting for him to continue.

"It's about knowing your place . . . my place, in the grand scheme of things. Example. When I was a kid we moved around a lot, so I never had a home place. Instinctively, I knew where I was from. I was born in Virginia and that was always where I felt the most comfortable. It was the trees and sky and the land; the smells, the taste in the air, the feeling of . . . home. These were imprinted on me from birth. But as we moved around, I began to understand that concept more and more. I wrote a poem once. "I was born on the road . . ." is the first line, and most of my poetry revolves around the land and my relationship to it. But I didn't realize when I first started writing that the sense of place and land and story were so connected to my identity.

"As I matured and developed my own voice, separate from yours and mom's, I was able to analyze with a critical eye how important the stories of home and my own home place were to me. I know it seems a roundabout way to justify my statement that it's about being connected, but the stories that you told me when I was young were about lessons for all time, not just when I was young. I find new ways to apply them even today. And at the core of all the stories I was told is knowing your place in the universe: how you relate to everything, everyone—all of creation. That's how it's all connected. That is how you draw the line from story to earth to creation to yourself. It's just connecting the dots.

"And I think that is true for all the stories of the People. About knowing your place or, more, being aware of your place in the universe. I am from Virginia. I am connected to the land in spirit, mind, heart, and body. Mostly it's just a feeling I get, but I can tell the minute I cross over the state line. Home. And my stories revolve around that home place. For me." (Lee Francis IV—Personal conversation—September 2002)

Working with urban Native students who take my classes is always a challenge. Whether I am teaching Native American Philosophy, Life and Thought, Spirit of Place, or Contemporary and Traditional Native Storytelling, the sad reality is that a majority of urban Native students do not have a clue about the trials, tribulations, joys, and hopes of the People. Few know about the treaties between the United States government and those from whom they are descended. Within weeks, however, they begin to remember the stories they were told as children. Stories their grandparents, elders, aunties, and uncles told them suddenly come into their conscious mind. They remember stories about generosity. Community. Caring for others.

The urban Native students in the class tell story about their lives. How they just knew that something they did or did not do was right or not. On further reflection, they remember "something my dad said when I was little" or "my grandma used to say . . ." A Native student in my Contemporary and Traditional Native Storytelling course wrote:

> I have always listened to the stories whispered to me by the trees, by the flowers with their sleepy heads drowsing in the sun, by the wind as it journeys from one part of the planet to another. I have seen the beat of the butterfly's wings and heard the story of the hurricane it would someday cause.
>
> I have also wondered for most of my life what people who do not have stories in their heads do have in there. If they are not listening to the stories that are constantly being told, what are they hearing? Is anything going on inside their heads? Is it like the snowy screen of a station that is off the air? Is it the sound of static on AM radio? Is it just a blue screen?
>
> I also have to wonder if they hear the stories that are passed on from blood to blood. When we told our origin stories, I told not only what I had experienced in my lifetime but what my mother and father experienced with my conception and my birth. Though I was just an un-united egg and sperm at the time, I know inside me the joy and love my parents felt at my making. I have listened to that story for my entire life.

The student ended her paper talking about her son.

> Here, then, I have told another story of understanding and loss. Those who have not seen their children grow up urban will not understand my sorrow of what he has lost due to the choices that I made. They will not understand that I still

hope within me that someday I will be able to show him these things [about life]. (Stormy Stogner, Critical Analysis Paper #1, 9 September 2002).

In instance after instance, urban Native students complete the semester filled with a new sense of purpose about their harmonious place in the order of all creation. They have a renewed sense of their identity. I don't have to, nor have I ever had to, force urban Native students to remember. They do that all by themselves. I don't have to harangue them about the evils of alcohol, drugs, and violence. They remember the ancient stories. They remember the stories of the past and tell them. And they interweave the lessons in stories of the past as they begin to tell story about the present and the future. In the process of remembering and telling, they discover their core identity.

Urban American Indian youth need to understand that one's identity is not about me, me, me, me. It's about we, the People.

# INDIANS IN THE ATTIC

## Joel Waters

**Dear Aunt Therese**

*You wanted to borrow money from me*
*But I never lent it to you.*
*We both knew you'd never be able to pay it back.*
*But you jumped headfirst into the idea*
*Without seeing how deep it would go*
*And I am much too shallow sometimes.*
*And yes, you have it hard*
*Moving away so many times*
*That you leave bits of you in those towns*
*Like a story you started*
*Just never knew how to finish.*
*And I know it's hard*
*Living in towns*
*Filled with people you don't know.*
*And yes, I do understand*
*When it gets too hard, too overwhelming*
*To build from nothing*
*And it's comforting to know*
*You can always go back to Grandma's house*
*Back to the reservation*
*And find security in poverty.*

*No expectations, no worries*
*'Cause we all work with pennies there*
*And everyone gets shortchanged.*
*Your run-down car*
*Looks the same way you feel.*
*It's okay if it breaks down*
*You're used to it.*
*And it's okay if you want to run away from this.*
*You're just going in circles.*

I grew up on and off the Pine Ridge and Rosebud Sioux reservations in South Dakota. It was always strange to make the transition of leaving the reservations and moving to a city, and coming back was equally as difficult.

The earliest memories I have are my mom taking us away from Pine Ridge (which was the place I spent most of my childhood years). There was always a sudden relief, like I was going to a special place, but we never went very far. My mom, a single parent of five children at the time, would move to the towns nearest the reservation. Some of those places were Rushville, Nebraska; and Rapid City, Buffalo Gap, and Hot Springs, South Dakota. All were within a hundred-mile range of Pine Ridge. I don't think we had much capital to get farther than that.

The reasons we kept moving back to Pine Ridge were mainly financial. My mother couldn't afford the places we lived in even though they were low-income housing; plus finding a good-paying job and a baby-sitter was always hard. As a child, my spirit felt wounded when I had to go away from those good schools and nice neighborhoods with clean parks and friendly people and move back to the slums of the reservations into an already crowded house filled with other family members. It was a horrible feeling to face as a child, going back to the place where nothing changes.

It was always the same old worries: Are we going to have enough food? Who's going to come drink beer, cause a fight, and scare everybody? I tried not to blame my mother for bringing us back to this because I knew she was struggling also. When I was two years old, my father died in a car accident. She has never fully gotten over this. Regardless of where we went and what happened, my mother always managed to take care of us. It must've been hard for her to give up trying to make it on her own in a world beyond the desolate reservations. It was also hard for us children to change schools and to lose our friends.

As a child, it was shameful for me to go back more than it was for me to stay in white towns and face the racism, because when I was very young I didn't really understand racism. Even though white kids said cruel things to me, or their moms didn't want their kids to play with me, it never hurt me as much as it would now.

I didn't start feeling the effects of racism until we moved off the reservation to Hot Springs. I was a teenager when my "disillusioned by innocence" world was peeled away and I was awakened to the way society really works. It became increasingly hard for me to avoid being hurt by racist comments made by non-Indians. But looking back, I realize just how much I chased after those white teenagers I wanted so much to be like. Even though they were rude and looked down on me, I still thought the world of them. Like other Native American teenagers living in Hot Springs, most of us were ashamed to be called Indians, and some, like my older sister, avoided being seen with other Natives.

I knew a couple of Indian teens from high school who flat out denied they were even remotely Native American. I was kind of hurt when a girl I knew and liked told me she wasn't Native American, and claimed to be white, even though it was very clear her features were more Native than white. Inside, I also felt ashamed but I didn't know what to do. No one ever told me at the time not to be ashamed of my culture. It was as though the whole town had a one-track mind. It was like "Yeah you can be Indian, but just don't act like it." We were the white man's Indian, and because we ignored our true selves, we were only acting, acting white.

"Why do you act so white?" "Why do you talk like you're white?"

I first heard these questions, which I thought were nonsense, when I moved back to the Rosebud Reservation in eighth grade. Obviously those living there thought I acted too good for them. It was because I didn't see myself as one of them, and I never saw them as important. Without acknowledging it forthright at the time, I was ashamed of being Native American, ashamed of my own people. Whenever I would return to Rosebud after living in other locations, I always felt contrite about the place. I associated the reservation with all my problems, and spent most of my years trying to avoid it because I still wanted to be white. I've now realized that shaming of one's self is a personal struggle and one can choose to stay that way or change. I'm not saying that wanting to be like white people is a bad thing, but if one destroys one's own heritage and denies one's own race just to be like the majority of people, it's not healthy for one's survival.

On the two reservations I've lived on, I've seen young Native Americans absorbing modern black culture in the way they dressed, with baggy clothes and such, and in the rap music they listened to. I can understand now why some go that way. Whether it is positive or negative, the point is most Native Americans tend to relate to black culture, and other nonwhite cultures as well. These cultures have common bonds because of the history of slavery and other human devastations caused by white Europeans.

I try not to get angry about America's history concerning Native peoples, but it's hard not to. It wouldn't be so bad if the relations today between whites and Native Americans were better in this state and other locations, but they are not. There is still racism and hatred of Native Americans, although not all white people feel this way. I have non-Indian friends who like me for who I am, but it does not change the reality of racism in this state. These friends can go only so far with me on these issues. They cannot stop the watchful eyes of white store clerks and cashiers; they cannot stop the businesses that hire only young white, smiling, pretty blondes; and they cannot stop the criminal justice system from being biased against Indians.

Many Native Americans are dealing with similar struggles, and I cannot help but wonder if I'm going to get a good job after graduating college because I am a Native American living in South Dakota. One has to be realistic about this state, as the fact is that most places prefer to hire whites. No amount of well-meaning white people can change my way of experiencing these things, because the reality of stereotypes, racism, and ethnocentricity is so obvious and oftentimes overwhelming.

In the state of South Dakota, it's hard for Native Americans to change any of this because the ball isn't in our court. The majority of Native Americans have little or no faith in the laws that are supposed to protect us, or the government that is supposedly here to help us. It is as though we are America's flowers in the attic. For the longest time we were not seen, we were a secret locked away, abused. So many past atrocities were committed, and now that we have been let out of the attic, we're supposed to trust and readily forgive those who kept us there? Even now white people tell us "get over it," and "your side lost, so quit complaining." One even hears it in the media from celebrities and politicians who run their mouths thinking they are funny or witty. These are the reasons that we need to keep our identities as Native Americans. We need to find ways to restore our pride; otherwise we will continue to be brushed aside and to be America's big secret.

While attending college in Rapid City, I began to experience a new atmosphere. There were so many Native people there who were speaking and advocating truth in Indian-and-white relations. I was amazed how many were sick of being labeled and stereotyped and wanted change. I also had the opportunity to meet several Native American authors, who inspired hope in me and helped me find my purpose in this world. That purpose is to write as they do, and try to change the way the world perceives Native Americans. As I underwent this change, even my amateur writings of angst-filled poetry changed. I used to pride myself in believing I was an individual, but I've realized over the past few years that I have to be a part of something, and that starts with first finding my own identity. My culture is part of my identity, and being Native American is an honor to me because I know what my people have gone through in the past. And I know most of the hardships my people are dealing with today. We are always fighting—we are warriors—but now we are warriors of words because that is our biggest strength.

Now whenever I go back to the Rosebud Reservation, where my mom still lives, I no longer feel ashamed, nor do I feel a heavy burden. It is my home for as long as my family lives there. Although it is not much, I want to try to change that for my family. I want to try to be their voice, because I am strong enough to do so, and I have opportunities they don't. I've gone through many obstacles to stay in school and to get this far. I don't want to be the only one to accomplish this, however, and I hope some of my family will join me in getting an education. We need more Native

Americans in college. The tribes could also do more to advocate education and to keep Native Americans in schools. There is never enough money to sustain Natives in college. There needs to be more funding and scholarships, because the ones in school are the ones who will be changing the way society sees us.

There's more to being Native American than skin color and stereotypes. It's how one feels and thinks that really defines one as Native American. We need to stop being ashamed of who we are as a people, even though some of us are poor. We need to try to get educated, because knowledge is our best defense against racism and stereotyping. Those of us who aren't on the reservations anymore must never forget our families who are. Even though the reservations are dirty and in bad shape, it's still the only place where Native Americans are allowed to be themselves, and our culture is best preserved there because that's where most traditions and elders are. We need to stop being ashamed of our culture-given names, because they are beautiful gifts from our past with important meanings behind them. It seems many Indians prefer to use white-sounding names because non-Indians prefer to hire someone named Williams or Smith to Weasel Bear or American Horse. My name was incorrectly written on my birth certificate, and because of this I have had to use Waters as my surname. My true name is Joel Aaron American Horse. I am proud of being of this bloodline, as I am proud of being Lakota Sioux, no matter where I am.

**Jamie**

*She stares out through dim eyes*
*Squinting at scenery that's not worth seeing.*
*I remember making fun of her when I was a teenager*
*Not caring that she had problems of her own*

91

*Like not knowing where to go.*
*She had a baby when she was seventeen*
*Now she strolls downtown with her mistake in hand*
*Or maybe, it wasn't a mistake.*
*Maybe this child will save her and give her a reason*
*To go on in this dump of a town.*
*And I could believe, I could go along with it*
*If I didn't know she was pregnant again.*
*I watch her crack open beer cans*
*The way children open presents*
*And she knows, and I know, that the fun lies*
*Somewhere in that 24-pack of cheap beer.*
*So we wait for the buzz that gets us all laughing*
*And having the time of our lives*
*And just for a little while we're all kids again*
*Not caring that we're poor and sitting in a shabby trailer house*
*Where the water doesn't run*
*And where the trash and roaches*
*Seem to be attached to everything.*
*And she tells me things like "Why should I be sober?"*
*"What do I have to look for?"*
*And for a moment, I understand her*
*Because I'm sitting here in poverty*
*And not in control.*
*"Why should I be sober?"*
*When our dreams fall like the cigarettes we flick to the*
*ground*
*Making a big ashtray out of a clean and perfect world.*

# America's Urban Youth and the Importance of Remembering

## Dave Stephenson

The urban maelstrom threatens to suck us into its depths. It beckons; it bewitches; it ensnares and obstructs our flow. We find ourselves swirling about in the inner-city madness. We struggle to retain our identities. And we endeavor to achieve successes based on criteria imposed by America's colonial culture. We scramble to attain wealth. We make Machiavellian lunges for power and hedonistic dives for individual pleasure. Too often, we lay inveterate traditions by the wayside. We begin to lose sight of who we are; and all too often we abuse our spirits, minds, and bodies. The seductive allure of the modern American world and its imperatives of affluence and power can easily overcome our innate aversions and draw us into a rip current of greed and regret. As mass American society burgeons about us, profiteers and charlatans exploit our ancient cultures and traditions. Cruel media stereotypes and cartoonish mascots whirl in the depths. Native America's urban youth have been torn from our own cultures and thrust into fast-paced worlds rife with commitments and temptations.

Due to forced and voluntary assimilation and quests for conveniences, refuge, or anonymity, sixty percent of America's Native people now reside in urban areas. We drift. We run. We abandon our communities with little forethought or fanfare. We plan. We coordinate. We accept jobs and attend colleges. Sometimes, we hitch rides and stumble upon urban landscapes. They are teeming Emerald Cities that at once hold bright promises of affluence and dark promises of disconnection. Some of us were carried to cities by our parents when we were infants. Many of us were born in cities. Even then, our spirits perceived a profound sense of displacement.

The second great displacement of Native America commenced in the 1950s, at the start of the Termination Era. Natives were forcibly moved to urban areas or given incentives to relocate voluntarily. By transplanting families and terminating tribes' special relationships with the federal government, the dominant culture hoped to definitively eradicate Native peoples. The eagerly anticipated denouement was that, deprived of recognition and thrust into multiethnic urban neighborhoods, we would breed out our blood and lose our identities. Our memories would falter; we would be cast adrift. Anglo America would be freed from an uncomfortable reality and could pursue its invented identity and illegal occupation of America with renewed ardor and absolution.

I was born in urban America, a product of assimilation. My maternal grandmother, a strong and gentle Tlingit woman whose Indian name was Kaax̱ kwéi, and her daughter, my mother, who was still but a girl, left Southeast Alaska in the 1960s, at the height of the Termination Era. Like so many Natives during that period, they left their ancestral homeland and waded into the turbulent urban river. And like so many Native families, their urban wanderings were eventually accompanied by offspring; ergo, my generation grew up in cities and became America's contemporary urban Native youth. Our lives have been bombarded by mixed messages and riven identities. We are at once Native and mainstream, at once urbane and yearning for tradition. Like all Native Americans, we are torn between two worlds, but perhaps the cuts are deeper, the alienation more profound for young urban Natives. Reservation or village life is more traditional than urban life; cultural and language programs and familial osmosis ensure that the youth of traditional communities are exposed to ancestral wisdom. Urban Indian youth are often denied exposure to traditional intuitions and institutions.

When I was born, I was given an Indian name from back home, a name that is unadulterated, a name that buttresses identity and invokes pride; many young urban Natives have only an Anglo name. Sometimes we are taught words from our native tongues, words that awaken a distant memory and summon self-awareness and intrinsic pride; sometimes English is our only tongue. We are told stories from back home, stories that are placid pools in a raging river, stories that are ancient, real, and profound. I was told timeless bear stories that contain invaluable lessons and fundamental truths. Our stories are juxtaposed with the faux yarns that blare from omnipresent media, from which so many Americans receive artificial knowledge and messages. Mainstream media threaten to supersede and usurp our memories; they suck us ever deeper into sorrowful depths.

The Termination/Forced Assimilation Era was accompanied by the advent of television and a massive proliferation of new media sources. John Ford westerns and foolish Indian caricatures flickered from cathode-ray screens and were smeared on the pages of glossy magazines. John Wayne and his fellow Indian fighters galloped to celluloid greatness by committing theatrical genocide, leaving impressionable viewers reveling in their dust. As urban Indians became more entrenched and accustomed to unfamiliar communities, media invalidations also became more imaginative and deep–rooted. But contemporary electronic media and mass-produced publications are simply an outgrowth of antecedent means of communications, and contemporary Indian stereotypes simply put a new countenance on some very old ones: We are tragic yet noble savages worthy of pity and condescension; we are vicious reprobates who drink, steal, and stab; or we are fawning companions to whites, faithful Tontos and Pocahontases who recognize the error of our ways and seek only to facilitate the inevitable progression of Anglo civilization.

Concomitant with malevolent media stereotypes are promotions of avarice and mass consumerism that are antithetical and foreign to all Native life ways. Many young urban Indians have been instructed solely by these injurious messages; we grow up confused and deluged by media messages that promote negative self-images and foster greed and self-interest and solipsistic nihilism. It is against everything we know. We are an unselfish people, devoted to our families; traditionally, we lived in extended kinship groups. These are our memories, and we struggle to retain them against a ferocious undertow of cruelty and mass-marketed sophistry. Material pursuits and solitary avarice are methodically engendering a great forgetting. We are slowly losing our memories and sections of our souls.

During my boyhood, I didn't watch television, nor did I immerse myself in other forms of mass media. The majority of my entertainment came from reading, play, and board games. But, notwithstanding my remoteness from mainstream media, I was surely impacted by and part of an urban world that receives its protocols and admonitions from the mass media. It etches messages into the stone of its collective psyche. The messages become immutable law. I knew I was Indian, and I was proud. I flowed with my identity. But I was also cognizant of a certain Indian stigma that members of the dominant culture could perceive quite distinctly, a bright blemish on our auras that engenders looks of distaste or incites ridicule. The Indian mark is promulgated by omnipotent and sorcerous messages disseminated by both mainstream media and American mythology.

Once when I was a boy in elementary school, the teacher left the classroom to take some papers to the office. A group of boys surrounded me and stuck a pigeon feather in my hair.

"Big Squaw," they jeered. "Big Squaw!"

"Goddamned fucking Indians," one boy spat out.

The throng of boys hurried back to their desks when the teacher reentered the classroom. She didn't notice the feather. I left it there for several minutes; it was a tangible mark, a stigma I could feel.

Shortly thereafter, my family moved across town. I began to attend a new school. I befriended a group of boys with whom I played football during recesses and lunch breaks. One day I walked back to class with one of my newfound friends.

"You look American Indian. Are you Indian?" he asked.

"No way." I looked away.

I was embarrassed at my lie, uncomfortable at my embarrassment, confused. I fought the current and was pulled closer to the turbid eddy.

My grandmother was a BIA employee for twenty-five years. She was a voracious reader, and loved all American novels; she collected American stamps; she lived in America's metropolitan areas for many years. But she was principally and foremost a Kaagwaantaan Tlingit woman, an Eagle, a Wolf. She told me many, many times, starting when I was very young, that she was "Indian first, American second." Grandma didn't disdain Anglo America; she appreciated urban conveniences and loved to travel and sightsee. She took a federal job because she wanted to see the country. She also sought to eschew the hardships she had experienced back home. But she always retained her indomitable pride and identity. When the BIA school in Stewart, Nevada, closed due to Reagan-era cutbacks, she returned to live with my mother, brothers, and me.

Grandma always wore a dazzling red windbreaker. Its back was emblazoned with the words "Stewart Indian School." It was adorned with Native art. Grandma was a diminutive woman, and her jacket was oversized; it hung to her thighs and she had to roll the sleeves so they didn't dangle well past her wrists. Her jacket swelled in the coastal breeze. She was small and taciturn, but her jacket shouted with enormity and pride.

I'm Indian first, she proclaimed.

In the midst of ruthless messages and myriad offenses, we must retain our identities and memories. We struggle against a treacherous undertow.

I knew a young Native man whose identity slowly faded. He had no family, no cultural or land-based connections. His memories were crushed under the onus of the chemical poisons he deluged his bloodstream with each day. He struggled and hustled and ran urban streets. Perhaps he succumbed to the aforementioned media mores of self-gratification and insatiable acquisition. He sought false and fleeting respites with bitter poisons imported from South America and Mexico. Many times I saw dull spikes pierce his tattered veins and carry him to a fleeting calm that quickly progressed to dark depths. Chemicals crudely packaged in Baggies and glass bottles are ubiquitous in the urban madness. They hold false promises of potential comfort; they afford temporary lulls and moments of soothing silence in the urban din; they slash and destroy.

The United States cavalry has replaced its Gatling guns, diseased blankets, and Springfield carbines with .45 pistols, lead-filled wooden truncheons, and twelve-gauge scatterguns. Their mounts are now Fords and Chevrolets and Kawasakis. The urban police are domestic soldiers and still pursue and persecute Native Americans with the same zeal as their nineteenth-century progenitors. The young man I knew was often in their crosshairs. He was arrested for countless narcotics violations. Once, the police handcuffed him, forced him to the floor of a holding cell, and kicked him into unconsciousness. Invariably, he was released after a few days due to overcrowding, lack of evidence, or an unwillingness or inability to investigate. Narcotics sales charges were dismissed or reduced to simple possession. He always returned to his whirling abyss; he continued to search for distant remembrances that were always just out of reach. They faded with him into a deep vortex. One year he was arrested fifty times, a citywide record and a dubious honor that earned him a spot on the evening news. I watched that night and saw his eyes blaze at the camera and sweep the courtroom.

"You're going to reduce the charges to simple possession. So just let me go," he challenged, and glared at the black-robed judge.

Perhaps he again subscribed to the aforementioned media stereotypes. Look at me. I'm a bad Indian. I'm tough, mean, and vicious.

The judge rebuked his insolence with twenty-seven months in a house of barbed wire, concrete, and steel. He would be annealed in additional violence and schooled in bigotry and continued addictions. He lost his memories and was deprived of an identity.

He was caught in the maelstrom.

I know a young Canadian Indian woman whose canvases come alive with brilliant splashes of light and color. She paints placid rivers and tumultuous volcanoes. She paints songs and stories; they croon from her easel like love songs and lovers' tales. The woman adores her babies as only a Native mother is able, and carries them with her everywhere. She is always happy, comfortable, proud. Like her art, she is vivacious and colorful and sensuous.

Frequently she and her babies return home to a small town on a small reserve. There, her family is as lengthy and stalwart as the St. Lawrence Seaway. Her parents, aunts, uncles, brothers, sisters, nieces, nephews, and cousins greet her and the babies with smiles and boundless familial warmth whenever she returns. Her elders hug and greet her, and she listens to them intently.

Even the land is delighted to see her. It smiles and receives her. It embraces her. The reunited family trades wisdom and warmth and stories; they share their pleasures, hopes, and sorrows. In short order, sorrows fade and smiles remain. The woman knows who she is, where she comes from, and where she belongs. She recognizes the offensive nature of the semiotics and messages we are so incessantly bombarded with but isn't embittered. She returns to the city rejuvenated and possessed of endless inspiration. Again she transforms stark white canvases into scenes of unsurpassed beauty and emotion. The woman's passions pour out of her soul and become visual poetry. If she feels the tug of the undercurrent and begins to falter, she always returns home to the warmth of her land and family.

The woman always remembers.

Native American thought and cultures are ineffable. Contemporary Native wisdom-speakers like Vine Deloria, Jr., Paula Gunn Allen, and Oren Lyons have eloquently explained many of our truths and understandings. Innumerable anthropological tomes have been written on our cultures and histories. But there is always a facet of our life ways that remains indefinable. It can perhaps best be described as a smooth flowing, a continuity of the land and its animals and ourselves, an uninterrupted progression. We are a part of the totality, and we are confident the totality will always remain.

The land completes us. It makes us whole. Always we flow with it.

• • •

I returned to my ancestral homeland within the verdant spruce forests and timeless straits of Southeast Alaska's Alexander Archipelago. Inside and among the fjords, glaciers, and towering peaks are reflections of life and fortitude inextricably intertwined with and dependent upon a land so bountiful and blessed that our vitality can only be regarded as an extension of it. The land always remembers us, as we remember the land. Our land, people, and memories remain one.

I scaled an Alaskan mountain that rises straight from the fertile tidewater. I stood on a precipice on the cusp of an ancient, impenetrable ice field above the tree line. I reclaimed memories and an identity that had always whispered softly from the spruce boughs and fertile earth. I flowed slowly to the fork where the rivers meet. The maelstrom roiled in my distant wake. I heard my grandmother whisper Bear stories from a distant stand of cedar and hemlock. Perhaps her grandmother whispered around her.

Always remember who you are.

# Three

## NATIVE LANGUAGES:
## WHERE WILL THEY GO FROM HERE?

*Thousands of distinct American Indian languages have been silenced for-*
*ever due to pandemics of smallpox and other diseases brought by Euro-*
*pean contact, acculturation, and total annihilation. Some linguists studying*
*Native languages estimate there are maybe fifty years left before all Native*
*languages are completely gone if they continue to dissipate at the rate they*
*have over the past hundred years. In the 1800s the government began an*
*official policy of forcing Indians to attend boarding schools in order to*
*wipe out all "Indianness." This doctrine resulted in almost an entire gen-*
*eration not passing on language skills. Now, with the third generation*
*emerging into adulthood, many Indian people are determined to revive*
*their Native languages. They are doing so in various ways such as teaching*
*language classes and encouraging their descendants to speak their native*
*tongues. There are also those who are proudly proclaiming their Indian*
*names with the intention of preventing the death of the spirit of their lan-*
*guages. For the remaining Native languages to survive, concentration*
*must now center on "how to keep our languages alive," instead of "who to*
*blame for the decimation."*

# SONG, POETRY, AND LANGUAGE—
# EXPRESSION AND PERCEPTION

## Simon J. Ortiz

My father is a small man, in fact, almost tiny. I think it must be the way that the Pueblo people were built when they lived at Mesa Verde and Pueblo Bonito. That's a long time ago, around A.D. 800 to 1200. One thousand years ago—this man? He's very wiry, and his actions are wiry. Smooth, almost tight motions, but like currents in creek water or an oak branch in a mild mountain wind. His face is even formed like that. Rivulets from the sides of his forehead, squints of his eyes, down his angular face and under his jaw. He usually wears a dark blue wool cap. His hair is turning a bit gray, but it's still mostly black, the color of distant lava cliffs. He wears glasses sometimes if he's reading or looking closely at the grain swirls of wood he is working with.

My father carves, dancers usually. What he does is find the motion of Deer, Buffalo, Eagle dancing in the form and substance of wood. Cottonwood, pine aspen, juniper, which has the gentle strains of mild chartreuse in its central grains—and his sinewed hands touch the wood very surely and carefully, searching and knowing. He has been a welder for the Atcheson Topekan and Santa Fe railway [ATSFRY] railroad and is a good carpenter, and he sits down to work at a table that has an orderly clutter of carving tools, paints, an ashtray, transistor radio, and a couple of Reader's Digests.

*His movements are very deliberate. He holds the Buffalo Dancer in the piece of cottonwood poised on the edge of his knee, and he traces— almost caresses—the motion of the Dancer's crook of the right elbow, the way it is held just below mid-chest, and flicks a cut with the razor- edged carving knife. And he does it again. He knows exactly how it is at that point in a Buffalo Dance Song, the motion of elbow, arm, body, and mind.*

*He clears his throat a bit and he sings, and the song comes from the motion of his carving, his sitting, the sinews in his hands and face and the song itself. His voice is full-toned and wealthy, all the variety and nuance of motion in the sounds and phrases of the words are active in it; there is just a bit of tremble from his thin chest.*

I listen.

*"Stah wah maiyanith, Muukai-tra Shahyaika, duuwahsteh duumah- sthee dyahnie guuhyoutseh mah-ah. Wahyuuhuunah wahyuuhuu huu nai ah."*

Recently, I was walking with a friend who is enrolled in a Navajo language course. She is Navajo, but she does not know how to speak Navajo. That is the story at present with quite a number of Indian young people who use English as the language with which they express themselves. English is the main language in which they experience the meaning and the uses of language.

She made a comment about not being able to learn Navajo easily. She said, "I can't seem to hear the parts of it," referring to inflections and nuances of spoken sentences and words.

I referred to a remark I made sometime before: "The way that language is spoken at home—Aacqu, the tribal people and com- munity from whom I come—is with a sense of completeness. That is, when a word is spoken, it is spoken as a complete word. There are no separate parts or elements to it." And I meant that a word is not spoken in any separate parts, that is, with reference to linguistic structure, technique of diction, nuance of sound, tonal quality, inflection, etc. Words are spoken as complete words.

For example, when my father has said a word—in speech or in song—and I ask him, "What does that word break down to? I mean breaking it down to the syllables of sound or phrases of sound, what do each of these parts mean?" And he tells me, "It doesn't break down into anything."

For him, the word does not break down into any of the separate elements that I expect. The word he has said is complete. The word is there, complete in its entity of meaning and usage. But I, with many years of formal American education and some linguistic training, having learned and experienced English as a language—having learned to recognize the parts of a sentence, speech, the etymology of words, that words are separable into letters and sounds and syllables of vowels and consonants—I have learned to be aware that a word does break down into basic parts or elements. Like my Navajo friend who is taking the Navajo language course, I have on occasion come to expect—even demand—that I hear and perceive the separated elements of Indian spoken words.

But, as my father has said, a word does not break down into separate elements. A word is complete.

In the same way, a song really does not break down into separate elements. In the minds and views of the people singing at my home or in a Navajo religious ceremony, for whatever purpose that song is meant and used, whether it be for prayer, a dancing event, or as part of a story, the song does not break down. It is part of the complete voice of a person.

Language, when it is regarded not only as expression but is realized as experience as well, works in and is of that manner. Language is perception of experience as well as expression.

Technically, language can be disassembled according to linguistic function, which mainly deals with the expression part of it. You can derive—subsequently define—how a language is formed, how and for what purpose it is used, and its development in a context. But when the totality is considered, language as experience and expression, it doesn't break down so easily and conveniently. And there is no need to break it down and define its parts.

Language as expression and perception—that is at the core of what a song is. This relates to how my father teaches and sings a song and how a poet teaches and speaks a poem.

*There is a steel vise at one end of the table my father works at. He clamps a handling piece of wood in it. This pine is the torso of an Eagle Dancer. The Dancer is slim and his chest is kind of concave. The eagle is about to fly aloft, and my father files a bit of the hard upper belly with a rasp. Later, he will paint the dancing Eagle man who was emerged out of the wood.*

*My father built the small house in which we sit. The sandstone was quarried near Shuutuh Tasigaiyamishrouh, on the plateau uplift south of here, toward Acu. This is his workshop. It has a couple of windows and a handmade door because he couldn't find the right size door at the lumberyard in Grants, where he trades. The single room is very secure and warm when he has a fire built on cold days in the woodstove, which is one of those that looks like a low-slung hog.*

*There are a couple of chairs on which we sit and the table with his work and bed in a corner. There is a stock of shelves against the eastern wall. My mother stores her pottery there. The pottery is covered with some cloth, which formerly used to sack flour. I think there is a box of carpentry tools on the floor below the lowest shelf. Against another wall is a bookcase, which doesn't hold books. Mainly, there are pieces of wood that my father is carving—some he started and didn't feel right about or had broken and he has laid aside—and a couple of sheep vertebrae he said he is going to make into bolo ties but hasn't gotten around to yet. And a*

*couple of small boxes, one of them a shoebox, and the other a homemade*
*one of thin ply board in which are contained the items he uses for his*
*duties as a cacique.*

*He is one of the elders of the Antelope people, who are in charge of all*
*the spiritual practice and philosophy of our people, the Aacqumeh. He*
*and his uncles are responsible for things continuing in the manner that*
*they have since time began for us, and in this sense he is indeed a one-*
*thousand-year-old man. In the box are the necessary items that go with*
*prayer: the feathers, pollen, precious bits of stone and shell, cotton string,*
*earth paints, cornmeal, tobacco, and other things. The feathers of various*
*birds are wrapped in several-years-old newspaper to keep the feathers*
*smoothed. It is his duty to insure that the prayer songs of the many and*
*various religious ceremonies survive and continue.*

*My father sings and I listen.*

Song at the very beginning was experience. There was no division between experience and expression. Even now I don't think
there is much of a division except arbitrary. Take a child, for
example, when he makes a song at his play, especially when he is
alone. In his song he tells about the experience of the sensations
he is feeling at the moment with his body and mind. And the song
comes about as words and sounds—expression. But essentially, in
those moments the song that he is singing is what he is experiencing. The child's song is both perception of that experience and
his expression of it.

The meaning that comes from the songs as expression and perception comes out of and is what the song is.

"Stah wah maiyanith, Muukai-tra Shahyaika, duuwahsteh
duumahsthee dyahnie guuhyoutseh mah-ah. Wahyuuhuunah
wahyuuhuu huu nai ah."

This is a hunting song, which occurs to me because it is near
deer-hunting season. I look around the countryside here, the

pinion and the mountains nearby, and feel that I might go hunting soon, in November. The meaning the song has for me is in the context of what I am thinking, of what I want and perhaps will do. The words are translatable into English.

"My helping guide, Mountain Lion Hunting Spirit Friend, in this direction, to this point bring the Deer to me. *Wahyuuhuunah wahyuuhuu huu nai ah.*"

The latter part of the song is a chanted phrase that is included with all hunting songs. The meaning—the song for the hunt, asking for guidance and help—is conveyed in English as well. There is no problem in deciphering the original meaning, and I don't think there ever really is when a song is taken to be both expression and perception.

The meaning for me is that I recognize myself as a person in an active relationship—the hunting act—with Mountain Lion, the spirit friend and guide, and Deer. It is a prayer. A prayer song. The meaning that it has, further, is that things will return unto me if I do things well in a manner that is possible, if I use myself and whatever power I have appropriately. The purpose of the song is first of all to do things well, the way that they're supposed to be done, part of it being the singing and performing of the song, and that I receive, again well and properly, the things that are meant to be returned unto me. I express myself as well as realize the experience.

There is also something in a song that is actually substantial. When you talk or sing with words that are just words—or seem to be mere words—you sometimes feel that they are too ethereal, even fleeting. But when you realize the significance of what something means to you, then they are very tangible. You value the meaning of the song for its motion in the dance and the expression and perception it allows you. You realize its inherent quality by the feeling that a song gives you. You become aware of the quietness that comes upon you when you sing or hear a song of quiet quality. You not only feel it—you know. The substance is emotional, but beyond that, spiritual, and it's real and you are present in and part of it. The act of the song, which you are experiencing, is real, and the reality is its substance.

A song is made substantial by its context—its reality—both that which is there and what is brought about by the song. The context in which the song is sung or that a prayer song makes possible is what makes a song substantial, gives it the quality of realness. The emotional, cultural, spiritual context in which we thrive—in that, the song is meaningful. The context has not only to do with your being physically present, but also with the context of the mind, how receptive it is, which usually means familiarity with the culture in which the song is sung.

A song can be anything or can focus on a specific event or act but includes in it all things. This is very important to realize when you are trying to understand and learn more than just the words or the technical facility of words in a song or poem. This means that one has to recognize that language is more than just a group of words and more than just the technical relationship between sounds and words. Language is more than just a functional mechanism. It is a spiritual energy that is available to all. It includes all of us and is not exclusively in the power of human beings—we are part of that power as human beings.

Oftentimes, I think we become overly convinced of the efficiency of our use of language. We begin to regard language too casually, thereby taking it for granted, and we forget the sacredness of it. Losing this regard, we become quite careless with how we use and perceive language. We forget that language beyond its mechanics is a spiritual force.

When you regard the sacred nature of language, you realize that you are part of it and it is part of you. You are not necessarily in control of it, and if you do control some of it, it is not in your exclusive control. Upon this realization, I think there are all possibilities of expression and perception, which become available.

*This morning my father said to my mother and me, "On Saturday I am going to go hunting. I am telling you now. I will begin to work on Tuesday for it." He means that he will begin preparations for it. He explained that my brother-in-law will come for him on Friday, and they are going to hunt in Arizona. This is part of it, I know, the proper explanation of intention and purpose. I have heard him say since I was a boy.*

*The preparations are always done with a sense of excitement and enjoyment. Stories are remembered.*

*Page was a good storyteller. I don't know why he was called Page—I suppose there is a story behind his name but I don't know it. Page was getting older when this happened. He couldn't see very well anymore, but he was taken along with a group of other hunters. "I was to be the kuus-teenhruu," he said. The camp cook sticks around the camp, sings songs, and makes prayers for the men out hunting, and waits, and fixes the food. Page got tired of doing that. He said, "I decided that it wouldn't hurt if I just went out of camp a little ways. I was sort of getting tired sticking around. And so I did; I wasn't that blind."*

*He walked a ways out of their camp, you know, looking around, searching the ground for tracks. And he found some, great big ones. He said, "It must be my good fortune that I am to get a big one. I guess I'm living right," and he reached into his corn food bag and got some meal and sprinkled it with some precious stones and beads and pollen into the big tracks. He said, "Thank you for leaving your tracks, and now I ask you to wait for me, I am right behind you." And putting his mind in order, he followed the tracks, looking up once in a while to see if the large deer he was already seeing in his mind was up ahead.*

"I was sure in a good mood," Page said, and he would smile real big. "Every once in a while I sprinkled corn food and precious things in the tracks. They were big," he said, and he would hold out his large hand to show you how big, "and I would sing under my breath." He followed along, kind of slow, you know, because he was an old man and because of his eyes, until he came down this slope that wasn't too steep. There was an oak bush thicket at the bottom of it. He put his fingers upon the tracks to let it know that he was right behind, and the tracks felt very warm.

He said, "Ah haiee, there you will be in the thicket. There is where we will meet," and he prayed one more time and concluded his song and set his mind right and checked to make sure his gun was ready—I don't know what kind of rifle he had but it was probably and old one too. And he made his way to the thicket very carefully, very quietly, slightly bent down to see under the branches of the oak. And then he heard it moving around in the thicket, and he said quietly, "Ah haiee, I can hear that you're a big one. Come to me now, it is time, and I think we are both ready," just to make sure that his spirit was exactly right. And he crouched down to look and there it was some yards into the thicket and he put his rifle to his shoulder and searched for a vital spot, and then it turned to him and it was a pig.

"Kohjeeno!" Page said, his breath exhaling. He lowered his rifle, cussed a bit, and then he raised his rifle and said, "Kohjeeno, I guess you'll have to be my kquuyaitih today," and shot the pig. He cut the pig's throat to let the blood and then on the way back to camp he tried to find all the precious stones he had dropped in the tracks of the pig.

After that, until he went back north—passed away—his nephews and grandsons would say to him, "Uncle, tell us about the time the kohjeeno was your kquuyaitih." And Page would frown, indignant a bit, and then he would smile and say, "Keehamaa dzee, we went hunting to Brushy Mountain . . ."

The song is basic to all vocal expression. The song as expression is an opening from inside yourself to outside and from outside yourself to inside but not in the sense that there are separate states of yourself. Instead, it is a joining and an opening together. Song is the experience of that opening or road, if you prefer, and there is no separation of parts, no division between expression and perception.

I think that is what has oftentimes happened with our use of English. We think of English as a very definitive language, useful in defining things—which means setting limits. But that's not what language is supposed to be. Language is not definition: Language is all expansive. We, thinking ourselves capable of the task, assign rules and roles to language unnecessarily. Therefore, we limit our words, our language, and we limit our perception, our under-standing, and our knowledge.

Children don't limit their words until they learn how, until they're told that it's better if they use definitive words. This is what happens to most everyone in formal educational situations. Education defines you. It makes you see with and within very defini-tive limits. Unless you teach and learn language in such a way as to permit it to remain or for it to become all expansive—and truly visionary—your expressiveness and perceptions will be limited and even divided.

My father teaches that the song is part of the way you're sup-posed to recognize everything, that the singing of it is a way of rec-ognizing this all—inclusiveness because it is a way of expressing yourself and perceiving. It is basically a way to understand and appreciate your relationship to all things. The song as language is a way of touching. This is the way my father attempts to teach a song, and I try to listen, feel, know, and learn this way.

When my father sings a song, he tries to instill a sense of aware-ness about us. Although he may remark upon the progressive steps in a song, he does not separate the steps or components of the song. The completeness of the song is the important thing, how a person comes to know and appreciate it, not to especially mark the separate parts of it but know the whole experience of the song.

My father may mention that a particular song was sung sometime before or had been written for a special occasion, but he remembers only in reference to the overall meaning and purpose. It may be an old, old song that he doesn't know the history of or it may be one he has composed himself. He makes me aware of these things because it is important, not only for the song itself, but because it is coming from the core of who my father is, and he is talking about how it is for him in relation to all things. I am especially aware of its part in our lives and that all these things are a part of that song's life. And when he sings the song, I am aware that it comes not only from his expression but from his perception as well.

I listen carefully, but I listen for more than just the sound, listen for more than just the words and phrases, for more than the various parts of the song. I try to perceive the context, meaning, purpose— all these items not in their separate parts but as a whole—and I think it comes completely like that.

A song, a poem, becomes real in that manner. You learn its completeness; you learn the various parts of it but not as separate elements. You learn a song in the way you are supposed to learn a language, as expression and as experience.

I think it is possible to teach song and poetry in a classroom so that language is a real way of teaching and learning. The effort will have to be with conveying the importance and significance of not only the words and sounds but the realness of the song in terms of oneself, context, and the particular language used, community, the totality of what is around. More complete expression and perception will be possible then.

*Yesterday morning, my father went over to Daibuukaiyah to get oak limbs for the Haadramahni—the Prayer Sticks. After he got back he said, "The Haadramahni for hunting are all of hardwoods, like the hahpaani." The oak grows up the canyons, which come out of the lava rock of Horace Mesa.*

*And at his worktable, he shows me: "This is a Haitsee—a Shield if you want to call it that—and it is used as a Guide." It is a thin, splinted strip of hahpaani made into a circle, which will fit into the palm of your hand. "There is a star in the center—I will make it out of string tied to the edges of the circle. This is a guide to find your way, to know the directions by. It is round because the moon is round. It is the night sky, which is a circle all around in which the stars and moon sit. It's a circle, that's why. This is part of it, to know the directions you are going, to know where you are at."*

*He shows me a stick about the thickness of his thumb. The stick is an oak limb split in half, and he runs the edge of his thumbnail along the core of the wood, the dark streak at the very center of the wood. The streak does not run completely straight, but it flows very definitely from one end to the other. And my father says, "This is the Heeyahmani. This is to return you safely. This is so you will know the points on your return back, the straight and safe way. So you will be definite and true on your return course. It is placed at the beginning of your journey. This line here is that, a true road."*

*And then he explains, "I haven't gotten this other stick formed yet, and it is of oak also. It is pointed on both ends, and it is stout, strong." He holds up his right hand, his fingers clutched around the stout oak limb. "It's for strength and courage; manliness. So that in any danger you will be able to overcome the danger. So that you will have the stamina to endure hardship. It is to allow you to know and realize yourself as a man. It is necessary to have also."*

*He tells me these things, and I listen. He says, "Later, we will sing some songs for the hunt. There is a lot to it, not just a few. There are any numbers of prayers. There are all those things you have to do in preparation, before you begin to hunt, and they are all meant to be done not only because they have been done in the past but because they are the way that things, good things, will come about for you. That is the way that you will truly prepare yourself, to be able to go out and find the deer, so that the deer will find you. You do those things in the proper way that you will know the way things are, what's out there, what you must think in approaching them, how you must respond—all those things. They are all part of it—you just don't go and hunt. A person has to be aware of what is around him, and in this way, the preparation, these things that I have here, you will know."*

My father tells me, "This song is a hunting song, listen." He sings and I listen. He may sing it again, and I hear it again. The feeling that I perceive is not only contained in the words but there is something surrounding those words, surrounding the song, and it includes us. It is the relationship that we share with each other and with everything else. And that's the feeling that makes the song real and meaningful and which makes his singing and my listening more than just a teaching and learning situation.

It is that experience—that perception of it—that I mention at the very beginning, which makes it meaningful. You perceive by expressing yourself. This is the way my father teaches a song. And this is the way I try to learn a song. This is the way I try to teach poetry, and the way I try to have people learn from me.

One time my father was singing a song, and this is what the instance in which this—perception by/expression of—became very apparent for me. He was singing this song, and I didn't catch the words offhand. I asked him, and he explained, "This song, I really like it for this old man." And he said, "This old man used to like to sing, and he danced like this." Motioning like the old man's hands, arms, shoulders, he repeated, "This song, I really like it for this old man."

That is what the song was about, I realized. It was both his explanation and the meaning of the song. It was about this old man who danced that way with whom my father shared a good feeling. My father had liked the old man, who was probably a mentor of some sort, and in my father's mind during the process of making the song and when he sang it subsequent times afterward, he was reaffirming the affection he had for the old guy, the way "he danced like this."

My father was expressing to me the experience of that affection, the perceptions of the feelings he had. Indeed, the song was the road from outside himself to inside—which is perception—and from inside himself to outside—which is expression. That's the process and the product of the song, the experience and the vision that a song gives you.

The words, the language of my experience, come from how I understand, how I relate to the world around me, and how I know language as perception. That language allows me vision to see with and by which to know myself.

### Addendum, April 2003

The status of the Acoma language is that it is a strong, continuing language, but like all other Native languages it is affected also by the constant, overpowering, sometimes overwhelming dominance of the English language. People my age and older are strong speakers, a good number of them fluent in the language. Sadly, the following generations, including our children, are not so fluent, and in cases do not speak Native languages at all. There is, however, an insistence by the tribal community on the use of the language, including the teaching of it in tribal language programs.

# X. ALATSEP (WRITTEN DOWN)

## Joseph Dandurand

I was so proud the first time I heard my Indian name called out to witness the work that was to be done. I stood tall and completely at ease as the family doing the work walked over to me and each member placed two quarters into my hand, and thanked me for witnessing the work they were doing that night in a longhouse far into the woods of British Columbia.

That is how that is done, this ritual. Old and repeated like tradition over and over and over again. Other rituals repeated the same. Not talked about. That is true spirituality, true and untouched by history that has been kept hidden and still stays hidden. Only those who live the life and the old ways know the truth.

My name means Written Down and was given to me by our people, the Kwantlen, a small group of river people, fishermen, on the Fraser River. There were twelve of us who were given names. Mine came from my grandfather's side, from the Nooksack tribe just down below us across the border in Washington State. It was then written in our language and translated by a group of elders upriver from our village. No one here at the time spoke our language.

We, the Kwantlen, used to number in the thousands. Now we are one hundred fifty and counting. Our elders are young and most do not know their language nor do they know their traditions. It is sad but it is a reality of what happened here and continues to happen. The greatest destruction to us—residential schools, alcohol, welfare, fishing laws, development—were passed off as attempts to assimilate us. But we struggle onward.

**One Year**

> there seemed to be a quiet moment
> here on this island.
> not sure why.
> maybe because the Indians
> all left long ago.
> just bodies of drink and smoke
> re-telling tales
> of woe and false glory.
>
> (he drops the rope down far enough
> so they cannot see him hanging there.
> he jumps and snaps away his worries.
> little children place flowers on his grave
> and try and remember who he was:
> a father? a son? a man?)
>
> (she covers her baby in wet leaves
> and sharpens the fishing knife for
> her own throat and slips away from
> the desperate voices that yell at her
> to just go ahead and die.
> no children come to her grave.
> old people come and shake their
> heads in disbelief and try to remember

*this girl and her child and they try*
*to remember the old days when*
*dying was so much quicker.)*

*this is one reserve of a thousand others.*
*here they fish and laugh and hide*
*from the spirits that walk and fly in*
*and about the cedar trees.*
*the world and water passes by.*
*the moon and sun creep over mountains.*
*animals and birds talk and stare.*
*everything is quiet in this moment.*

*a small girl walks towards the river filling*
*her pockets full of ancient stones.*

*she steps over the edge and is gone forever.*

There is that struggle within that is kept hidden. What about abuse and alcohol and lost spirituality? I see it every day. I see lost people drunk or angry and unable to get past it all. What about their names? What were their names?

In my village we try to do the best we can, but we are limited by the connection we have with a greater society, which ate us up and continues to eat us up. It just does it in a quieter way. The quiet revolution of the not-talked-about assimilation of Natives. I feel those Natives who do not live where their ancestors live are in trouble and are unable to fulfill their true destinies.

For me, I came home seven years ago and discovered my reason. It was to become a good man, a good father. It was to discover that I *am* Indian even after thirty years of calling myself Indian. I was given a name and I stand proud every time someone calls me X.alatsep.

I have a hard time now going into the city or taking part in the conferences on Native literature, or even trying to publish or produce one of my plays. I feel I do not belong to that. I feel that is a part of the greater society, one that on the one hand glorifies my history and on the other attempts to oppress me. The greater society's history represses me. Its life attempts to threaten my survival.

### Fort Langley

you can see the fort from where I live.

wooden walls,
trees,
desperate voices.

they call to me,

"come on over,
come on over,
come on."

"shut up, shut up and
stay over there." I say.

used to drink at their bar,
used to sip whiskey,
used to fight,
used to be blind from it all.

*now*
*I stare at their walls.*
*wooden walls.*
*thick with history.*

*many men and women never made it home.*
*they found them trying to climb over the walls.*
*whiskey bottles broken and empty roll down to the river,*
*laceless shoes sit silent as if waiting to fit someone else,*
*a picture of someone's mother blows away and over the walls,*
*the gate is closed.*

*the fort.*
*over that way.*
*over past the mass grave.*
*smallpox.*
*you ever seen smallpox?*
*pretty ugly.*
*not as pretty*
*as wooden walls.*

## Before Me

*read a book about the past.*
*it seemed real enough for me to go there.*
*so I went.*
*1900, something or other.*
*old time.*
*back then.*
*before me.*
*before.*

*river looked the same,*
*treacherous,*
*silent,*
*unforgiving.*

*more trees than now.*
*more eagles,*
*deer,*
*salmon,*
*humans with faces.*

*saw them.*
*they wore the paint,*
*not like now,*
*not like humans now.*

*I tried to talk to them*
*but the river came and got me,*
*it took me down,*
*shit,*
*I think my shoes fell off.*
*my toes touched the bottom.*

*I woke up as the ones with paint*
*came to me and told me never,*
*never tell.*

*"tell what?"*

*no answer.*

*"tell what?"*

*only water.*
*I found my shoes,*
*they were next to my bed,*
*right where I left them.*

*the past.*
*before.*
*before me.*
*so clouded,*
*so uneven.*

*future.*
*after.*
*after me.*
*eternity,*
*I think.*

*eternal water.*
*the paint.*
*faces.*
*humans with paint on their faces.*
*brothers and sisters.*
*crying the song,*
*drumming the past.*

*never.*
*never read a book about your past.*
*it becomes you.*
*you become it.*

*my face,*
*it has the paint.*

*my voice,*
*it has my song.*

*my eyes,*
*they have never,*
*ever,*
*let go.*

What about my history? What about my spirituality? I cannot and will not ever write it down. True Native spirituality is not talked about, is not shared with those who cannot truly be a part of it. The only way you can learn about true Native spirituality is to become a part of it. To leave this world and go to the other side.

It is so sad that another's religion has clouded my village's beliefs. We are shrouded in shame. Not shame of religion but that of selfish demons within religion, and there are many. We still hear about them today. The abusers. The pedophiles. The angry nuns and the abusive priests. Their torment continues today as I hear the footsteps coming down the hall. The footsteps of one man abused by another in a residential school. He smiles his toothless smile as he stinks of abuse and weed. His sixty-five-year-old mind destroyed by drugs and alcohol. His weary child smile stinks of assimilation.

### St. Mary's I

*night.*
*all the little christians are in their beds.*
*except for muh.*

*a little guy of about 10 or 11.*
*skinny.*
*brown.*
*short hair.*
*cut by god.*

*he stares out the window.*
*the moon.*
*full.*
*talks to him.*
*tells him that his mother is sick.*
*dying.*
*smallpox.*
*killing her slow.*
*the moon rises.*
*getting farther away.*
*harder to hear.*
*hear the words.*
*the song.*
*the drum.*

*"hey, muh."*

*"quiet"*

*"hey, muh."*

*"what?"*

*"what're you looking for?"*

"nothing."

he goes back to his small bed.
pulls his blanket over him.
his brown feet peek out at the bottom.
he's growing big.
just like father.

the moon comes to the window.
lights all the little christians.
their skinny feet poking out of blankets that are too small.

muh falls asleep.
he dreams of his home.
his father cutting wood.
making the fire.
the little house warm for the night.
mother sleeps quietly on her bed.
she moans.
the sickness killing her slowly.
killing her.

the moon.
the moon is on fire.
little christians.
little boys and girls beneath blankets that are too small.
beneath it all.
away from sickness.
away from god.

away from the window

*where*
*a*
*fire-moon*
*burns.*

## St. Mary's II

*a young girl is screaming.*
*screams in the chapel.*
*broken hands.*
*she has been whipped for stealing a smile.*
*told to speak,*
*to speak a tongue not her own.*

*quiet.*
*mass is over.*
*drank the wine.*
*raped the savage.*
*told them to look upon god.*
*to speak only to god.*
*speak his tongue.*
*cross.*
*blood.*
*guilt.*
*pain.*
*anguish.*
*savage.*
*cross.*
*nailed.*
*nails.*
*no screams.*

brother on top of a little girl from up that way.
screams beneath pillow.
moan.
groan.
pain.
cross swings from his sacred chest.

"you are my gift from the lord, my little child."

screams.
alone in her bed.

"hey, puh," muh whispers.

"hey, puh!"

no answer,
only silent screams.
pain.
anguish.
savage.

the ripping of the cross leaves
its distinguishing mark upon this girl.

later.
much later,
when she hangs from that tree,
you swear she looks
like a hungry crucifix
as it

*gently*
*swings.*

## St. Mary's III

*"next time, young man,*
*you will shovel until morning*
*mass is over. Do you understand?"*

*"yes, Father."*

*"good. now carry on."*

*st. mary's res. school.*
*catholics with a vengeance for extracting*
*the severest of all confessions from*
*little brown kids.*
*little indians.*
*savages.*

*"hey, muh." no answer.*

*"hey, muh."*

*"what?"*

*"you save any bread from breakfast?"*

*"yes."*

*"can I have a piece?"*

*"sure."*

*a small hand,*
*brown,*
*breaks a piece of bread in half*
*and passes it to another small hand,*
*the hand of a savage.*

*"thanks, muh."*

*winter on the west coast.*
*rain.*
*cold.*
*1954.*
*laughter in the trees away from the school.*
*laughter of children.*
*they're playing a game of tag.*

*"you're it."*

*"you're it."*

*"no way."*

*"yes."*

*"no."*

*"yes."*

*"you're it."*

*"no way."*

*giggles.*
*laughter.*
*silence.*
*everyone hiding.*
*black robes appear.*
*a bible in hand.*
*a cigarette in the other.*
*brother john.*
*his big belly rumbles.*
*not enough bread for breakfast.*
*lights the smoke.*
*blows it into the coolness of the winter morning.*
*no laughter.*
*brown eyes staring through the wet trees.*
*branches swing with cold wind.*
*brother john smokes his smoke,*
*unaware of the children.*
*unaware of the eyes upon him.*
*he begins to whistle,*
*he stops,*
*he puffs,*
*he exhales,*
*he stamps his feet.*
*his big belly bounces up and down.*
*a child giggles.*
*the others place their hands around the giggling child's*
*mouth.*
*silence.*
*rumbling of a big belly.*

*need more bread.*
*need more bread.*
*cigarette stamped out.*
*black robes walks away.*
*giggling child pulls away from the others.*

*"you're it."*

*"you're it."*

## St. Mary's IV

*1955.*
*down by the river.*
*puh and muh fishing.*
*quiet sunday afternoon.*
*all the chores have been finished.*
*catholics are in the fields searching for lovely flowers to pick,*
*to smell,*
*to taste.*

*puh hooks the first one.*
*her little arms holding on,*
*holding,*
*pulling,*
*pulling.*
*the fish snaps up into the air and looks around.*
*its eyes staring right at her.*
*little indian girl.*
*little fisherman.*
*little gift from above.*

*her hands grasp the pole,*
*her eyes widen,*
*her breath quickens.*
*flowers picked out of earth.*
*snapped at the stem.*
*noses sniffing the air,*
*searching for the scent of god.*
*all his creations.*
*now devoured by humans.*
*flowers,*
*fish,*
*little indians with crosses around their necks.*
*flowers.*
*lovely flowers.*
*fish.*
*it jumps once more and snaps the line.*
*going down to the bottom.*
*down where the water is calm.*
*it rests.*
*swallows the fat worm.*
*unaware of the creation.*
*unaware.*

*muh gets a nibble.*
*the hairs on his arms stand up.*
*catholics singing in the fields.*
*songs about glory and salvation.*
*muh dances the worm.*
*singing his song beneath his breath,*
*soft enough so the nuns do not hear him.*

*he shuffles his feet,*

*trying to remember his dance.*

*worm dances beneath the water.*

*a salmon spots it.*

*swims towards it.*

*hunger.*

*dance.*

*song.*

*shuffling of bare brown feet.*

*fields of flowers.*

*fields of salvation.*

*river.*

*water.*

*fish takes the worm.*

*fields of song.*

*worm becomes a hook.*

*the salmon snaps its head to the left and then to the right.*

*hook goes deeper.*

*muh pulls.*

*his little indian arms pulling.*

*his song getting louder.*

*his feet quickening to the beat of the drum inside his head.*

*he pulls,*

*he sings,*

*he shuffles his feet like the old days,*

*like the days back home.*

*he pulls the fish out of the water.*

*he takes a small club-like branch*

*and snaps the fish on top of the head twice.*

*fish stops.*

*muh pulls the hook and what is left*

*of the worm out of the fish's mouth.*
*drops it back into the river.*

*fields of flowers.*
*songs of glory and salvation.*

*two indian kids on the river's edge.*
*1955.*
*worms on hooks.*
*songs.*
*drum.*
*paint.*
*memories of home.*
*silently breathing songs of glory.*

So, with my name that I carry so proudly and the spirit that I now have I walk onward, trying my best to soothe the worries of the less fortunate. I help those who cannot help themselves. I try my best to protect my family from harm from the outside world and the world that we live in. I try to walk the good life. I am gentle to those who do not understand. I do my best to teach those who wish to listen.

That is greatest lesson of all, one that I learned on my journey to where I am now. The greatest lesson we can all learn is to listen, to open your ears and listen and learn. If you never listen, how can you move forward? Listen and learn and take care of yourself and your spirit.

My name is X.alatsep (Written Down).

## Feeding the Hungry
*blue jays nest beside my legs.*

flying to eat winter bugs juicy with nectar.
black birds squawk at me and my day.
telling me that I should've stayed in bed.

spring.
day.
mid-afternoon.
quiet.
no one about.
just me and the island.
no one drunk on the side of the road,
not even me,
not even my spirit.

blue jays eat big worms.
choking on their hunger.
chewing too quickly.
throwing up the day.
the day.
quiet.
no one dead.
everyone alive.
even the old ones in the trees.
they squawk at the warm wind.

blowing dust into the eyes of birds:
blue and black.
tired and hungered by the length of the winter months.
skinny birds nest in swampy waters,
their wings too weak to fly.

*they stand and stare at the owl as she dives for unsuspecting*
*mice.*
*the cracking of their skulls echoes around this island.*

*this island where everyone is alive.*
*this island where spirits eat you.*
*you can hear their songs pounding in the trees.*

*can you hear them?*

*quiet.*
*owl dives.*
*cracking bones.*
*drum.*
*whispers of the old ones.*
*something touches my arm.*
*I open my eyes.*
*it was my spirit.*

*someone forgot to feed him.*

# DON'T TALK, DON'T LIVE

## Carol Snow Moon Bachofner

The story I am about to tell is a harsh one, telling how my own family was ashamed to be what they are: Abenakis. I know this denial was for survival, to keep away insults and disrespect. So for their sakes I must begin with the traditional Abenaki apology, to show that I don't wish to offend or misrepresent my relatives: *Anhaldam mawi kassipalilawalan* (Forgive me if I have wronged you). But I believe that silence is more destructive and deadly than protecting oneself. So I must tell it.

Even in private, our family didn't often discuss being Indian, although my great-grandmother smoked her clay pipe openly at the dinner table and we knew why. Whenever a child would ask why, there would be the curt reply "Well, Nana is an Abenaki Indian, and Abenaki women smoke," along with a reminder that this was private and we should not talk about it. We were told that we shouldn't tell people we had any Indian blood, we should just say we're French Canadian.

I was never okay with the subterfuge in our family. I kept asking questions of my great-grandmother, who was happy to talk to me. Whenever my mother and father were out of the room, Nana B. allowed me to pinch the special tobacco mixture into her pipe and light it for her. When I said it smelled funny, she told me how the Creator made the tobacco for our people and that it was special, not like what people smoked in cigarettes or cigars. She also let me help carry plates of food outside to the edge of the woods behind the house for the little people who lived there. She told me that these little people always helped our people in times of trouble and that we needed to thank and help them. Whenever I picked blueberries, I'd tuck the fattest ones under the bushes for these folks, thinking maybe they were so small, they couldn't reach up high enough to pick their own. Later, when I was told stories of leprechauns in Ireland, I wondered if these were our little people who had to move to Ireland because we didn't thank or help them enough.

Nana B. told me to be proud to be an Abenaki, and that the Abenaki people were alive, living through her blood in me. She also told me in one of the saddest voices I've ever heard that our language was dying. I remember the tears in her eyes when she whispered that to me. I wondered how a people could be alive and their language be dead. She said, "Don't talk, don't live. It's that simple." I wanted to learn to speak the Abenaki language so it wouldn't die, so I wouldn't die.

In each generation it seemed that one child stood out boldly in family photos as darker, more "Indian-looking" than the rest. In my generation I was the "designated papoose" in the group pictures. My eyes and hair were a deeper shade of brown, my cheeks rounder, and my smile distinctly different and more serious. I also became the one who got to know the old stories and gain exposure to the old way of talking, however limited. I craved going to visit my great-grandmother and hear about how we came to live on this continent and how kind our people were, how they loved to dance and sing and tell stories. I loved the music in the words she whispered to me, like a prayer only she and I were lucky enough to say.

I was surprised at how very French the words sounded. Nana B.

explained to me that during King Philip's War the Abenaki were under attack all over New England, and many fled over the invisible border between Canada and the United States. There were already many Abenakis living near Quebec at Odanak, and our people were happy to be together and safe. In fact, there are still a few Native speakers living near Odanak today, but precious few. Once the war was over, many tribal families from New England returned home. Nana said that this exodus caused the language to take on a clearly more French sound. I asked if maybe that was the Creator's way of providing protection, giving us a cover. She nodded. "Ohn, hohn."

Living in Maine in the fifties and sixties, it certainly was easier to be "French Canadian" than to admit being Abenaki Indian. In my hometown of York, there is a famous "massacre site," Snowshoe Rock, which somehow became the focus of schoolroom discussion in our Maine history classes every year. Teachers, well-meaning to be sure, pointed out how the "bloodthirsty" Abenaki Indians came sneaking into town in the middle of a winter night to kill the men and capture women and children. The story tells how the Indians leaned their snowshoes against the rock and made their way several miles through the deep snow to town to do their ill deeds. Of course this story is not even logical. No Indian who needed snowshoes to travel would abandon them at a point far from his intended destination. But stories about Indians' misdeeds are rarely accurate, and the wilder they are, the more they make for exciting lore. Exciting or not, I didn't want to be known as a bloodthirsty Indian, so I went deep into the family cover story. I was French Canadian.

In eighth grade, in a class on the geography of Maine, I ran smack-dab into the Abenaki language. One of the requirements of the class was that we each had to memorize the name of every river and lake in the state, along with the names of the towns. Our teacher said that the names were hard to say because they were originally Indian names. I was fascinated. He told us that the original inhabitants of the land knew nearly every river or lake or pond by words that described them. I knew that the name of the road where my house was had an Abenaki name because my mother told me. Organug Road. It sounded wonderful in my ears. But now I was hearing lots of Abenaki words in the names of the ponds, lakes, rivers, streams, towns: *Piscataqua, Androscoggin, Norridgewock, Mooselukmeguntuk, Khatadin*. The words were so musical, so mystical, so very magical in my ears. While others in the class struggled to pronounce them, these words seemed to roll right off my tongue as if they had been sleeping there in my throat, waiting to get out. Still, I didn't dare to say it: "I am Abenaki." My teacher said I had a flair for languages and should probably take French in high school.

When I was still a young girl, Nana B. gave me her special little brown basket, telling me it held stories, language. She said that the basket held all I'd need to be a good Abenaki woman someday. It looked empty to me. I admit that I started believing what everyone said: that she was old and addled. But I never gave up my little basket, my *abazenoda*. I kept treasures and necessities in it, things like prized shells, buttons, bobby pins, hair ribbons, little feathers or pebbles I found on the beach. I took the basket with me when I went away to college. Somewhere deep inside I think I knew that someday I would find something special in there, something Indian, some clue about the real me, the Abenaki me. After Nana B. died, I wondered if I would ever hear any Abenaki words again. I wondered if the language had died with her. I looked around me and all I saw was white, all I heard was English and French. I kept looking into the basket, waiting to see or hear something Abenaki.

By age forty I was fully involved in the Abenaki culture to the extent one can be at a three-thousand-mile distance from home country. I was living in California and part of an intertribal circle. As part of the circle, I fasted twice a year for four days and took part in traditional pipe ceremonies and sweats. At a fast on tribal lands near Palm Springs, I heard someone speaking distinctly like Nana B. An Ojibwe priest was speaking Ojibwe. It sounded so much like Nana's language. I was happy to hear the rolling throaty sounds. I wanted more. I told him what Nana had said and asked him how I could find a way to learn Abenaki. He gave me the best possible advice: Start with the word for the Creator and He will slowly give you the rest. Father John gave me the names of people I could contact, Gordon Day and Jeanne Brink, who were working on an Abenaki dictionary. I tucked the slip of paper he gave me into Nana's basket and breathed the name of the Creator aloud in the sweat lodge that night. I had begun my journey back to life. Father John called me cousin. I was proud. I was happy. I set out diligently to reclaim my own culture. And I have. Talk, live. I contacted Jeanne Brink and got language lessons, tapes, and eventually the dictionary. I searched out every Abenaki I could find and begged for whatever bits of language they knew.

But I am still discriminated against at every turn. Four years ago, I was registering at a local college for a couple of classes I needed to complete a degree program. I dutifully and proudly checked the box "Native American Indian" and presented the forms to the lady at the registration window. She took an eraser and unchecked the box, checking instead "Caucasian." I must have checked the box in error and she had fixed that for me. I told her I had not made an error, and she said, " Well, you don't *look* Indian." No beads, feathers, or hooked nose: obviously not Indian. I offered to go to my car and bring her my Jay Treaty papers, to show her that the

United States government had admitted I am Abenaki, authentic as Sitting Bull. I told her I smoked a pipe like my great-grandmother and that I didn't wear my feathers around campus. My level of sarcasm was rising by the minute along with my level of hurt. She grudgingly changed the form.

Now in graduate school, I am planning to write my thesis on the Native poets of the northeastern tribes. I want to show that they are not second-class citizens in the world of literary accomplishment or talent. This school is prestigious and is located in an area fairly near where the Abenaki live. It amazed me, however, that no one there seemed aware that there are any Indians anywhere close by. In fact, the former governor of Vermont had recently asserted that "there are no Abenakis in Vermont today, only Vermonters." His weak and demeaning remarks may be interpreted by some to be generous and inclusive. But they are the same disclaiming and wounding remarks as ever. They are remarks that serve to wipe out a culture.

Despite the proximity of this college to tribal lands and Abenaki people, and despite my assertion that I have a responsibility to my culture, of the college I attend, the faculty adviser to whom I first mentioned the proposed topic failed to see its importance or seriousness. He attempted to hold me off from getting started on it, and referred to it as my "little Native American project." At one point he actually told me that I didn't have a proper grasp on how to write within the culture, suggesting changes that made the poem distinctly white in outlook and style. Age fifty-six and still the discrimination, the cultural genocide, continue. I have since found an adviser who is not only sensitive but also encouraging of my thesis planning. He is urging me on in my reading and my writing. He appreciates when I include the Abenaki language in the poems I write. And Father John was right: The words are really flowing now.

Speak, live. One word at a time I keep my people alive, and I honor my grandmother. I honor the land, *Ndakinna*. And I will continue to write from my heart, the heart of an Abenaki woman, *Alnobaskwa*. I will strive to put my people in the best, most truthful light. I will not suffer discrimination anymore because I choose not to suffer, but to correct. *Ktsi Wliwini*, great thanks.

# Iah Enionkwatewennahton`se`:
# We Will Not Lose Our Words

### James Aronhiotas Stevens

"The Mush Hole," also known as the Mohawk Institute; founded in 1831 in Brantford, Ontario, Canada, by the New England Company, a Protestant mission based in Britain. Renovated as Woodland Cultural Centre.

Thomas Asylum for Orphaned and Destitute Indian Children, later known as "Thomas Indian School," was founded in 1854 in Irving, New York, Cattaraugus Seneca Reservation by Philip E. Thomas, a wealthy Quaker merchant of Baltimore, Maryland. Main building standing but windowless.

Language in the Burnham and Bero families; dismantling begun in the late nineteenth century. Structure unsound and listing badly, but possibility of future renovation.

The loss of the Mohawk language in my mother's family began with her paternal grandfather, my great-grandfather, or *Double-Totah*, as Mohawk kids might say today. *Totah* is the word for any respected elder but is most often used for a grandparent. My great–grandfather James Burnham was born on the Six Nations Reserve, bordering the city of Brantford, Ontario. Orphaned as a child, he was schooled at "the Mush Hole," and grew up not speaking his own language, *Kanienkehaka*, or Mohawk. Later he would marry Ida Anderson. Ida was from a farming family in Oshweken and still spoke Mohawk fluently, but as English was the language of their interpersonal communication, the children, including my grandfather Earl, did not learn it.

My grandmother, Esther Bero, was born at the Saint Regis, or Akwesasne Mohawk Reservation in Upstate New York. Her mother, Harriet, died when my grandmother was fifteen, with six children even younger. The three eldest, Esther, Mary, and Irene, were old enough to stay with their father. The next three, Thomas, Ray, and Leona were sent away to the Thomas Indian School on the Cattaraugus Reservation, where their language was dissolved. My aunt Lena at Akwesasne adopted the baby, Eva, born while my great–grandmother was bedridden. Her language remained intact, along with that of the three eldest children.

At the age of seven, while my iron-working great-grandfather had taken his family to Syracuse, a white man abducted my grand–mother, the *Totah* in my family. At seven she spoke no English other than her name and address, not her true name, *Kanarathakwas*, but Esther Bero. As the man dragged my grand–mother through the side streets of Syracuse, they passed a young couple and my grandmother was able to tear away from her abductor and cling to the legs of the passing woman, repeating her name and address over and over. The man, of course, took the opportunity to escape. This event most likely signaled to Esther's parents the importance of learning English.

My grandparents, Esther and Earl, met at an Indian Defense League function in Niagara Falls, New York. My grandfather's family from Six Nations, though no longer Mohawk-speaking, was very active in Indian rights, especially concerning border issues, since his whole family had by then moved stateside. Meanwhile, my *Totah*'s father had brought her and her siblings to live in Nia-gara Falls. Totah and Grandpa met for one date, then Totah had to leave to go back to Akwesasne; however, they remained in touch and were married after her return. My mother, Judith, is the first of six children born to them. Though involved in Indian functions, the children were never taught Mohawk. Again, English was the shared language between their parents. Certain phrases have survived, such as *Kanaron'kwa* (I love you); *She'kon, skennonkowa?* (Hello, are you well?, in the great peace); and others, but there is no fluency.

The transliteration of Mohawk to English letters, while making the language more accessible to non-Native scholars, actually aided in its deterioration. Most people I know who are fluent in the language do not read it in its written form, as the chosen letters don't function in a way that makes sense to them. My *Totah*, who can readily say *Kanaron'kwa* in her mother tongue, writes *Gonalunkwa* on birthday cards. Why is it that a word as simple as the word for yes, *hen*, can confuse a reader? Because the word is pronounced as two trochaic syllables with a nasal, sounding more like *huh'uh*. Hello, or *she'kon*, is pronounced *say'go*. These are the small words. Imagine how daunted one feels on encountering a word like *enionkwatewennahton'se'*, meaning "We will lose our words."

Early dictionaries, before it was settled upon that *t* and *th* equal *d*, *k* is *g*, *r* is *l*, and so on, are often easier to read, as they are simply written phonetically; although, one must take into account the rules of the translator's language, for example the Dutch *j* as *y* in the following texts, beginning with a short Mohawk vocabulary list written in 1624 by Nicolaes Janszoon van Wassenaer. This would be followed by van den Bogaert's 1635 text, and Johannes Megapolensis's list of 1644. These brief lexicons are of very little use to modern-day Mohawks for two reasons. First, many of us have become familiar now with the accepted transliteration system, and secondly, lexicons such as Megapolensis's are full of phrases indicative of missionary zeal.

For example: *Tkoschs ko aguweechon Kajingahaga kouaane Jountuckcha Othkon* means "Really, all the Mohawks are cunning devils."

This phrase has never come in useful in my own life, nor have I found much more in Megapolensis's text useful. This example is from one of the two dictionaries I had available to me as a teenager. The other is actually a small pamphlet, which was compiled at Akwesasne in 1975. The words are only roughly in alphabetical order, with corrections made in pen before photocopying.

At least twenty years during my childhood and young adult life were spent visiting my grandparents' home on the Tuscarora Reservation, six miles from my own family's home. Though surrounded by great leaders and activists like their neighbors Chief Clinton Rickard and Mad Bear Anderson, my ancestral language—obviously a key element in language acquisition, did not surround me.

Due to the availability of work at factories in Niagara Falls, and my grandfather's job at the Carborundum Company, my grandparents sought a place to live at the nearby Tuscarora Reservation. This push toward the cities in order to find work is responsible for much of Native American language loss. In particular, so many Iroquois and Anishnaabe men left for the cities to find ironwork. My grandparents were lucky, as they could at least live surrounded by Iroquois culture, if not language. The Tuscaroras, one of the six nations of the Haudenosaunee Confederacy, readily accepted them, and they stayed for a period of some twenty years. In the time I spent on that reservation while growing up, I don't remember hearing anything other than English, unless it was at an official gathering such as the Tuscarora picnic, a much-anticipated event with its nighttime fireball game. Now the Tuscarora School has implemented a language program, and signs on the reservation, including traffic signs, are written in Tuscarora.

Ironically, I first became seriously interested in the Mohawk language upon moving to New York City after high school. I lived in the Williamsburg section of Brooklyn before its gentrification, and although I had originally moved to the city in order to attend the School of Visual Arts, monetary problems forced me to withdraw and I took a job at a café. I later began to work at the Museum of the American Indian—Heye Foundation, now relocated from its Spanish Harlem site to the old New York Custom House and soon to move to the Washington Mall as the Smithsonian's National Museum of the American Indian.

Being surrounded by other Natives who were employed there, Potowatomis, Cherokees, Aymara, Salish, and Hunkpapa Lakota, I was quickly reabsorbed into the Indian world. I began attending powwows at the YMCA and became involved in the American Indian Community House on Broadway and their gallery in SoHo. I was exposed to Spider Woman Theater and the Shinnecock Drum. It was obviously a very different Indian world, dancing on a basketball court at the McBirney Y, but nevertheless, it was Indian.

I began reading as much translation as I could, fascinated by the more comfortable structure of Native languages. I began writing at this point, and *Blue Mesa Review* published the first three poems I wrote, "3 Songs of the Medicine Bundle." This style of writing became more developed when I attended the Institute of American Indian Arts in Santa Fe. By the time I reached graduate school at Brown University's Creative Writing Program, I was working on poetic forms that involved direct translation from Mohawk, meaning instead of translating a word like *akohsa'tens* as horse, I translated it as its linguistic parts, the that aside. This alludes to the way Mohawk people first saw this animal, as reined together, pulling wagons and plows. Ironically, everyone thought I was deeply influenced by "language poetry."

My first book, titled *Tokinish*, a single poem, began formulating in my mind during graduate school. I worked briefly at the Narragansett Tribal House on Friendship Street in Providence as a data collector for a program called Wahteauonk. It was designed to keep children off the city streets after school by providing classes in Native tradition. Many of the children spoke Spanish, but none of them spoke a tribal language. I remember being surprised at two children who were, at least hereditarily, from the Acoma Pueblo. They had never been there and I recall their delight when I showed them photographs I had from a feast day I had attended at the pueblo.

I was interested in the fact that the Narragansett words I saw written on the after-school projects were taken from Roger Williams's 1636 dictionary of Narragansett. People were left to choose Indian names from Williams's *A Key into the Language of America*, as there were not fluent speakers. This forced loss of language has affected the self-identity of countless tribes. I began to relate it to the loss of individual identity in personal relationships also. What happens when we first call another person *mine* and begin our own colonization process? This question, using the Narragansett language as a guide, became *Tokinish*.

Most recently I have used the Mohawk language in a series of poems from my book *Combing the Snakes from His Hair*. These poems stem from a project I deemed *Sui-translation*, translations for the self. These translations are executed in a way that allows for the words to change, in order to create relevancy in one's own life. The following is an example, beginning with Mohawk words, followed by the literal translation, and the sui-translation:

## Canoe Song

*Teiohonwa:ka ne'ni akhonwe:ia. Kon'tatieshon iohnekotatie.*
*Wakkawehatie, wakkawehatie.*

*The canoe is very fast. It is mine. All day I hit the water. I*
*paddle along.*
> *I paddle along.*

> *I am the hull—rapid against your stream.*
> *Birch beneath the ribs*
> *Circumnavigating your body.*
> *Endless propeller of my arm*
> *As it circles to find the flow.*
> *I move this way against you.*
> *I move this way.*

This traditional song is originally intended to be sung while paddling, much like work songs that developed in African American slave communities, rhythmic tunes to help one get through a task. Seeing as I don't often have to travel any distance by canoe, this song could be written off as being useless to me. However, it can and should change in order to become relevant to my life. This goes against what ethnographers and anthropologists have imposed on us since they first began to study us.

As early as the 1930s anthropologists like Elsie Clews Parsons in her two-volume work *Pueblo Indian Religions* were declaring tribes such as the Laguna Pueblo lost causes, due to the fact that their stories had changed since the earliest recordings. That it is one of the tenets of the oral tradition that stories must evolve to create relevancy was never even considered by anthropologists.

How is a canoe song relevant to my life? Every day I move against a stream of other lives, currents of emotion, eddies of fear or pain. Each day my arms reach for another, birch ribs under skin, trying to find a flow of unity. This is how a canoe song helps me. This is what I am trying to show in my work, specifically in the work that relies on Mohawk language for imagery and meaning.

In a recent interview with Mark Anthony Rolo in *The Progressive*, Ojibwe author Louise Erdrich states: "The real life, blood, and guts of a language is in the everyday interactions between people" and "If it's not taught in the home from the very beginning, is that a real language, or is that an academic exercise?"

I wholeheartedly agree with Erdrich, and sadly, I recognize my own knowledge of my language as academic exercise. I love the sound of Mohawk, and its construction is so beautiful to me, but I am a professor, and college teaching positions are not available on the Mohawk Reservation, or even close enough that I could immerse myself in the language. Presently I teach between the Cattaraugus and Allegheny Seneca reservations, to whom I'm indebted for the opportunity to attend occasional lacrosse games and socials; however, I find myself in a place not unlike that of my grandfather and great-grandfather, moving for job opportunity and forced to sacrifice language, if not culture.

In 1997 I moved to Lawrence, Kansas, where I taught at Haskell Indian Nations University for five years until moving back to New York in 2001. I saw many students go through courses in the Choctaw and Cherokee languages, and it was clear the pride with which they would greet me or say good-bye in these languages, but I never knew any of these students to actually have a group in which to converse or move beyond useful phrases. The fact that these courses are offered at all is a great step toward preservation, but the main element lacking in language preservation is a base of Native speakers large enough to support daily conversation. I envy the Diné for their Diné language radio station. And although many of my Diné friends have also ended up in urban areas to find work, there is a large community to return to for interaction with their language.

Recently I did a reading at the University of Maine in Orono, and was glad to see an exhibit at the Hudson Museum concerning the Penobscot Primer Project, where a Native speaker was shown pictures and asked to describe them in Penobscot. The spoken language is recorded and also transliterated on a computer screen. While this provides a record of the language, I feel that until there are committed people willing to create "language nests," as Erdrich calls them, communities of people speaking a single language and passing it on, we are all in danger of losing the thing most important to our tribal identities.

Dorothy Ann Lazore writes in *Iehatien: tere'skwe'* (Prophecy) in the anthology *Kanien'keha' Okara'shon: 'a*: Mohawk Stories:

> On: wa' ki' wenhniserá: te kerihwaién: tere's oh nahó: ten' rati:ton'. Ne kí:ken kén' nón:we nikaná:taien' tenwatté:ni'. Iáh ó:ni' onkwehonwehnéha' thenhshako'nikonhrotákwen iáh ó:ni' ónhka' thaonsaiontatíhseke' nonkwawén:na' enionkwattewennáhton'se' ok ó:ni nonkwaianerénhshera' tenwatté:ni'. O:nen ki' tiotáhsawen tsi teiottenionhátie'.

> (Now, today, I understand what they meant by these stories. This very place will change. We Indians will no longer speak our language, and, along with our words, we will lose our law. Even now it has begun. It is changing.)

• • •

In looking through this book of Mohawk stories today, I come across one of the most beautiful phrases, and it haunts me as I write this—*Ó:nen iehióhe naienenhstaienthó:ko'* (Now is the time, when one should unplant the corn). This idea of harvesting as *unplanting* what one has planted is one of those typical linguistic structures I admire. It is the time for us to unplant our languages, to gather together what has been sown in the generations before. May the prophecy go unfulfilled as we all work toward its *unfulfilling*.

# THE SPIRIT OF LANGUAGE

## Neil McKay

Hau mitakuyepi! Owasin cantewasteya nape ciyuzape do. Cantamaza de miye. Bdewakantunwan Oyate hematanhan k'a Mniwakan Oyate heciya omawapi. Homaksidan heehan, Dakota iwaa owakihi sni. Dehan Dakota waunspewicakiya hemaca. Dakota iapi k'a nakun Dakota wicohan tewahinda. Ho, hecetu do.

Hello my relatives! It is with a good heart that I greet each and every one of you with a handshake. I am Ironheart. I am from the Sacred Lake Dweller nation of the Dakota and I am enrolled at the Spirit Lake Reservation in North Dakota. When I was a boy, I could not speak Dakota. I am now a Dakota language instructor. I cherish the Dakota language and also the Dakota way of life. It is so.

My English name is Neil McKay and I am currently the Dakota language instructor at the University of Minnesota. I am thirty-three years old and I started learning Dakota when I was twenty-five. My mother is an enrollee of the Turtle Mountain Ojibwe Nation. My father is Dakota and attended boarding school at Fort Totten (Spirit Lake) and to this day can speak some Dakota words and phrases. When my father was a boy, he asked his mother why he wasn't being taught Dakota, and like so many Dakota children before him, he was told he would be better off without it. Despite all of this, my parents have taught me well.

I have had many teachers throughout the years, but I must acknowledge Franklin Firesteel, who first taught me not only the Dakota language but also started me on my journey of what it is to be a Dakota man. He also taught me how to view the world from a Dakota perspective and I believe this reason alone is why we need to learn our own language.

Before the coming of the Europeans, the people indigenous to North America lived side by side and could speak each other's languages. It was not uncommon for an individual to be multilingual. We see this today in Europe. One of the advantages of speaking more than one language is having more than one perspective on the world.

Viewing the world from a Dakota perspective comes from immersing oneself in the language and living among the people and their way of life. There is no substitute for learning from a speaker of the language. I believe language books, CDs, and cassettes are good learning aids. However, the Dakota language is within the people. Hearing a speaker and witnessing the spirit of the language is quite the experience.

The Dakota language also paints pictures as it is being spoken. I have always been a visual learner, and when I am speaking or listening, I am watching everything unfold. I try to pass this on to my students because the visuals of the language can be very humorous even when a mistake is made. One of the benefits of being an instructor is having the opportunity to share my own mistakes. Hopefully, those whom I am teaching will benefit and not make the same errors.

I remember my first time speaking with *Kunsi* (Grandmother) in

Dakota. I had been learning Dakota for only two weeks and she taught me some new words, including *hohpi*, meaning "hair." I was so proud I remembered the words she taught me that I went back to school and immediately started teaching them to my classmates. I told Franklin about my new words, and when I pointed to my head and said *hohpi*, he looked puzzled and said Kunsi was teasing me. *Hohpi* does not mean "hair," it means "nest." Maybe I was having a bad hair day when she taught me that word.

When my wife and I discussed having children, we talked about what languages we would teach them. We decided I would teach them Dakota and she would speak English. (Since we are both proficient speakers of German, we would keep German as our "secret" language.) As a Dakota, I was taught to sing and speak to the child while he was in the womb—so I did. I used complete sentences instead of baby talk. We now have a four-year-old named Ian and a two-year-old named Daryn who can both speak and understand Dakota and English.

When Ian started to walk, I first noticed he understood everything I was saying to him. His first complete sentence caught me off guard. I was changing his diaper and he happened to peek at the soiled diaper and said, *Nina cewasdi* (I really went poop!). The humor is endless, and soon even the little ones pick up on it. With the threat of our Native languages vanishing, to hear Dakota come out of those tiny mouths is a treasure.

Much of what I have learned by teaching my sons I am taking and successfully applying to the adult learners in my university classes. I think one of the most difficult ideas to convey is the thought process behind the language. As a second-language learner, I have been told that I may never think in Dakota the way someone does who grew up with the language. At one time I was concerned about this, until I witnessed something that I will always hold very dear to me. I was reading from a Native newspaper and there was the word *okolakiciye*. I said it out loud because I like to expose my sons to Lakota and Nakota. This will get them used to the beauty of all the different ways of speaking the language. (In the dialect I speak, the "l" is replaced with a "d.") When I said *okolakiciye,* my wife asked what that meant and I thought about how to explain it. Before I could say anything, Ian said, "It's where you go to make friends or be friends with one another." I wondered how this little three-year-old could respond so quickly and precisely upon hearing the word for the first time. It soon occurred to me that he was thinking in Dakota.

I later learned about the process of internalizing the language. It is said that children by the age of three are already fluent in their language(s). From birth (or while in the womb), children imprint the mechanics of the language itself (the grammar, vocabulary, voice inflection, et cetera.) and prepare it for future use in communicating. They have the Native thought process and intuition within them. I have heard many times that the only way to bring back the Dakota language is to raise a generation of fluent speakers. An Ojibwe elder said when the people could no longer speak Ojibwe, they become only descendants of the Ojibwe. I believe this is true of any language. If we raise our children speaking Dakota, they will be able to think as our ancestors did. This is why we need to teach our children while they are still infants.

In the American school system, a second language is traditionally taught in high school. If we teach a language while children are in their early years, the results will be visible much sooner. On a recent visit to the Maori in New Zealand, I was visiting with Dr. Graham Smith and shared with him some stories about my boys. I told him how well Ian was doing with math in Dakota and how well he can use a computer. Dr. Smith said it's a benefit of teaching him more than one language. Ian has figured out math and the computer because they are other languages. By learning more than one language, along with expanding his insight and perspective on the world, he is learning how to crack codes.

All our teachings are intertwined in the Dakota language. The traditional way of life goes hand in hand with learning and teaching the language. Our relationship with the Creator and all of creation, how we conduct ourselves, certain basic protocols like introductions, and even the "let's see how fast it takes us to figure out how we're related" game are all part of the language. There are rules of conduct that are monitored by the language. As a result of language loss, many of these rules are unknowingly being overlooked.

In the city it is hard to keep a connection with one another and continue to use the Dakota language. English constantly surrounds us. When we speak our language in public, we are often given strange looks. There is a sense of community in various places where the language is used. Unfortunately, there is no place for young people to be immersed in the language for a lengthy time. But today home language nests, community classes, and immersion schools are starting to take form in the urban areas and communities.

As a student of Dakota, I am in a race to gather as much information as possible from speakers, most of whom are elderly. Visiting with speakers while living in the city can be difficult. In the state of Minnesota, there are four Dakota communities. As of two years ago, there were only twenty-nine fluent speakers of the Dakota language in these communities and all of them were elderly. (This does not include those speakers in the Twin Cities area or account for other Dakota reservations and communities in the United States and Canada.) The health of the speaker becomes a factor in learning Dakota. Many of our elders constantly remind us that they will not be around forever, so we need to move now to learn from them. I once visited with Iola Columbus from Morton, Minnesota, or *Cansayapi*. She told me that as an elder, she is still learning. She said that when someone comes to learn from her, she also learns from them, and that is why we need to visit with our elders.

It is necessary to be around as many speakers as possible because each speaker has her or his own way of conveying thoughts in the language. In the days before European contact, if someone spoke differently, it identified the speaker's community. This is still true today. An elder recently told me that differences in language are acceptable. We tease one another about the differences within our language. This form of teasing is also a good teaching tool because when the differences are discussed, there is always a good lesson to learn.

I have made a personal goal to be familiar with the many different ways our relatives speak the language. As I am learning the language, I am also taking time to learn the morphology and etymology of the words I am speaking. I believe this gives an insight into the worldview of the Dakota. I have always been taught that I should be fully conscious of what I am saying in the language. Learning the deeper meaning of the words helps with this.

An elder recently proposed a question to group of speakers and students. Will the people still speak Dakota in the year 3000? It was at that moment I knew I could not plan just in terms of what I can do for the language in my lifetime, but I must plan for the generations to come. I ponder this question quite often, and it brings me back to the children and the elders. We cannot move ahead without either. We must take a stand and teach our children. What message are we sending if we have our children learn Dakota and we ourselves do not speak it? We must take responsibility and learn alongside them to give them community and life in which to speak Dakota. Raising a generation of fluent speakers is the start of ensuring that our people will speak Dakota in the future.

I have witnessed many times that Dakotas are very encouraging of others learning Dakota language. A speaker once went on for almost an hour about how well a student said *pidamayaye do* (thank you). I was told that no matter what someone's speaking level is, they are speaking Dakota and that is all that matters.

I am honored by the stories and experiences that many Dakota people have taken the time to share with me. I will continue to teach the language for the rest of my life. When I hear my sons speak Dakota, I know that the language will be passed on. When I hear my elders give those words of encouragement, I know that the teaching will be done in a good way. I would encourage anyone who is interested in learning his or her language, no matter what it is, to simply visit with a speaker. Experience listening to a speaker and witness the spirit of the language.

*Hau mitakuye owasin!* (All my relatives!)

# A Different Rhythm

## H. Lee Karalis

"A degree from UC Berkeley will never change the fact that I cannot understand my grandfather when he asks for more coffee."

—Esther G. Belin (Navajo) from *In the Cycle of the Whirl.*

L illie sits in front of her computer at the Choctaw Tribal Complex in Durant, Oklahoma. She looks into the monitor with its built-in camera and speaks to me, to us, her Internet students from D.C. to Menlo Park, California.

"*Halito! Chim achukma!*" she says with her easy smile. "Welcome to Chahta Anumpa. Let's see who's here tonight."

Some of the students are even newer to the language of our relatives than I am. That gives me solace.

"*Halito, Lillie!*" I return her greeting to the monitor while she is looking at the list of those who have signed on tonight. "*Achukma hoke, chishnato?*" I continue. I really do feel good tonight, though it is ten P.M. on a Thursday, and I am exhausted from a day's teaching and grading and prepping. The truth is, I don't always make it to her class.

As the lesson begins, Lillie demonstrates again the aspirated "hl," whose sound is still confusing some students. I proudly make the sound, puffing air around the sides of my tongue as I pronounce *hlampko,* meaning "strong." But no one hears me.

Some of the students in this on-line class have mothers and grandmothers in their homes who do speak the language, and I am jealous. My mixed-blood Choctaw-Irish grandparents died years before I was born. My father is a decade gone now, my uncles and aunts long before that. I am trying to claim what I never had but what I felt my father owed me. He can't give it now, so I must do it for myself. I am angry at him. And my grandfather. And the world as it was then for making them hate themselves, for making them assimilate.

> *He was a toe-headed-mixed-quarter-blood*
> *after the Kaiser's Great War*
> *running barefoot*
> *through the range grasses*
> *with homma-toned boys—Chahta*
> *speaking the People's words—Chahta*
> *his wide light face shining*
> *free of the Reservation's tattoo*
> *his father's dark skin*
> *reflecting the blood and the tongue*
> *and the People his father hated*
> *for losing the land he now rented.*

My father spoke Choctaw . . .

"*Chahta,*" Lillie says, dropping the hard lone "c" that does not appear in our language.

. . . as a boy in Tishamingo, Oklahoma, and was well acquainted with the stories, the ceremonies, and the dances. I doubt he was fluent in the language, as my grandfather, Poppy, would not have allowed him to speak the language in the house. He was one who felt that survival made it necessary to assimilate, to leave the past behind. In fact, it sometimes seemed that he had come to hate Indians. Once, he got down out of the wagon he was driving and in front of one of my young uncles proceeded to beat up an Indian who was drunk, stumbling along the road, bothering no one. Poppy cursed the cowering man with each blow. My uncle had to finally pull him off. I think Poppy hated what he thought we were becoming, how he thought we were representing ourselves to ourselves and to the rest of the world. Poppy was a pragmatic man, determined to succeed in a world he did not make, transformed from the traditions his parents and grandparents knew. But the world he made for himself and for his family would be in his control. He did finally own his land and kept it when others lost theirs during the Great Depression. He was a successful rancher. He never took a handout, never felt he needed one. He put our "pedigree papers" away, never to use the government assistance that their existence promised—or cursed. He was proud. He would not be Indian. But he was.

Lillie begins working through kinship terms. The traditional terms, she tells us, may change depending on whether a male or female is speaking or being referred to.

"*Amafo*," Lillie says, "my grandfather."

Poppy, I think.

His weakness was, perhaps, his children, especially the youngest, my father. My father was in diapers when my grandmother Rose's heart stopped from the poisons of appendicitis. Poppy promised her never to let another woman raise her five children. A hard request in 1912. But he honored his promise long past the children attaining adulthood. It fell to my oldest aunt, Artie, not yet in her teens, to maintain the household and raise her younger sister and brothers. They all doted on my father, did all of his life. He got used to it, too used to it, expected it, especially from all the women in his life. And he usually got it. So my dad played with the darker boys of his blood and learned the Choctaw culture even as Poppy and my uncles turned away from it.

> *My father knew his name*
> *when his feet carried him away*
>
> *from the boys—Chahta*
> *and the tongue—Chahta*
> *and the father—Chahta*
> *to a western coast. My coast.*
> > *Where my first memory of being of the People*
> > *was watching feathered headdresses following*
>
> > *rhythms of voices and drums as deer skinned dancers*
> *asked tourists to join in.*
> > *I was a tourist.*

"*Aki*," says Lillie, "my father."

By the time I came along, my father was well into his forties, selling, ironically, real estate in the then-endless backcountry of California. It was a place well removed from his heritage in Oklahoma, but the rolling grasslands with horses and cattle were familiar. I think he teased me with only a few words of our language when I was a child. I don't know what they were. I remember only the sounds rolling quickly off his tongue. I did not push to learn the words or their meaning. Because my parents were not together and I didn't spend much time with him, I was shy with my father, the stranger I adored. Tall, lean, with a voice as resonant as the powwow drums I would later come to know. And I think he felt awkward around me too. The one female in his life who did not jump into his lap and smother him with kisses. So he would quickly begin to speak of my schooling or my mother or my love and his of horses. Through horses we could speak a little. We would go riding together, not saying much. Not sharing. The tradition our family had accepted.

> *You're an Indian*
> *my father said to me*
> *Go dance with 'em.*
> > *He pushed my small body*
> > *into the smiling rhythms*
> > *But I did not know them.*
> > *Or my name.*
> > *I remember his disappointment*
> > *as I walked away from the crowd*
> > *embarrassed by his words*

"*Vllatek*," says Lillie, "girl child."

My own childhood was West Coast beaches and waves and copper sunsets shrouded in the smell of salty air and seaweed. Very far from the Oklahoma creeks my father fished as a boy. My house was near a slough with its many seabirds nesting in the backwaters of the bay, over the hill from the Pacific Ocean, where pelicans fought their extinction from DDT. So far from the rolling Oklahoma hills of my father and the sweltering southern Mississippi woods of Poppy. I knew I was Indian, at least a part of me was, but there was no one around me who could tell me what it meant to be Indian, to be Choctaw. . . .

"*Chahta*," says Lillie.

. . . The kids would say, "Okay, if you're Indian, speak Indian." I didn't know what they meant, so they war-whooped around me and I punched them. My father dismissed my complaints of them with a wave of his hand. But that didn't tell me who I was—though I gained respect on the block as the girl who could and would beat up boys.

> *Some Indian you are*
> > *But my father's feet did not join the dancers.*
> > *They turned and followed mine*
> > *away from the tourists*
> > *and the music.*
>
> *My father knew his name*
> *but he never gave me mine.*

Lillie tells us during one of our discussions of Chahta history that as a child she spoke Chahta in her home as her first language. But then she was sent to boarding school, where she wasn't allowed to speak the language of her family.

"I came home from boarding school at the age of ten," she says, "and went to the public school. Choctaw was spoken at home in the evenings, but during the day I spoke English at school. My siblings had also been affected by the 'boarding school syndrome,' so we weren't able to speak to one another in Choctaw."

When her parents died, her everyday connection to Chahta Anumpa was gone. But teaching the language to others brought that connection back. So she has patience with us, those of us who are trying to learn—for the first time.

"I grew up in a household where Indian was spoken all around me but never to me. I would sit on the periphery, unable to comprehend, though I did manage to learn a few words. This experience precipitated my love of language."

—Gloria Bird (Spokane) from
*Breaking the Silence: Writing as "Witness."*

I grew up loving the written word and the worlds each word opened for me. Books. I devoured them. I would hide in them because I didn't seem to fit in with the real world around me. Nobody understood. Not even me.

I grew up with Spanish all around me, but I do not speak it well, though I can read it—a bit. I was afraid to let the Spanish words fill my mouth and explode with the culture that surrounded me. I was not Spanish and was afraid of ridicule. I am an Indian-white mixed-blood, neither here nor there, afraid of speaking Chahta— and of sounding foreign to it. But I am.

I grew up in a Greek stepfamily, was adopted into it, and saw how language fed relationships, made connections, made you whole. During his life my adoptive grandfather was as patient with me as Lillie is now. He told me stories of growing his garden each year in the Imperial Valley, of fighting the Turks as a young man in Greece, of my step/adoptive father as a troublesome boy, and he had great fun teaching me how to curse in Greek. He wrapped his culture around me as best he could, but it didn't fit well. Yet he remains with me in small ways. I garden each year as he once did, and my youngest son is as troublesome as my adoptive father once was. As my own father once was being the much-spoiled baby of the family. And I have not forgotten how to curse in Greek.

> My father's own dreams of death
> brought him into my life again.
> But he could share so little

*of the People*
*and the land*
*in his final months.*
*The bridge his bones supported*
*between what is white in me*
*and what is not*
*had narrowed with time*
*and brittled with cancer*
*and then vanished*
*in the crushing space*
*between our dreams—*
*which never touched.*
*My father knew his name*
*but he left me without the song of mine.*

After he died, I didn't know what to do. My cousins didn't speak the language. They had been raised to ignore our Indianness, to succeed "in spite of it." And they did. This was the doing of my grandfather, who didn't want his children to suffer for their/his Indian blood. I don't know why my father was the one allowed to veer from the white path as a child—maybe because he was the baby and the last reminder of my grandmother.

"I sometimes imagine that I am my ancestors. That as I write I am speaking what my ancestors spoke or would speak through me."

—N. Scott Momaday (Kiowa) from *Ancestral Voice:*
*Conversations with N. Scott Momaday.*

After my father died, I got out my Chahta dictionary and began playing with the words to try to build phrases. I wanted a piece of the culture denied to me, and I knew the language was an essential part of it. I did that for years but was terrified that I was doing it all wrong. I understood that the best way to learn was through immersion, but I knew no Choctaws and was too intimidated to look: I would never be accepted. I was a border dweller, between two cultures, more white than Indian. I resented myself. Then I discovered an on-line Chahta language course through the Oklahoma Choctaws.

> "Ojibwemowin is a marvel; the more I know the less I know
> . . . I'll always be a beginner in this language, as it is surely
> one of the most complex on earth."
> —Louise Erdrich (Ojibwe), interview from
> *An Emissary of the Between-World.*

I am a perpetual beginning Chahta Anumpa student. I see the words on the page and they comfort me because the written word has always comforted me, given me a place to go without being judged. But when I hear Lillie speak the words, I become frightened. She is so easy with the rhythms and stresses, so patient and confident with us. I take a deep breath, repeat the sounds, and slowly I begin to understand the words. I am, once again, a three- or four-year-old *listening* to the adults around me speak. I was always a listener, even then. And now these rhythms are becoming faintly familiar, but sometimes they extend beyond what I can absorb. As a child, I listened to the musical nature of the words and the speaker. I learned to make my own music on the page because my spoken voice was often nervous and uneven. And now there is a different rhythm whirling in my head, playful and challenging. I can begin to hear my grandmother and the songs she might have sung to me, to my father. And my understanding of this music is encouraged to grow.

People don't war-whoop around me anymore, but they do still ask me if I speak Indian. I resist the urge to punch them. Now I simply say that I am learning Chahta.

"*Chahta iskitini anumpuli li.*" "I speak it a little."

"*Kamomi.*" "Very little," but the nasal "a" comes more easily these days.

Lillie is smiling even as the class has run twenty minutes over with questions and confusions about pronounciations and context. But finally she says, "If there are no more questions"—she looks at the screen and into me—"I will end this session of Chahta Anumpa. I'll see you next time. *Yakoke.*" And the video portion of the screen fades around her smile.

*Yakoke.*

# NAMES BY WHICH THE SPIRITS KNOW US

## Sean Lee Fahrlander

*aniin, Niizho-migizi-wag indigo. Migizi indoodem.*

My name is Sean Fahrlander and following in the tradition of my people I've introduced myself in my own language, Ojibwe.

My introduction translates, "Hello, Two Eagles is what the Spirits call me." Eagle is my clan. It may fly in the face of some people's convention for me to share this much information, but I was told to share. Unfortunately, nine arguments out of ten in Indian County (I use the term Indian County broadly—in essence, wherever an Indian person is standing) are about what I know versus what you know. With that said, I want to stress that what I'm saying applies only to what I've been taught.

I received my name from an old man on the White Earth Reservation in northern Minnesota. He's no longer with us, and out of respect I will not mention his name. He was a rare individual and assumed the role as my namesake with the same passion that he lived his life. He became my surrogate father as well as a teacher. When I left the military and came home to the reservation, I would often show up on his doorstep late at night, find the spare key, let myself into the house, and crash on the couch. In the morning I would wake to the smell of breakfast cooking and hot coffee. He never turned me away.

The day he named me will never be far from my mind. I had asked him to do this because of the esteem I had for him. In the old days it would have been left up to my parents to choose someone to be my namesake. A lot has changed since then. However, my generation is one of the first to start the long walk back to our traditions. I passed tobacco to the old man and asked him to be my *wen'enh*, or namesake. He used my tobacco to ask the Spirits to reveal to him what it was that they called me. After receiving the insight, he shared it with me in front of several people from the community and my family. He then smoked his pipe and we feasted my new name.

It was the start of a great journey and thankfully it has not ended. One of the important things I've learned on this trail is how names come to be. Part of my understanding is as we pass through life, most of the time we are blissfully unaware of the Spirits that exist along with us. I'm certain that we grow away from the ability to interact with them. In a way, I think we have lost the awe that allowed us to see. Even if we don't let ourselves be aware of the Spirits, I'm sure they are aware of us. I like to think of this like gravity. We live our whole lives never seeing gravity, just its effects. We trip and fall; we drop things and at times even defy gravity for our own purposes. But in the end gravity is what keeps us grounded.

I believe that the Spirits act in the same manner. We don't and can't understand Spirits. Most of the time, we ignore them. We even defy the Spirits for our own purposes, but still they keep us spiritually grounded. And when the Spirits talk about us they call us by the names they have for us. That is why my people use the term *indigo*, which literally translates, "the Spirits call me."

It's strange how many people feel that they are not worthy or ready to care for an Indian name. This is very confusing. One hundred fifty years ago we all had Indian names. We were born into our Native tongue and therefore given Indian names. I'm pretty sure that we didn't go around calling all the men "he" or "him" and all the women "she" or "her." Surely all our aunts and uncles, cousins, and grandparents had names, and those names were reflections of their Spirits.

This is not to say that we wouldn't be given another name later in life. This sometimes happened. I remember a story about a grass dancer who was getting on in years and couldn't keep up with the younger dancers. I was in the arena when he quit dancing in the middle of a song. He walked out of the arena, took off his outfit, and gave it to a young man. I asked later what this was all about and a friend explained. It seems the man had been told as young boy that when he gave up dancing he was to take his elder name and become a teacher. I was honored to be there when he reached this transitional place in his life.

Sometimes I doubt that I'm worthy of the name I carry. It's at this point that I divorce myself from my name and split off from the grace that was granted me. If you're wondering about what I mean, look up the word "grace."

It's interesting that I had no more control over my Indian name than I did over my white name. There's an old saying, "A name is what you make it." To me, this means that a person is judged not by his or her family but rather by his or her actions. We determine who we are.

In the 1800s in Wisconsin, there was an Ojibwe man by the name of Bezhigo. His name translates into "The One Alone" or "By One's Self." He lived back in the deep woods and didn't interact with his neighbors very often, preferring to keep his own company. On the occasion of war with the Fox people, Bezhigo would come out to battle. Bezhigo was such a powerful warrior that the Fox were never able to win on a day he was involved in the fighting. This became so apparent that the Fox warriors would call out before battle, asking if Bezhigo was with the other Ojibwe. If he answered them, the Fox would quit the field. Bezhigo is remembered to this day for his actions as well as for his name.

The questions raised by this little slice of history cause me to wonder if Bezhigo was named at birth or did this name come later when he chose his solitary lifestyle. More important, did the man make the name or did the name make the man? I'm really not sure.

I've seen Indian people struggling to find themselves. Hell, I struggle. I've sat in judgment of myself, evaluating and criticizing. I've punished myself for not living up to my potential, and even gone so far as to believe that I was unworthy of the things that I've received in life. I've even felt guilty for not living up to the promises of my Indian name. I know some people reading this might say that I was unready or even undeserving. That's okay with me. It took me a long time, but I have learned that I have value.

Some twelve years ago I went on my first fast. I was sitting on the ground way back in the bush. On the second morning something happened that clarified my place in the creation. Just as the sun was breaking over Strawberry Mountain, I discovered myself. It was early fall and the frost hadn't yet driven away the insects. I was wearing black jeans, and as I watched the morning start, I looked down. Crawling on the grass next to me were hundreds of bumblebees drinking the dew. As I watched, some of the bees left the grass and started to crawl on my legs. Soon I had over fifty bees drinking the dew off my pants. At first I was scared to move, but as I continued to watch, I didn't want to move. My fear had been replaced by awe.

As the day warmed and the bees flew away on their business, I sat in wonder. "What does this mean?" For the rest of the morning this question ran through my head repeatedly. Around noon it hit me. To those bees I was just another piece of grass. I existed on the same level as any other part of the world, not above or below, but with. I was another part of creation and not the creation itself.

I don't want to give the wrong impression, because that would only cheapen the event. Many other things happened during my fast that I choose not to talk about and keep to myself. They have become my touchstones and remind me of the balance that exists in creation, and I find myself returning to them often, just to reflect. These happenings still teach me.

I think in many ways that Indian people are buying into the stereotypes of the dominant culture. It's that "bill of sale" offered to the public at large and contains the typical connotations of Indians being spiritual people and in touch with the wholeness of the universe. On one hand this is true, but only if the individual chooses it. On the other, it's a misconception that can be attributed to the fractionalization and loss of our culture as well as the picking up of our culture by non-Natives. I believe spirituality is not an event or ceremony, it's a choice.

In saying this, I know that some will disagree, but that's the beauty of the human condition: our right to choose, to question and to doubt. I often find myself at odds with some of my elders because of my questioning ways. I've found it hard to just accept. I have the need to experience. I don't want to walk aimlessly through life; instead, I want to experience it, to live it. It's in these experiences that I find myself and have no illusions about who I am.

An old man from Red Lake once told me the difference between knowledge, experience, and wisdom. He said knowledge can be sought, experiences had, but wisdom comes only by combining the first two with reflective thought and then applying it to your life. I've watched people who in their rush to "become" get lost. It's like they're trying to complete a "résumé of Indianness." Find my name, find my clan, learn my language and everything I can about my culture, and then I'll be Indian enough. I've seen people spend so much time "becoming" instead of "belonging" that they never allow themselves just to "be."

I was taught that by the right of being born, we belong. We belong to our family, we belong to our clan, and we belong to our people. All the shit in the world can't change that.

I also think that becoming is not a static event. It's linear and fluid, like time. Everything we see, smell, touch, or otherwise sense adds to our experiences and changes our perspectives and us. We can exercise very little control over an event. And in many ways, it just happens. But we do have control over being. We have to choose to be. We can allow ourselves just to be who we are, and live in the moment.

For me this is almost impossible to do. I have to make that conscious choice to let things happen. I find myself having to shut out the electronic noise that has become so much of my life. This is much harder than it sounds. I've gone to great lengths to divorce myself from silence. The cell phone, Internet, TV—all this white noise drowns out the quiet whispers of the creation trying to remind me that I belong.

I've been to the other side too. I used to spend all my free time at or in ceremony and was losing touch with myself. I had gotten to the point that ceremony had taken me over. I was like an alcoholic who sobers up and finds that he is incapable of living life without A.A., and then A.A. becomes his fix.

Me, I became a ceremony junkie.

This went on for over a year before my elder pulled me to the side and told me that life was not a ceremony. He said when ceremony is over, go out and live life for a while. I had spent so much time inside the bubble of ceremony that I quit doing the things I enjoyed. It took time for me to feel comfortable doing the hunting, fishing, and hiking I loved, because I thought that I was cheating on ceremony.

What does this have to do with naming? Well, in a word, balance. Any kind of extreme is unhealthy. And to place more importance on any one facet of our lives forces us to ignore the rest.

For my people a name is a key that opens doors, but we must walk through them. Once through the doorway, we find that the road has many forks and we must choose which way to go. A name can't do that for you. You must do it for yourself. The name is not the journey, just the beginning of it.

One morning, about seven years ago, I was driving to work at the Northwestern Minnesota Juvenile Center, where my job was to develop culturally oriented programming for American Indian youth. It was spring, and life was just waking up in the earth, and I started to cry. There I was, driving to work, when it dawned on me. Of all the things in creation that the creator could have made me, He chose to make me human. He could have made me a rock, a tree, a bird, or an animal, but He didn't. He made me a man, and an Indian man at that. In that moment I understood gratitude. I was grateful for what the creator had chosen for me. I wasn't looking at what I didn't have or what I hadn't accomplished but only at what I'd been given. It was a very good day.

When I'm asked to talk with people, one of the things I encourage them to do, if they haven't done it yet, is to seek a name. It's our names that allow us to be familiar with the Spirits and give us a strong sense of selves as Indian people. I also explain that all of the things I'm sharing with them belong to them just by the simple fact of being born Ojibwe. I explain it's their birthright. And the only people who can take it from them are themselves. I want to share the knowledge that they are an integral part of creation and they belong. And even though I don't understand the whys of it, I have to believe that the creator knew what He was doing when He breathed life into the first human being. *Miigwech.* (Thank you.)

# Four

## INDIANS AS MASCOTS: AN ISSUE TO BE RESOLVED

*For many years, the dominant society has admired the mythological Indian but rarely the genuine person. Many today still look upon Indians as people of the past. These two beliefs have perpetuated the idea that using Indians as mascots is permissible. If one uses a term that is offensive to others without realizing it is offensive, this action can be considered stereotyping. But, if one becomes informed that the term is offensive and continues to use this term, this is pure racism. After all, American Indians are human beings, not animals, and not a people of the past. Therefore we should not be used as mascots.*

*Though many feel there are issues of more importance and relevance that American Indian people must deal with, this issue is one that is perpetuated on a continual basis: one that strips our youth of self-assuredness. It is definitely an issue that begs to be handled in a diplomatic, respectful manner.*

# Symbolic Racism, History, and Reality: The Real Problem with Indian Mascots

### Kimberly Roppolo

The stadium lights starburst above the misty football field. The band blares and pounds out the school's fight song like only a hometown high school band can do. Blond, perky cheerleaders clap as they hop from foot to foot, rousing the fans to a controlled roar. Two of them hold a huge sign, painted painstakingly while sprawled across a dusty, linoleum-lined corridor. The men of the hour prepare to enter the arena of combat. They begin a slow trot, then burst through the paper to shouting cheerleaders—"Kill the Indians!" they scream.

Many people would say I am overreacting to be offended by this scenario. After all, what's more American than high school football? What could be a more wholesome activity for young people in today's age, when so many more dangerous temptations beset them at every side—drugs, alcohol, unprotected sex, and gang activity? I think the danger of this situation is that it is so precisely American. Americans in general see the Indian mascot controversy as "silly," and there are admittedly American Indians who see it the same way. Having taught the mascot controversy as a topic for my argumentative research-writing course at the community college where I am a professor, and having discussed it with some of my family and friends, I realize that many people see no problem with the use of American Indians as sports mascots. However, I think the danger of this use is more than just its potential to offend. It is representative of an endemic problem: racism against America's First Peoples. Despite the fact that racial problems still exist in our country, for the most part we are in a day and age where racial tolerance and tolerance for all kinds of diversity has increased. But this is not the case with racism against American Indians, largely because racism against American Indians is so ingrained in the American consciousness that it is invisible.

Dr. Cornell Pewewardy of the University of Kansas calls this kind of racism "dysconscious racism," or, in other words, racism that the people themselves who exhibit it are unaware of. The use of American Indian mascots falls under this category. The grossly exaggerated features of the Cleveland Indian, the cartooned vicious savages decorating high school spirit ribbons, the painted, dancing, fake-buckskin-clad white kids running down the sideline doing tomahawk chops, are all unintentionally stereotypical and aren't even perceived by most Americans as negative. They fall in the same category as rock singer Ted Nugent's ridiculous stage antics in a fluorescent mockery of a Plains chief's headdress. They fall under the same category as cigar store Indians topping car dealerships. They fall under the same category as words like "squaw," "papoose," "wagon burner," and "Indian giver." They fall under the same category as Disney's painted bombshell Pocahontas and the 36-24-36 asking-for-it Aztec seductress from *El Dorado* or her grotesquely depicted male counterparts. They are no more meant to be offensive than the standard moniker "chief" for any American Indian male a redneck encounters in the army, the workforce, or anywhere else in America. The average American engages in this behavior without ever being aware of it, much less realizing that it is racism.

Every semester I ask my students what is in the front foyer of

Applebee's restaurant. None of them, not even if they work there, are ever able to tell me there is a statue of an Indian man, in non-specific tribal attire, often with a "special of the day" sign around his neck. Applebee's claims this statue "points to the next nearest Applebee's"; I guarantee that if a major restaurant chain placed a statue of an African American man in supposed tribal dress in the front of each of its restaurants pointing to the next nearest one, people would realize these statues were inappropriate. In the same way, as many others have pointed out, if we had sports teams named the New York Niggers or the Jersey Jigaboos, Americans would know this was wrong. The average American, who would clearly perceive the Louisville Lynched Porch Monkeys as a problematic name for a team doesn't even realize the Washington Redskins emerges from a history of the literal bloody skins of American Indian men, women, and children being worth British Crown bounty money—no one's skin is red. American Indian skin is brown, at least when it is on our bodies and not stripped from us in the name of profit and expansionism. African Americans, thank God, have raised the consciousness of Americans enough through the civil rights movement to keep the more obvious forms of racism usually hidden, though it took publicly armed Black Panthers, the burning of Chicago, and even the riots of Los Angeles to get this point across. American Indians are frankly so used to being literally shot down if we stick our heads up, we aren't nearly as likely to do so. In fact, from our own civil rights movement with AIM, we still have Indians like Leonard Peltier, who stuck their heads up although incarcerated for over twenty years when even the FBI admits its evidence was fabricated.

Racism against American Indians is so intrinsically part of America's political mythology, the truth a group of people agrees to believe about itself, that without it this country would have to do something it is has never done: face colonial guilt. Everything we see around us was made from stolen American Indian resources, resources raped from this Earth that we consider sacred, an Earth in danger of global disaster from imbalanced greed. We live like no people in the history of the world have ever lived. Our poorest are rich in comparison to the world's average citizen. We all—Indian, Euro American, Asian American, African American, or Chicano—have benefited at least in some material way from the murders of an estimated one hundred million people, crimes that are still going on in this hemisphere, in Mexico, in Argentina, in Oklahoma, in South Dakota, in New Mexico, Arizona, Montana, and more. These acts, along with innumerable rapes, along with untold numbers of sterilizations of women even up to the past few decades, along with the removal of children without cause from their parents' homes, from their cultures, along with the destruction of language, with the outlawing of religious freedom up until 1978, constitute what is defined as genocide under the United Nations Convention on Genocide's definition, a document never signed by the United States, because under it, that very government owes restitution to both American Indians and to African Americans, an estimated forty to sixty million of whom were killed during the slave trade before they ever reached the shores of the "New World."

An estimated six million Jews died in the atrocities committed in Nazi Germany, being treated before and after death in ways the world will never forgive—starved, herded naked like cattle, poisoned to an excruciating death, made into curios—lampshades, little collectibles for the Nazi elite. But this we recognize as inhuman, not the kind of behavior we as people can tolerate. We see the sins of Germany and the sins of Bosnia, where former students report seeing little girls with dolls still in their arms, dead with open eyes in mass graves, for what they are. But unlike the rest of the world, we as Americans cannot see our own. We are not taught in school that Columbus's men smashed babies' heads on rocks in front of their mothers. We are not taught that they sliced people in two for fun, in bets over whose sword was the sharpest. We are not taught they tied men up after slaving in silver mines all day, threw them under their hammocks, and raped their wives above them. We aren't taught that the Pilgrims were called the "cut-throat people" by the Indians, who taught them survival and feasted with them because, at one meal the good Christians invited them to, those very Christians took their knives and slit them from ear to ear. We aren't taught that our "forefathers" roasted Pequot men, women, and children alive in their beds. We aren't taught that Thomas Jefferson promoted miscegenation as a means of eradicating the "Indian problem." We are not taught that American soldiers collected labia and breasts and penises for curios after slaughtering women, children, and old men on what must be considered, when we look at the primary evidence of American history, a routine basis. The list goes on and on. We aren't, indeed, taught a lot of things. And we aren't taught them for a good reason. We aren't taught colonial newspapers created fictitious accounts of Indian attacks to encourage annihilation to open lands for settlement. We aren't taught that the beloved creator of *The Wizard of Oz*, L. Frank Baum, wrote the kind of "kill 'em all" editorials that led up to the slaughter at Wounded Knee. We aren't taught that California newspapers openly advertised the sale of female Indian children as sex slaves, children whose parents had been legally murdered, making them, as orphans, into legal chattel. The average American would be appalled at our own history.

American Indian Nations are the only sovereign nations the United States government has ever broken over five hundred treaties with, violations that Russell Means rightly suggests gives these nations the legal justification to issue one huge eviction notice to the United States, the only nations whose citizens are owed, even with the outright thefts *not* taken into account, even with the restitution the United Nations Convention on Genocide should mandate under international law *not* taken into account, billions of dollars in money that was held in "trust" for Indians thought incapable of being responsible for it, billions of dollars that same United States government has lost. Despite this, American Indians serve this country in its military forces in higher numbers per capita than any other ethnic group—and have in every war since the American Revolution. Despite this, American Indians on the whole maintain a huge amount of respect for this country and the flag that flies above it.

The real problem with the kind of dysconscious, symbolic, abstract racism that is perpetuated today by sports mascots and the kind of historical, intentionally inculcated, politically motivated racism that enabled the near total genocide of American Indian peoples is that it enables very real, very concrete, and very conscious acts of violent racism that American Indian people still face in this country and this hemisphere on a daily basis. It is our conceptualization of people that dictates our behavior toward them. Most Americans don't come into contact with Indians on a daily basis because of that very genocide, or when they do, because of the campaign of rape and encouraged miscegenation through intermarriage, they don't realize they do. To most Americans, American Indians themselves are invisible. Those who appear to be "full bloods" are historicized—they are, even when mainstream Americans come into contact with them, the ephemeral reminders of their "savage" ancestors, those frozen in time by inaccurate depictions in Hollywood's movies and television serials; they are today's "noble savages," seen as "in touch with nature" and "spiritual," ghosts alive only to kindle a sense of an exotic Wild West past, to prompt the notion that we must save the planet the capitalism and materialism brought by Europeans is rapidly destroying, or to lead spiritually void New Agers on "vision quests." We who are of Indian ancestry mixed with either whites or African Americans are not seen as "real Indians." But for Americans who live near or on reservations or tribally controlled lands and for our neighbors to the south, who very much still realize an Indian presence in "their" countries, the western hemisphere's Indigenous Peoples are very much still present, and because of the atmosphere of hatred that the dysconsious racism of the rest of the country allows and even promotes, violence abounds.

This is not to say that no other group in America is still subject to prejudice-induced violence. There are occasionally still unspeakable acts against African Americans like the one in Jasper, Texas. There are also unfortunately incidents of violent bigotry against homosexuals, like the one in Laramie, Wyoming, that led to the creation of federal hate-crime legislation. But the fact is that American Indian women are twice as likely as black men to die of homicide. White males commit most of these murders; most involve alcohol sold by white proprietors on reservation borders; many are never prosecuted. Like the murders in the 1970s that instigated the American Indian movement to begin with and the rash of Indian killings that followed it, these murders go largely unnoticed by mainstream America. So do the beatings. So do the rapes. If "real" Indians don't exist in the American mind, then hate crimes against them have no room in the American imagination of possibility. And the media, the same media that descends from that which actively promoted the extermination of Indians through the early 1900s, don't cover

that continued extermination now because of their early effective-
ness in our erasure.

This kind of violence is so common that in one week this
summer, in a class of five Cheyenne and Arapaho college students,
three of them were directly affected by it. Two girls had a female
cousin close to their age murdered, murdered by her white
boyfriend and several of his friends because the girl was pregnant
with his child, a little "half-breed" he didn't want his middle-
upper-class white parents or the nice white folks in his rural Oklahoma community aware of. One young man had his brother
nearly beaten to death—his skull cracked open, not just cracked—
when several bouncers at a local nightclub had to control his
"rowdy" behavior. And this was just the violent racism. This
doesn't include the kind of daily humiliation that Indians are subject to—the stares my colleague and I, both "invisible breeds,"and
more obviously Indian students endure while trying to share a
pizza, the turned-up noses we get from convenience store clerks,
the rejection by potential employers, the whispered "Hey, did you
see that Indian" we hear when we become visible in more "mainstream" America.

Perpetuators of conscious racism in more Indian-populated
regions of this country will justify their behavior with accusations
that Indians themselves act in such a way that it encourages the
negative stereotype—we are all unemployed, government-money-
grubbing drunks. Yes, as well as having a higher rate of homicides,
American Indians have a higher rate of every cultural malaise that
can be imagined—a higher rate of unemployment, a higher rate of
high school dropouts, a higher suicide rate, a higher rate of drug
abuse, a higher rate of alcoholism, a higher rate of teen pregnancy,
a higher rate of infant mortality . . . but one must consider the kind
of low self-esteem that both conscious historical racism and

dysconscious contemporary racism in the form of things like sports mascots brings about. Not only do Indian people have to deal with the fallout of being "conquered" people, the "survivor guilt" from being alive and suckered in by colonialist capitalism when so many were butchered in its creation, the shame of being men who descended from those unable to protect our women and children in the face of a demonic killing machine we could have never envisioned in our traditional cultures, the shame of being women who descended from those raped and tortured, or those who married or enconcubined themselves to European men as a means of survival. We have to deal with images of ourselves that do not match who we are—human beings. Moreover, Indian people *themselves* sometimes unconsciously internalize the stereotypical images projected on them by mainstream culture—"of course I can't succeed, I'm an Indian. I ought to either be dead or dead drunk." In comparison, the noble-savage ideal promoted by those who claim to be honoring Indians by using mascots based on Native peoples seem complimentary. No wonder some Indians find no problem with racially based mascots. American Indians are *not* all stereotypical unemployed drunks. Most are hardworking, struggling, long-suffering individuals who despite the rarity of opportunity for mainstream success fight daily to keep alive what proud cultural and spiritual traditions we have remaining after the near extermination of our peoples, fight daily to minimize the risks of the negative impact of colonization on our children and promote education for them both in our traditional ways and in the mainstream ways that will ensure their success in both of the worlds in which they must live. No, we are not all dead. Neither are our extremely diverse cultures. And far from being the beneficiaries of government welfare, the average American Indian lives far below poverty level—if you have never visited a reservation like the Northern Cheyenne live on in Lame Deer or that Lakota people live on in Pine Ridge or Rosebud, then you have never seen what poverty in this country really is, not even if you have lived in the poorest of poor urban ghettos. American Indians weren't paid for this land, and though some government "handouts" like commodity cheese, the far-below-standard medical treatment dispensed by the Indian Health Service, or money distributed to the tribe for housing or other needs is dispensed, it falls way short of the government's promises to Indian peoples—that our ancestors and their descendants (us, even those of us with the lowest blood quantums) would be provided for in perpetuity in exchange for our means of providing for ourselves: our lands, the lands that we cultivated for agricultural products, the lands we obtained our game from, the lands our ancestors lived on for centuries and our cultures are tied to, the lands our ancestors rest in. We are more than aware of what we have lost—and cartoonish depictions that make light of both those very losses and us do nothing to encourage mainstream "achievement" among our peoples. And though money from casinos has recently created an influx of capital that some tribes are using to promote economic development, it has by no means enriched the average Indian, and the existence of the casinos themselves, which the tribes as sovereign nations under the United States Constitution have the right to legally create on their own ever-shrinking land bases, is continually under attack from the states, which have no legal jurisdiction over the tribes or their lands.

Sports mascots might indeed seem to be a small issue in light of all of this. And while, admittedly, American Indians have much greater problems to worry about, I would contend that the mascots are both symptomatic of racism and promote it. Some contend that other mascots, like Notre Dame's Fighting Irish, are based on racial identity and that no other group has raised issue with this. However, I would suggest that this is because the creation of "white" as an ethnicity in America's great melting pot has both cooked off cultural identification and a strong sense of heritage for the descendants of late immigrants and early indentured servants and erased colonial guilt for the still-at-the-top-of-the-heap descendants of those who actually engaged in active genocide. The descendants of Irish American immigrants—me included, as some of my ancestors were Irish, along with those who were Cherokee, Choctaw, Creek, German, and Welsh—aren't offended by the Fighting Irish because they don't have a great stake in Irish identity, unlike those who live in Dublin and deal daily with what being Irish, much less Catholic Irish or Protestant Irish, entails. For those who do identify strongly with one of the groups depicted by other ethnic mascots, the answer may be different. The two Scottish female golfers who play for our community college team and are taking my English courses, for instance, admit to finding our mascot, the Highlander, very strange, as it is tied to a heritage and history that has nothing to do with the rest of our athletes. In short, it is offensive if for no other reason simply because it is misappropriated by those who have no right to it. Michael Jordan doesn't give the right to use his name to athletic shoe manufacturers for free and doesn't give them total laissez-faire in regard to their manipulation of his image—why should the Seminole tribe grant this to Florida State or the Cherokee Nation (and the Comanche and the Apache and the . . .) tolerate this kind of use by Jeep/GMC or other corporations?

Not only has the National Education Council denounced the use of mascots based on ethnicity, the abolition of such mascots could really be accomplished relatively easily. Simply change them. Yes, schools would have to sacrifice some of their precious traditions, but what are these traditions compared to the traditions American Indian *cultures* have been forced to sacrifice in the wake of colonization and genocide? Are school traditions really more important than the elimination of images just as racist and offensive as "Sambo"? Can you imagine cheerleaders dressed as a sexed-up version of Aunt Jemima? No, but put one in braids, face paint, and a fringed miniskirt, our college, university, and high school alumni will picket to defend her right to this travesty of what Indian womanhood is and was really about. Others complain about the exorbitant costs that changing a mascot would incur for schools that might do so. But if racist memorabilia like cast-iron segregated beach signs and little black concrete yard boys brings the prices collectors are willing to fork out for them, can you imagine what authentic "Redskins" jerseys would bring on eBay?

After all of the offenses our peoples have suffered throughout the history of Europeans in the Americas and in light of the kind of racism to which American Indians are still subject, it seems a small thing to me that some of us ask that sports mascots that depict American Indians be eliminated. After all, it is not that we are asking for what we will never receive—we aren't asking for a return of our stolen lands or even payment for them, we aren't asking that all of the broken treaties be honored or that the United States pay full restitution to us under the United Nations Convention on Genocide. We aren't even asking for a formal apology by a United States president for the atrocities our ancestors suffered. We are simply asking for the same respect that other ethnic groups receive in this country. We are simply asking to be recognized as people, not as television images, not as cartoons.

# Indians as Mascots: Perpetuating the Stereotype

### Alfred Young Man

Some years ago Oneida comed'jun Charlie Hill—who jokes that people call him a "One eye duh"—took the piss out of American sports teams who use Indians for mascots in one of his many brilliant comedic routines. He said that the Atlanta Braves have a guy on the baseball field decked out in some kind of ridiculous-looking "Indian" outfit who does an equally idiotic "Injun" dance around his tipi every time his team scores. That kind of moronic antisocial behavior is not particularly endearing or surprising coming as it does from Ted Turner's tomahawk-chopping fans, if not Ted himself. This questionable behavior has a way of reducing otherwise dignified human beings to the level of village idiots, in both senses of the term. Applied here, the old adage "Never argue with a fool because people may not be able to tell the difference" has never rung more true. I have never personally witnessed this infamous, grotesque dance performed, if performance it can be called, and I would never go so far as to say that it was a dance anyway—but then again, I am not that big a fan of, or fool for, what I consider to be racist sports or games or entertainment anyway. I use these terms liberally here, as synonyms, whether the sport or game or form of entertainment is baseball; football; hockey; horse racing; golf; wrestling; making movies; boxing; comedy; naming automobiles; fox hunting; fishing; Monopoly; cock- and dogfights; goldfish swallowing; cricket racing; flea, frog, or turtle racing; engaging in late-night-talk-show babbling (e.g., Letterman/Leno nonsense—have I left anything out?) or any other reality TV, sport, game, or entertainment activity.

Sports should be about improving upon one's moral and spiritual integrity, or fiber, above all, about testing your agility, strength, skill, talent, courage, vigor, and intelligence against that of your fellow man or woman, classmates or team. These things are only sports, games, or entertainment after all, so why take them so seriously? Have some fun! Games have been played for thousands of years in Native American cultures and they are still being played at all stages of a Native individual's life from early childhood to old age. It is only comparatively recently, in terms of Native history on this continent anyway, that sports, games, and entertainment in North America have taken on the negative racist overtones they have and which they have now become known for the world over, having gone astray in the last five hundred years or so. That is a relatively short time in terms of the North American Indian's long tenure on this great continent. It was only a scant five hundred plus years ago that Columbus's henchmen cut the breasts, arms, hands, and feet off Taino women to use as objects to toss about in a macabre game of catch, a ritual of the white soldier that has been carried down to our times.

I believe that sports should fundamentally be about learning how to gain your opponent's respect, to test and judge their mental and physical abilities and skills. Bad-mouthing another race is hardly the way to gain anyone's respect. Sports should be about testing your opponent's spiritual strength of character, their moral character. Sports should never be about the need to express individual or collective naked political aggression toward your fellow man or woman, nor should it be about boasting who is the tougher person or who has the meanest brawling hockey or base-ball team or who is the most self-righteous or who gets paid the most money or who is the winningest team ever. Nor should any of this be about silver cups or champagne or about advertising Nike shoes or beer or pizza or fashion or ownership of the most lucrative baseball franchise, nor about personal egotism, crass patriotism, racial superiority, religious doctrine, class differences, paternalism, and least of all that God made you the greatest player there ever was so "Hot damn! Ain't I great?" I doubt very much that whatever God there is even takes the time to watch sports, nor would such a God engage in such obviously trivial pursuits. The latter attitude, when selfishly expressed in sports, amounts to sheer conmanship, therefore is absolute baloney. It is entirely possible that whatever God there is in fact does not work in the affairs of ordinary sports or mundane entertainment and probably never has. I am sure that God has more important things to worry about than whether or not such and such a quarterback, tight end, wide receiver, or halfback scores so many touchdowns or end runs or passes in a season or whatever the hell the case may be. And if God is so preoccupied with such ordinary affairs, then I think that he/she has far too much time on his/her hands so we may therefore consider the world to be in deeper doggy doo than anyone has ever imagined. Surely, with the likes of Osama bin Laden and his army of crazies hell-bent on world destruction, all of them being on their own selfish quest for collecting their own nine virgins from God after they commit suicide, I would think that any rational God would be worrying more about the inno-cent lives these senseless people want to extinguish than toying about with some egotistical ball carrier or switch hitter. (Yeah, you got it right.)

Sports should be about respecting and gaining respect for one's fellow human being and through earning that respect about learning how to honor ourselves as human beings who are living on a tiny, definable, fragile, totally destructible planet in an unimaginably immense universe. Whether the opposing team wins or loses is hardly the point. The phrase "It's not whether you win or lose, it's how you play the game!" although now widely knocked, still holds currency in this day and age. Sports should not be driven by anything other than respect and honor for everyone involved in the activity whether it be acknowledging the rights of players, fans, families, children, referees, umpires, and yes, even Native Americans. Rioting in a stadium, whether it be in hockey, baseball, rugby, soccer, should be seen for what it is, namely, being the height of antisocial madness. Indeed, it is sheer lunacy, anarchy, childish and juvenile backward and stupid, barbarous, brain-dead, airhead behavior that endangers innocent lives. Fighting of any kind should never be encouraged let alone condoned by those who are the leaders of sports teams or by those who make the rules. When we excuse that sort of behavior we diminish ourselves as human beings, we give up our privilege of living in a civilized society, and we may just as well hang up our bats, gloves, hockey sticks, jockstraps, helmets, or whatever else and go home.

"Indians love baseball," jokes Charlie Hill, "but we don't set up camp in the ballpark! Hey, if the Atlanta Braves think that using Indians as mascots is simply harmless fun, then why not have them dress up some white guy in a three-piece suit and have him shuffle around a mobile home parked in the middle of the outfield every time their team scores a hit? Or how about changing the names of a few of these sports teams? Why not have the Atlanta White Boys or the Kansas City Caucasians or the Chicago Negroes, the Washington Jews or New York Rednecks?"

My hat is off to Charlie since the truth is in his humor, which is undoubtedly lost on many a non-Native. But then again, this mascot stuff is a very old, even clichéd issue by now, but even so, nothing seems to have fundamentally changed since Charlie did that routine in 1983, but then again, racism is old . . . stuff. It is a truism that racism grows old with racists and so with the generations. Will things ever really change? Well, probably not in and of themselves, for as one physicist remarked about the dilemma of why scientific ideas that are clearly anachronisms continue to be taught as suitable for science today, "Diehard believers in old ideas and concepts never change . . . you have to wait for these people to die off." I can hardly wait for the believers in the idea of using Indians as mascots to die off. They can exit this planet none too soon for this writer.

The Indian mascot practice is an utterly inappropriate and contemptible idea to Native people today, especially in light of what we now know about crosscultural education, psychology, racism, and political history, nor is it the harmless fun that Ted Turner, his fans, and others insist on saying it is. Muslims would certainly be up in arms if Mohammed were ever used as a mascot; indeed, suicide bombers would be unleashed by the thousands, all happily wrapped in dynamite vests, ready to blow themselves up on a moment's notice in packed sports stadiums across North America, all done to collect on their promised virgins in the next life. Wow, what a payoff! (I wonder what sort of "virgins" Mohammed promises suicide bombers who are female?) Jesus Christ, likewise, would certainly be a poorly chosen icon to use as a mascot, since Christians would be screaming bloody murder.

The point is, Indian icons should never be used as mascots, and doing so should never be thought of as simple harmless fun, nor should using Indian mascots ever be considered as a way of "honoring" Native Americans in some fashion. And if you persist in digressing along these paternalistic lines, then you either need to see a shrink, preferably a Native American shrink, or you need to move to another planet. Think about this for a moment: For a Native American to use a white or black person or icon as a mascot would certainly strike the average white or black sports fan as a most peculiar way of "honoring" white or black people. The depth of insensitivity displayed by owners of sports teams (and sports teams themselves who use Indians as mascots) can be matched only by the extreme greediness of such people whose only desire is to remain totally ignorant of the needs and wishes of Native people. Indian mascot supporters are nothing more than shallow individuals who will go to any length to keep American sports and games the mean, racist specter that such people have always made of them, which in turn breeds an ugly, obnoxious people who go to make up an equally unrefined and rude society.

It is an interesting irony that now that blacks have reached a critical mass in population density and growth as reflected in the United States census and in the sports and entertainment industry, racism against that particular segment of the American population seems to have diminished dramatically in the past thirty years or so. Of course, such forward movement and basic change seems to have had to first suffer the deranged assassination of several of the black population's most prominent and vocal political leaders such as Martin Luther King and Malcolm X by racist whites and blacks alike before any real change could occur. Black men and women had to, en masse and wholesale, change their "slave" names to those favored by their Black Muslim leaders. Michael Jackson, it seems, had to bleach his skin and cut off his nose to gain a modicum of space and respect for himself in the world of music. Incongruently, Jackson had to turn himself into something resembling the

Phantom of the Opera in order to awaken the American people to
the fact that racism is a dangerous cancer eating away at American
society and that things had better change and that blacks were real
people too! Martin Luther King's cry a generation before that we
should judge people by the content of their character and not by
the color of their skin largely fell on deaf ears. Interestingly
enough today, one rarely sees a television commercial, movie,
newscast, sitcom, or top political post that is not filled, staffed, or
features a prominent person of African ancestry with their cooler-
than-cool and hipper-than-hip jargon and attitudes. You gotta get
an attitude no matter how improbable those scenarios might be
in real life.

Out here in southern Alberta, great black and white social and
professional relations are next to nil and the relationships between
the red and white races are even more nil. We still live in a world
of social and political apartheid in Canada and, I dare say, the
U.S.A. I find it humorous that the black man's claim to political
and cultural sovereignty in sitcoms stopped just short of black
characters in the family sitcom adopting a white child and raising
it black. Comedian Steve Martin parodied just such an implausible
situation in the movie *The Jerk*. By contrast, Native Americans are
still very much the invisible man in all this, as if we do not exist as
real people, more like real Village People perhaps. Even the reflective poignant sculpture *The Wall*, which portrays a group of tired
but courageous soldiers huddled together, as a very central part of
that Vietnam War memorial on the Mall in Washington, D.C.—the
artist unfortunately missed the salient point that thousands of
Native Americans fought and gave their lives for the United States
in that war and in every war since that country became a republic.
Such crass political omissions in the history of America, not only
in its art but in its history, make it okay to use Indians as mascots,

for we remain invisible as a people . . . out of sight out of mind, and of course that has been said more times than I care to remember.

I was born—and raised—in a very small and rural backcountry community on the Blackfeet Indian Reservation in northwestern Montana, and lived there for the first twenty years of my life. Sadly, and in a surreal turn of events in my life, I am now being labeled an urban Indian by Indians and whites alike who have never even visited a reservation let alone lived on one, even though I routinely commute one hundred twenty miles each way nearly every weekend to where I was raised and where my family still lives. The issue of stereotyping is not new to me or to my family or to millions of other Native people who have had to live sometimes with absolutely backward and ludicrous claims and ideas about who we are, who have had to live with this racist stigma for all of our lives with no respite from the dominant society who seem to have forever awarded themselves the dubious title "the guardians of all true Native knowledge." It is as though they and they alone undoubtedly know who Native Americans are and how we feel about absolutely everything, whether it is about Indian mascots or treaties or the BIA or DIA, education or art or music or politics, race, spirituality, or death. No one asks for our opinion on these things, and when we do venture to speak out on them, we are immediately shouted down by those who "know better." This essay will no doubt meet that same fate.

When my son was between six and twelve years old, he played peewee and junior hockey for various teams in Lethbridge, Alberta, made up mostly of Caucasian children. Those children knew that my son was an Indian, although in their limited knowledge and worldly experience they failed to apprehend the "tribe" or, more correctly, Nation, he was from, so they simply assumed that he was a local Kainaiwa Indian. The Kainaiwa are the most discriminated against of all First Nations people in southern Alberta, if not Canada, although it is difficult to quantify this assertion since racism is racism no matter where it is found, and it is ugly. Back then I did not bother to or see any reason to tell these white guys that my son and I were in fact Cree Indians from Montana. But regardless, that would not have mattered to them in the least, since whites in this part of the world simply lump all Native people together for equal discrimination. In over twenty-five years of living in Lethbridge, I have found that to the average Canadian, First Nations people in Canada are pretty much all alike, since reserves have no boundaries when it comes time to discriminate. These people would never think to ask if such and such a Native person was from a Blood, Mohawk, Cree, Salish, Miq'maq, Iroquois, Huron, Dene, or Dog Rib reserve, for they know very little about Native people in Canada. Ignorance is something of a badge of honor in Canada, which boasts a Parliament full of politicians who like to keep it that way insofar as Native people are concerned. And why should they know anything anyway since Canada's racist Indian Act, with scant regard for the individuality of each Native person, has made all Native people nothing more than bureaucratic numbers. Such are the consequences of practicing the Canadian style of baldheaded racial politics regarding racism, religion, patriotism—such are the politics of the Canadian state and nationalism.

First Nations people are still thought by the majority of Canadians to act and think exactly alike. Most Canadians, for instance, actually believe that First Nation people do not pay taxes or work or have a culture or do art or even have written languages, and to top it all off, they believe that First Nations get everything free. Of course, nothing could be further from the truth, but needless to say, racists and unscrupulous politicians find these kinds of political fables far too convenient a tool to use against Native people when it comes time to steal more of their land and natural resources. Racist sports teams in North America more than do their part in helping such people achieve their questionable goals since Indian mascots manage to reduce all Native people to mere commodities ripe for exploitation. Powerlessness begets racism and racism destroys people and so, as Buffy Sainte-Marie sings, "The little wheels spin and spin, big wheel turns round and round."

The coach of my son's hockey team regularly called him "chief," unknown to me until I happened to be close by one day and overheard this racist bilge. Up to that point I had been simplistically teaching my son that racism was practiced only by people with a limited education and intelligence. I was counseling him that such people did not know any better. I knew full well, of course, that Nazis in World War II were fully educated and considered to be intelligent people but they were racist nonetheless. Understandably, my son was confused and torn between taking instruction from this lowlife coach and taking to heart what I taught him about such people. I was absolutely livid, of course, when I learned about this coach's attitude, and it took all my willpower not to take this guy out to the back alley and teach him a lesson or two in what we now call political correctness; however, the idea of being politically correct was still gaining currency, since there was no such thing as being politically incorrect. Back then racism was more direct, more visible, and either you said what you thought about such racist attitudes or you shut up altogether.

In the most diplomatic way that I could possibly muster, I finally calmed down and informed this moron that he was behaving as a racist in the manner in which he was addressing my son and that if he did not cease and desist immediately, I would take steps to do something about it, and failing that, I would see him in court. Similarly, and at about the same time, my son's junior high principal responded to my criticism that he should not let white kids call Native children racist names by retorting that the kids all did that to each other anyway so what was the big deal? That backward simpleton explanation in that man's eyes somehow made all that okay. That principal and principle is still working at that school unfortunately, still poisoning young minds with racist philosophy. Racism in education is not a new concept, and we may just have to wait for the old believers in these old and antiquated institutions to die before any real fundamental change can take place.

The truth of the matter is—racism comes in all shapes and sizes, colors, philosophies, creeds, political persuasions, and ideologies, and it is up to us as individuals and as sports teams, as nations, to watch the old believers die off, but we also have to prevent new racists from being born. I have been discriminated against by whites, Chinese, Japanese, blacks, Native Americans, Italians, neo-Nazis, rednecks, judges, professors, politicians, artists, waiters, doctors, secondary school principals, students, cops, merchants, homeless people, and men of the cloth, so the waiting may take some time. Meanwhile, we need feel no sympathy for the Indian mascot who literally dies on the field, for we can rejoice in the knowledge that an old idea has finally come to an end—and the times? . . . well . . . they may be a-changin' after all, we shall see.

# Invisible Emblems: Empty Words and Sacred Honor

**Steve Russell**

I could not tell if I was dreaming.

You know how it is. You wake up but something about reality doesn't seem quite right and you think you might still be asleep but you can't really tell. I stumbled out of bed, started the coffee machine burbling, and collected the newspaper from the front yard.

The sports page told me that the New Jersey Niggers had beaten the Boston Micks. Some player on the Houston Hebes had accused the San Antonio Spics of dropping their last game to get a higher draft pick. The league was expanding to Toronto, and since they had already honored African Americans, Irish Americans, Jewish Americans, and Hispanic Americans, they wanted to name a team to honor Native Americans.

They sent out notices to all the tribal leaders, and they told us we could have whatever we wanted: Prairie Niggers, if the New Jersey team did not object, Redskins, Savages, Warriors, Heathens, Braves, Bucks—and of course the cheerleaders would be the Squaws, unless we wanted to modernize the language and just call them the Cunts.

But the tribal leaders voted for a write-in candidate, the Treaties. "Toronto Treaties." It has a nice ring to it. But the league was puzzled. What kind of a name is that?

"If the United States and Canada want to honor the First Nations," said the tribal leaders, "honor our treaties."

And there was a sidebar story. It seems that the President of the United States and the Prime Minister of Canada had heard this and called a joint press conference. "We had no idea," they said, "that our countries have violated so many agreements with Native Americans. We have formed a joint commission to recommend how to make it up to the survivors, and we have each proposed legislation tendering a formal apology."

And it was at that moment I knew I was dreaming.

From Indian mascots to the Nuager Clan of the Great Wanabi Nation, the *yonega* (whites) are fascinated with connecting to Indians, Indians understood in some bizarre sense that escapes most of us. It's the same way in Europe, where grown people go prancing through the woods half naked, drumming at all hours, and building tipis in places where tipis would manifestly make no sense. Tipis were good shelter for places where wood was scarce; American Indians did not build tipis in the woods.

Many Americans believe they are the grandchildren of Cherokee (why does is always have to be Cherokee?) royalty, usually a princess, who came to them in a dream and told them to collect artifacts associated with Siouan peoples. At least Grandmother had a sense of humor.

My grandmother had a sense of humor too. She was Dutch, not Cherokee, abandoned as a young girl at the Sac and Fox Agency in Indian Territory, later Oklahoma. She was a bit racist, a product of her times except in regard to Indians, who had treated her well. Her daughter married a Cherokee and produced me.

Bessie VanHooser was left by her father Samuel at the Sac and Fox Agency so he would not be slowed down in his run for the last great piece of "free land," the Cherokee Strip. Locked into that phrase "free land" was the story of my people, a story that escapes the notice of the descendants of all those Cherokee princesses.

The "free land" came from lands declared "surplus" after the Curtis Act destroyed the reservations of the Five Tribes in Indian Territory: Choctaw, Chickasaw, Seminole, Muscogee (Creek), and Cherokee. The Dawes Commission took rolls, a census of those who would involuntarily receive a piece of the tribal homelands, a process that proceeded in spite of resistance led by the Muscogee Chitto Harjo and the Cherokee Redbird Smith.

The lands allotted by the Dawes Commission had been given to the tribes in perpetuity (and also involuntarily) in exchange for the lands of their ancestors in the southeastern United States. The Indians were removed at gunpoint in an ethnic cleansing noted if at all in American history as the Trail of Tears. Cherokees lost their sacred lands and a third of their people. My great-great-great-grandmother made that walk, a lucky survivor.

The Cherokee Strip, also known as the Cherokee Outlet, was given to the tribe as a guaranteed path to the rich bison hunting on the Southern Plains. That use of the land was rendered moot with the near extinction of the bison. The rush for the Cherokee Strip was for the purpose of converting bison habitat to *yonega* habitat.

As my Dutch immigrant great-grandfather was an unsuccessful participant in that land rush, my Cherokee great-great-grandfather was a victim of it. In the sixties, my father received a per capita payment of compensation amounting to, if memory serves, $2.36. Payments were split among the many descendants of Dawes enrollees.

As Samuel VanHooser made his unsuccessful attempt to snag a piece of Cherokee land, his daughter Bessie waited at the Sac and Fox Agency, later to meet my grandfather, who did not come for free land but rather to work in the oil fields.

## To My Grandfather
for Judson George Russell

I.

*I told him I wanted to be like Mickey Mantle,*
*who escaped the poverty of rural Oklahoma,*
*and appeared to own New York,*
*a grand place located near Oz.*

*Mickey Mantle got to play in the World Series every year,*
*which I took to be annual games*
*between the New York Yankees and the Brooklyn Dodgers*
*to determine possession of New York.*

*"What position do you want to play?"*
*"Just like Mickey Mantle. Batter!"*

*Grampa laughed and laughed*
*until the laughs found the smoke in his lungs*
*and turned to coughs.*

II.

*Grampa always wore a suit and tie to town.*

*He would walk to the post office, check Box 384, and head for*
*the Playmor pool hall. This was a men's place and Granma*
*did not approve.*

*It was cool and dark. If I was with Grampa, and if I was*

*quiet, I could watch the elders play dominoes around ciga-*
*rette-burned tables with brass spittoons at the corners.*

*I often lost track of who won among the tall stories of the oil*
*boom days and it took a long time for me to realize that the*
*elders lost track of who won, too.*

*I learned to play dominoes and to lose track of who won*
*at Grampa's elbow, sipping my Grapette,*
*uninterested in the stink of his Falstaff,*
*and oblivious to the clouds from his Pall Malls.*

*Once or twice I tried to come into the Playmor*
*without Grampa,*
*but they always chased me off.*

*III.*

*When I was fifteen*
*and at home alone,*
*my Aunt Eleanor called*
*to tell me that Grampa was right,*
*he would not be coming home from the VA Hospital in*
*Muskogee.*

*I raged.*
*I fought with myself over whether to follow him.*

*The old Scots-Irish roughneck came to me in the Indian way*
*and told me gently that I had work to do*
*and my grandmother needed me*

*and I should hold fast like the warrior I would be.*
*It was not a good day to die.*

*Some time after the funeral*
*I left the public school deathtrap for good*
*and for once I did not hide in the public library.*
*I walked into the Playmor alone*
*in the middle of the day*
*and nobody chased me off.*

*IV.*

*I left Oklahoma*
*and as the years accumulate*
*Oklahoma almost leaves me.*
*The road home is distant and dusty and even more unlikely*
*than the road here.*

*I have seen New York.*
*And Oz.*
*And College.*

*Soon I will play dominoes with my own grandchildren.*

*And although I still cannot tie a necktie, Grampa,*
*I have taken your name.*

*I have never held a job that did not interest me. I have never*
*been rich but I have never been poor.*

*I remember you blowing Pall Mall smoke in my ear*
*to soothe an earache*

*and how you walked an Indian child down Main Street,*
*not hearing that which should not be spoken,*

*and I want you to know*

*I am still playing batter.*

I first stepped up to bat in the U.S. Air Force. Military service is a given for Indian boys. For me, it was a way to escape the menial jobs for which the public schools believed Indians were predestined. I didn't think of it that way at the time, of course. My grandparents had lost the war with the schools for my self-image. I just wanted to get through boot camp so I would not get sent back to Oklahoma without honor.

As I write this, a film about Indians in the military, *Windtalkers*, is skulking out of the theaters. It purports to tell the story of the Navajo code talkers in the Pacific theater of World War II. In fact, the hero is a white guy under orders that violate the fundamental bond of honor among U.S. Marines, orders to kill "his" code talker if capture appears imminent. The Marine Corps, of course, flatly denied that any such orders existed.

Since I am now an Indian academic, I do not have to be persuaded that the United States government will lie. However, after reading the histories and interviewing living code talkers, I have satisfied myself that in this matter the government is truthful. White Marines were not ordered to kill Indian Marines. Many code talkers *were* assigned white "minders," it turns out, after several incidents where the Navajos were taken POW by American troops

from other units. The purpose of the white escorts was not to protect the code talkers from the Japanese but, rather, to protect them
from Americans.

None of the code talkers I spoke with reported any ill treatment
from other troops beyond the usual stuff that was awaiting me
when I enlisted in the sixties, such as the inevitable "chief"
moniker. For some reason, *yonega* either see us as all chiefs and no
Indians or they don't know that Indians do not customarily
address each other as "chief." Or "Geronimo," except for one guy I
knew whose name really *was* Geronimo, but he was a *Chicano*, an
Indian who got his identity taken by the Spanish rather than by the
English, so he did not know he was Indian.

**Not Juan Valdez**

> In Chiapas,
> a man rises and pulls on plain white garments
> scrubbed from the river

> En Chiapas se levanta un hombre
> y se pone su ropa sencilla blanca
> lavada en el río

> takes bandana and straw hat, a long drink of water,
> and heads to work before the sun

> toma su pañuelo y sombrero de paja
> un trago grande de agua
> y se va a trabajar antes que salga el sol

> stopping at the Catholic mission
> and again at a private place

to thank all gods that will listen
that his children are healthy.

parando en la misión Católica
y también en un lugar retirado
a darle gracias a cualquier dios que escucha
por la salud de sus hijos.

The green coffee beans flying through his nimble fingers
into canvas sacks
are stained by the steam from the humid plants
mixed with his sweat
and we know
that his name is not Juan Valdez.

Los frijoles verdes de café
pasando por sus dedos ágiles
a sacos de lona
contienen el vapor de plantas húmedas
mezclado con sudor
y sabemos que él
no se llama Juan Valdez.

In Seattle,
a man in Polo and Nike and Ralph Lauren

En Seattle
un hombre vestido de Polo, Nike, Ralph Lauren
sips Chiapas coffee,
bebe a sorbitos su café de Chiapas
barely touches his croissant and kiwi

*Muy poco come de su pan y kiwi*
*notes on the front of the international section*
*that Indians are being killed in Chiapas,*

*Lee en frente de la sección internacional*
*Que matan indgenas en Chiapas*
*wonders briefly what they have done to provoke this*
*turns to the business section*
*to check his portfolio*

*Se pregunta de pasada*
*qué habrán hecho para merecer esto*
*va a la sección de negocios*
*para revisar sus valores*

*congratulates himself for remembering*
*to have his secretary pick up something*
*for his daughter's birthday,*

*se felicita porque se acordó*
*decirle a su secretaria*
*que le traiga algo para su hija*
*que cumple año*

*waves down the waitress to refill his coffee*

*llama a la mecera que le dé más café*
*y él tampoco se llama Juan Valdez.*

*and his name is not Juan Valdez, either.*

● ● ●

My son was born in San Antonio, a military town before it was a tourist town. Raised in Austin by an Indian father with close political alliances in the Chicano community, Paul's decisions should not have surprised me at all.

## Young Warrior
for Paul Russell-White

> *I told him*
>> *his father told him*
>>> *go in this order:*
>>>> *Air Force*
>>>> *Navy*
>>>> *Army*
>>>> *Marines*

*So naturally, he went directly to the Marine Corps recruiter. When he aced the tests and the recruiter started talking technical school,*

> *I told him*
>> *his father told him*
>>> *go in this order:   Electronic*
>>>> *Administrative*
>>>> *Mechanical*

*So naturally, he told the Marine Corps recruiter "combat infantry." When the assignments were made,*
> *I told him*
>> *his father told him*
>>> *go in this order:   Stateside*
>>>> *Europe*

*So naturally, he volunteered for hazardous duty.*
*He is not Dragging Canoe, Stand Watie, Ira Hayes or a Diné*
*Code Talker.*
*That was then and this is now, and he is my son.*
*And naturally,*
*this is how Indian sons have always served the conqueror:*

*Semper Fi!*

*Semper fidelis,* always faithful. Fidelity to what, and why? We are in fact faithful to the government that gave us *Lone Wolf v. Hitchcock,* Indian treaty abrogation, and the famous words of Justice Hugo Black that Indian lawyers call the all-purpose federal Indian law dissent: "Great nations, like great men, should keep their word." Whenever we see those words from Justice Black, we know we are about to have some more of our treaty rights stripped away at the whim of Congress. And yet we still fight wars for the United States, recognizing that white Americans, while they may not always be the best of neighbors, are still neighbors. Our fate is bound to the United States, and honor demands our service.

**At the Vietnam Veterans' Memorial**
*How quickly the tears come*
*is a tribute to their valor and to Maya Lin*
*and the perfection of her vision.*

*I perform an experiment*
*for my students back in San Antonio.*
*Standing before each panel*
*near the casualty-rich center*
*I count the seconds*

*until my eyes find a name*
*that tells of Indian-Spanish heritage:*

*A thousand and one-Flores*
*A thousand and two-Gonzalez*
*A thousand and three-Zuniga*
*A thousand and one-Flores*

*It is a bad day for flowers*
*and I cannot exceed three seconds.*

> *The air cavalry burns another village to save it as*
> *the choppers clip the morning air over the scent of*
> *jellied gasoline and the sound of crying children*
> *the fresh troops fly in and the body bags fly out.*

> > *After they pulled down the tipi*
> > *an Arapaho elder*
> > *raised a trade goods hatchet-pipe*
> > *and the young officer who rode him down*
> > *turned to finish the old man*
> > *and was almost thrown for*
> > *not knowing that a horse*
> > *will try not to step on a human being*
> > *or not knowing that the elder*
> > *struggling to rise on his unbroken arm*
> > *was a human being.*

*Across the grass there is a new monument to the women.*
*One nurse holds a pressure bandage*
*on the chest of a fallen warrior*

*with the heel of her hand*
*another gazes skyward*
*for Med Evac.*

*The smell of powder and the haze it creates and the*
*constant din-din-din of automatic weapons fire*
*takes all the senses out of the world but for a*
*wild shout that cuts through all the overloaded*
*neural pathways and connects to the here and now:*
*"Medic! We need a medic!" Women were not supposed*
*to be battlefield medics, but they forgot to tell*
*the battlefield.*

*The young officer ended the encounter*
*with a pistol shot to the head*
*close enough to spatter*
*the blue coat red.*
*He had another for the elderly woman*
*ululating over the body.*

*The statue raised to placate*
*those who did not share Maya Lin's vision*
*is not as dreary as I expected.*
*Three young warriors, bone-tired,*
*seem to be regarding*
*the names of their fallen comrades.*
*I stand beside them, crying.*

A woman is walking, stumbling in a line of other people. It is cold. The path she walks is icy mud and there is snow drifted around the tree trunks. There is no sound even though there are lots of people, and when she looks down at her feet wrapped in rags, the mud looks like a pudding beginning to set: there should be a crunching sound.

The woman falls and she thinks a snowdrift beside the path looks like a soft, downy pillow. She is sleepy. There is no sensation of cold. She closes her eyes.

She wakes with a sharp pain in her side. A man is standing over her, a soldier. He has poked her in the side with the barrel of a rifle. He shouts something and menaces her with the rifle, but there is still no sound. She climbs laboriously to her knees and then to her feet and stumbles back into the line.

Sometimes I watch this scene from above, sometimes from up or down the trail. Sometimes I am the woman and sometimes the soldier. The other people are many but faceless.

When I am the soldier, I feel no hatred. I move with a dispassionate efficiency but with no more feeling than my grandmother had toward the chicken when she wrung its neck for Sunday dinner.

It was many years later and after many visions of this scene that I learned how my family got to Indian Territory, now called Oklahoma. They could have been Old Settlers, who moved to Arkansas to escape colonial expansion, clashed with the Osage, and wound up in Oklahoma. They could have been survivors of Duwali's band, massacred in Texas and chased north (the ones who ran for Mexico having been slaughtered).

No, my great-great-great-grandmother walked what the perpetrators have come to call the Trail of Tears, a loose translation from the Cherokee. It was even after learning that, and after getting a law degree, that I discovered how the Trail of Tears came in defiance of a United States Supreme Court ruling that the removal of the Cherokee people to Indian Territory was without legal authority. "John Marshall has made his decision," President Andrew Jackson is rumored to have said of the chief justice, "now let him enforce it!"

So it was that a people who were wealthier and better educated than their white neighbors were rounded up at gunpoint and force-marched through a winter for which they had not been allowed to prepare. So it was the wife of Chief John Ross died in Arkansas after, the story goes, giving up her blanket to another. So it was that a third of our Nation perished and that I was born in Oklahoma. If I am linked with that history as certainly as I am linked to the United States, what does it matter to how I walk in the world? Does honor really demand as much as Indian sons have given it?

## Seeing Off the Troop Train
for Bessie Lois Russell

*Going to war must be grand!*

*"Nobody elected Truman," Granma grumped, and I was too*
*young to know she hadn't voted for Roosevelt either.*
*All the important people were there, and the Indians too.*

*I watched from Grampa's shoulders as the shiny black engine,*
*impossibly tall, belched enough steam to rival the politicians*
*behind their red, white and blue bunting.*

*"We got no business over there," Granma grumped.*

*Every Indian boy of age was on that platform, all dressed alike*
*and all the girls in town, it seemed, were pouring forth hugs,*
*kisses and tears.*

*The high school band played marches, everybody cheered, and I desperately*
*wished myself old enough and wise enough to ride the train to Korea.*

*Twelve years later,*
*I still thought going to war must be grand.*
*What does an Indian high school dropout in rural Oklahoma do that is*
*(legal) (honorable) (sensible)?*

*"We got no business over there," Granma grumped,*
*"and nobody elected Johnson."*
*No band; no speeches; no steam trains.*
*By that time, I knew she hadn't voted for Kennedy, either.*

*The train that went to Korea didn't stop in Vietnam, so we*
*said our goodbyes at the airport in Oklahoma City.*
*Twenty-eight years later, my son is a volunteer soldier.*
*Nobody elected Bush or his crew of 20th century retreads.*
*Granma is not here to say, "We got no business over there!"*

*But I hear her anyway.*

# Five

## WHO WE ARE, WHO WE ARE NOT: MEMORIES, MISCONCEPTIONS, AND MODIFICATIONS

*Today, after five centuries of Eurocentrism, most people have no idea which American Indian tribes still exist and which have been totally obliterated. Nor are they sure what traditions belong to what tribes. Over the years the public has been inundated with various presentations of Indian stereotyping thanks to movies and literature depicting Indigenous peoples as spiritual gurus, pagan savages, Indian princesses, or pitiful burdens of society—all this always with a mishmash of tribal cultures and traditions.*

*Fortunately, over the past decade there has been a rising interest in the accurate depiction of Native cultures and histories, as well as present-day struggles. More and more people (Indian and non) have become interested and respectful of the truths that somehow evaded history books. Only those of Indian blood can successfully dispel the misconceptions surrounding who we are and who we are not, why and how we are not all the same. Only we can keep relating true accounts of our own personal histories—revealing disappointments as well as accomplishments—in an effort to be respected as human beings who have every right to exist in this world, regardless of blood quantums, the color of our skin, or where we reside.*

# Yellow Woman and a Beauty of the Spirit

### Leslie Marmon Silko

From the time I was a small child, I was aware that I was different. I looked different from my playmates. My two sisters looked different too. We didn't look quite like the other Laguna Pueblo children, but we didn't look quite white either. In the 1880s, my great-grandfather had followed his older brothers west from Ohio to the New Mexico Territory to survey the land for the United States government. The two Marmon brothers came to the Laguna Pueblo Reservation because they had an Ohio cousin who already lived there. The Ohio cousin was involved in sending Indian children thousands of miles away from their families to the War Department's big Indian boarding school in Carlisle, Pennsylvania. Both brothers married full-blood Laguna Pueblo women. My great-grandfather had first married my great-grandmother's older sister, but she died in childbirth and left two small children. My great-grandmother was fifteen or twenty years younger than my great-grandfather. She had attended Carlisle Indian School and spoke and wrote English beautifully.

I called her Grandma A'mooh because that's what I heard her say whenever she saw me. *A'mooh* means "granddaughter" in the Laguna language. I remember this word because her love and her acceptance of me as a small child were so important. I had sensed immediately that something about my appearance was not acceptable to some people, white and Indian. But I did not see any signs of that strain or anxiety in the face of my grandma A'mooh.

Younger people, people my parents' age, seemed to look at the world in a more modern way. The modern way included racism. My physical appearance seemed not to matter to the old-time people. They looked at the world very differently; a person's appearance and possessions did not matter nearly as much as a person's behavior. For them, a person's value lies in how that person interacts with other people, how that person behaves toward the animals and the earth. That is what matters most to the old-time people. The Pueblo people believed this long before the Puritans arrived with their notions of sin and damnation, and racism. The old-time beliefs persist today; thus I will refer to the old-time people in the present tense as well as the past. Many worlds may coexist here.

I spent a great deal of time with my great-grandmother. Her house was next to our house, and I used to wake up at dawn, hours before my parents or younger sisters, and I'd go wait on the porch swing or on the back steps by her kitchen door. She got up at dawn, but she was more than eighty years old, so she needed a little while to get dressed and to get the fire going in the cookstove. I had been carefully instructed by my parents not to bother her and to behave, and to try to help her any way I could. I always loved the early mornings when the air was so cool with a hit of rain smell in the breeze. In the dry New Mexico air, the least hint of dampness smells sweet.

My great-grandmother's yard was planted with lilac bushes and iris; there were four o'clocks, cosmos, morning glories, and holly-hocks, and old-fashioned rosebushes that I helped her water. If the garden hose got stuck on one of the big rocks that lined the path in the yard, I ran and pulled it free. That's what I came to do early every morning: to help Grandma water the plants before the heat of the day arrived.

Grandma A'mooh would tell about the old days, family stories about relatives who had been killed by Apache raiders who stole the sheep our relatives had been herding near Swahnee. Sometimes she read Bible stories that we kids liked because of the illustrations of Jonah in the mouth of a whale and Daniel surrounded by lions. Grandma A'mooh would send me home when she took her nap, but when the sun got low and the afternoon began to cool off, I would be back on the porch swing, waiting for her to come out to water the plants and to haul in firewood for the evening. When Grandma was eighty-five, she still chopped her own kindling. She used to let me carry in the coal bucket for her, but she would not allow me to use the ax. I carried armloads of kindling too, and I learned to be proud of my strength.

I was allowed to listen quietly when Aunt Susie or Aunt Alice came to visit Grandma. When I got old enough to cross the road alone, I went and visited them almost daily. They were vigorous women who valued books and writing. They were usually busy chopping wood or cooking but never hesitated to take time to answer my questions. Best of all they told me the hummah-hah stories, about an earlier time when animals and humans shared a common language. In the old days, the Pueblo people had educated their children in this manner; adults took time out to talk to and teach young people. Everyone was a teacher, and every activity had the potential to teach a child.

But as soon as I started kindergarten at the Bureau of Indian Affairs day school, I began to learn more about the differences between the Laguna Pueblo world and the outside world. It was at school that I learned just how different I looked from my classmates. Sometimes tourists driving past on Route 66 would stop by the school at recess time to take photographs of us kids. One day, when I was in the first grade, we all crowded around the smiling white tourists, who peered at our faces. We all wanted to be in the picture because afterward the tourists sometimes gave us each a penny. Just as we were all posed and ready to have our picture taken, the tourist man looked at me. "Not you," he said, and motioned for me to step away from my classmates. I felt so embarrassed that I wanted to disappear. My classmates were puzzled by the tourists' behavior, but I knew the tourists didn't want me in their snapshot because I looked different, because I was part white.

In the view of the old-time people, we are all sisters and brothers because the Mother Creator made all of us—all colors and all sizes. We are sisters and brothers, clanspeople of all the living beings around us. The plants, the birds, fish, clouds, water, even the clay—they all are related to us. The old-time people believe that all things, even rocks and water, have spirit and being. They understood that all things want only to continue being as they are; they need only to be left as they are. Thus the old folks used to tell us kids not to disturb the earth unnecessarily. All things as they were created exist already in harmony with one another as long as we do not disturb them.

As the old story tells us, *Tse'itsi'nako* (Thought Woman, the Spider) thought of her three sisters, and as she thought of them, they came into being. Together with Thought Woman, they thought of the sun and the stars and the moon. The Mother Creators imagined the earth and the oceans, the animals and the people, and the *ka'tsina* spirits that reside in the mountains. The Mother Creators imagined all the plants that flower and the trees that bear fruit. As Thought Woman and her sisters thought of it, the whole universe came into being. In this universe, there is no absolute good or absolute bad; there are only balances and harmonies that ebb and flow. Some years the desert receives abundant rain, other years there is too little rain, and sometimes there is so much rain that floods cause destruction. But rain itself is neither innocent nor guilty. The rain is simply itself.

My great-grandmother was dark and handsome. Her expression in photographs is one of confidence and strength. I do not know if white people then or now would consider her beautiful. I do not know if the old-time Laguna Pueblo people considered her beautiful or if the old-time people even thought in those terms. To the Pueblo way of thinking, the act of comparing one living being with another was silly, because each being or thing is unique and therefore incomparably valuable because it is the only one of its kind. The old-time people thought it was crazy to attach such importance to a person's appearance. I understood very early that there were two distinct ways of interpreting the world. There was the white people's way and there was the Laguna way. In the Laguna way, it was bad manners to make comparisons that might hurt another person's feelings.

In everyday Pueblo life, not much attention was paid to one's physical appearance or clothing. Ceremonial clothing was quite elaborate but was used only for the sacred dances. The traditional Pueblo societies were communal and strictly egalitarian, which means that no matter how well or how poorly one might have dressed, there was no social ladder to fall from. All food and other resources were strictly shared so that no one person or group had more than another. I mention social status because it seems to me that most of the definitions of beauty in contemporary Western culture are really codes for determining social status. People no longer hide their face-lifts, and they discuss their liposuctions because the point of the procedures isn't just cosmetic, it is social.

It says to the world, "I have enough spare cash that I can afford surgery for cosmetic purposes."

In the old-time Pueblo world, beauty was manifested in behavior and in one's relationships with other living beings. Beauty was as much a feeling of harmony as it was a visual, aural, or sensual effect. The whole person had to be beautiful, not just the face or the body; faces and bodies could not be separated from hearts and souls. Health was foremost in achieving this sense of well-being and harmony; in the old-time Pueblo world, a person who did not look healthy inspired feelings of worry and anxiety, not feelings of well-being. A healthy person, of course, is in harmony with the world around her; she is at peace with herself too. Thus an unhappy person or spiteful person would not be considered beautiful.

In the old days, strong, sturdy women were most admired. One of my most vivid preschool memories is of the crew of Laguna women, in their forties and fifties, who came to cover our house with adobe plaster. They handled the ladders with great ease, and while two women ground the adobe mud on stones and added straw, another woman loaded the hod with mud and passed it up to the two women on ladders who were smoothing the plaster on the wall with their hands. Since women owned the houses, they did the plastering. At Laguna, men did the basket making and the weaving of fine textiles; men helped a great deal with the child care too. Because the Creator is female, there is no stigma on being female; gender is not used to control behavior. No job was a man's job or a woman's job; the most able person did the work.

My grandma Lily had been a Ford Model A mechanic when she was a teenager. I remember when I was young, she was always fixing broken lamps and appliances. She was small and wiry, but she could lift her weight in rolled roofing or boxes of nails. When she was seventy-five, she was still repairing washing machines in my uncle's coin-operated laundry.

The old-time people paid no attention to birthdays. When a person was ready to do something, she did it. When she no longer was able, she stopped. Thus the traditional Pueblo people did not worry about aging or about looking old because there were no social boundaries drawn by the passage of years. It was not remarkable for young men to marry women as old as their mothers. I never heard anyone talk about "women's work" until after I left Laguna for college. Work was there to be done by any able-bodied person who wanted to do it. At the same time, in the old-time Pueblo world, identity was acknowledged to be always in a flux; in the old stories, one minute Spider Woman is a little spider under a yucca plant, and the next instant she is a sprightly grandmother walking down the road.

When I was growing up, there was a young man from a nearby village who wore nail polish and women's blouses and permed his hair. People paid little attention to his appearance; he was always part of a group of other young men from his village. No one ever made fun of him. Pueblo communities were and still are very interdependent, but they also have to be tolerant of individual eccentricities because survival of the group means everyone has to cooperate.

In the old Pueblo world, differences were celebrated as signs of the Mother Creator's grace. Persons born with physical or sexual differences were highly respected and honored because their differences gave them special positions as mediators between this world and the spirit world. The great Navajo medicine man of the 1920s, the Crawler, had a hunchback and could not walk upright, but he was able to heal even the most difficult cases.

Before the arrival of Christian missionaries, a man could dress as a woman and work with the women and even marry a man without any fanfare. Likewise, a woman was free to dress like a man, to hunt and go to war with the men, and to marry a woman. In the old Pueblo worldview, we are all a mixture of male and female, and this sexual identity is changing constantly. Sexual inhibition did not begin until the Christian missionaries arrived. For the old-time people, marriage was about teamwork and social relationships, not about sexual excitement. In the days before the Puritans came, marriage did not mean an end to sex with people other than your spouse. Women were just as likely as men to have a *si'ash* (lover).

New life was so precious that pregnancy was always appropriate, and pregnancy before marriage was celebrated as a good sign. Since the children belonged to the mother and her clan, and women owned and bequeathed the houses and farmland, the exact determination of paternity wasn't critical. Although fertility was prized, infertility was no problem because mothers with unplanned pregnancies gave their babies to childless couples within the clan in open-adoption arrangements. Children called their mother's sisters "mother" as well, and a child became attached to a number of parent figures.

In the sacred kiva ceremonies, men mask and dress as women to pay homage and to be possessed by the female energies of the spirit beings. Because differences in physical appearances were so highly valued, surgery to change one's face and body to resemble a model's face and body would be unimaginable. To be different, to be unique, was blessed and was best of all.

The traditional clothing of Pueblo women emphasized a woman's sturdiness. Buckskin leggings wrapped around the legs protected her from scratches and injuries while she worked. The more layers of buckskin, the better. All those layers gave her legs the appearance of strength, like sturdy tree trunks. To demonstrate sisterhood and brotherhood with plants and animals, the old-time people make masks and costumes that transform the human figures of the dancers into the animal beings they portray. Dancers paint their exposed skin; their postures and motions are adapted from their observations. But the motions are stylized. The observer sees not an actual eagle or actual deer dancing but witnesses a human being, a dancer, gradually changing into a woman/buffalo or a man/deer. Every impulse is to reaffirm the urgent relationships that human beings have with the plant and animal world.

In the high desert plateau country, all vegetation, even weeds and thorns, becomes special, and all life is precious and beautiful because without the plants, the insects, and the animals, human beings living here cannot survive. Perhaps human beings long ago noticed the devastating impact human activity can have on the plants and animals; maybe this is why tribal cultures devised the stories about humans and animals intermarrying, and the clans that bind humans to animals and plants through a whole complex of duties.

We children were always warned not to harm frogs or toads, the beloved children of the rain clouds, because terrible floods would occur. I remember in the summer the old folks used to stick big bolls of cotton on the outside of their screen doors as bait to keep the flies from going in the house when the door was opened. The old folks staunchly resisted the killing of flies because once, long, long ago, when human beings were in a great deal of trouble, Green Bottle Fly carried the desperate messages of human beings to the Mother Creator in the Fourth World, below this one. Human beings had outraged the Mother Creator by neglecting the Mother Corn altar while they dabbled with sorcery and magic. The Mother Creator disappeared, and with her disappeared the rain clouds, and the plants and the animals too. The people began to starve, and they had no way of reaching the Mother Creator down below. Green Bottle Fly took the message to the Mother Creator, and the people were saved. To show their gratitude, the old folks refused to kill any flies.

The old stories demonstrate the interrelationships that the Pueblo people have maintained with their plant and animal clans-people. *Kochininako* (Yellow Woman) represents all women in the old stories. Her deeds span the spectrum of human behavior and are mostly heroic acts, though in at least one story she chooses to join the secret Destroyer Clan, which worships destruction and death. Because Laguna Pueblo cosmology features a female Creator, the status of women is equal to the status of men, and women appear as often as men in the old stories as hero figures. Yellow Woman is my favorite because she dares to cross traditional boundaries of ordinary behavior during times of crisis in order to save the Pueblo; her power lies in her courage and in her uninhibited sexuality, which the old-time Pueblo stories celebrate again and again because fertility was so highly valued.

The old stories always say that Yellow Woman was beautiful, but remember that the old-time people were not so much thinking about physical appearances. In each story the beauty that Yellow Woman possesses is the beauty of her passion, her daring, and her sheer strength to act when catastrophe is imminent.

In one story, the people are suffering during a great drought and accompanying famine. Each day Kochininako has to walk farther and farther from the village to find fresh water for her husband and children. One day she travels far, far to the east, to the plains, and she finally locates a freshwater spring. But when she reaches the pool, the water is churning violently, as if something large had just gotten out of the pool. Kochininako does not want to see what huge creature had been at the pool, but just as she fills her water jar and turns to hurry away, a strong, sexy man in buffalo-skin leggings appears by the pool. Little drops of water glisten on his chest. She cannot help but look at him because he is so strong and so good to look at. Able to transform himself from human to buffalo in the wink of an eye, Buffalo Man gallops away with her on his back. Kochininako falls in love with Buffalo Man, and because of this liaison, the Buffalo People agree to give their bodies to the hunters to feed the starving Pueblo. Thus Kochininako's fearless sensuality results in the salvation of the people of her village, who are saved by the meat the Buffalo People "give" to them.

My father taught me and my sisters to shoot .22 rifles when we were seven; I went hunting with my father when I was eight, and I killed my first mule deer buck when I was thirteen. The Kochininako stories were always my favorite because Yellow Woman had so many adventures. In one story, as she hunts rabbits to feed her family, a giant monster pursues her; but she has the courage and presence of mind to outwit it.

In another story, Kochininako has a fling with Whirlwind Man and returns to her husband ten months later with twin baby boys. The twin boys grow up to be great heroes of the people. Once again Kochininako's vibrant sexuality benefits her people.

The stories about Kochininako made me aware that sometimes an individual must act despite disapproval, or concern for appearances or what others may say. From Yellow Woman's adventures, I learned to be comfortable with my differences. I even imagined that Yellow Woman had yellow skin, brown hair, and green eyes like mine, although her name does not refer to her color, but rather to the ritual color of the east.

There have been many other moments like the one with the camera-toting tourist in the school yard. But the old-time people always say, remember the stories, the stories will help you be strong. So all these years I have depended on Kochininako and the stories of her adventures.

Kochininako is beautiful because she has the courage to act in times of great peril, and her triumph is achieved by her sensuality, not through violence and destruction. For these qualities of the spirit, Yellow Woman and all women are beautiful.

# She's Nothing Like We Thought

## Molly McGlennen

Simultaneously: Poet/Mixed-blood/Granddaughter. The blur of blood and lilac, the unforgettable smells of a Minnesota summer. Wore my swimsuit from June 1 until the night before third grade, where I first heard S Winner's 1868 "Ten Little Injuns Comic Song and Chorus." *(Two little Injuns foolin' with a gun, one shot t'other and then there was one.)* I stand in ankle-deep water, the beginning of color, and sing my version:

**10 Little Indians**

> *1 is a troubled breed, traces bloodlines*
>> *to Anishinaabe grandmother with her right hand,*
>> *a French grandfather with her left.*

> *2 never knows what box to check, used to go to mass*
>> *every Sunday with blue jeans and a t-shirt.*

> *3 has blue eyes and an Irish name, wrote her first poem*
>> *in the eighth grade and got a C.*

> *4 occupies two homes, one where she sleeps at night*
>> *and one as memorized landscape, arrowheads*
>> *she found around the bluffs.*

*5 loves to swim the lakes of her childhood, water she knows by heart,*

> *has never told the secret of her hands, their sculling.*

*6 shoots baskets with her brother in the alley*
> *until the crickets come out.*

*7 dances salsa and tries to speak Spanish, legs like her*
> *aunts and grandma;*
> *she saves the holy cards they send her.*

*8 helps her mother cook wild rice, has known the recipe, never spoken,*
> *since she was small; her hair pulled into a ponytail.*

*9 resists explaining herself every time someone asks her,*
> *So, what are you anyway?*

*10 takes her time, speaks slowly, is careful*
> *not to be misunderstood.*

Now bar patrons ask me: "What *are* you?" The room moves with iconic delineations of who I am supposed to be. My identity is emotion.

Both the midnight
and blinding white
of blue.
This happens all too often: locally, globally.

**Synonymous**

*They say in each country* la manera *is different*
*here, the shake of his shoulders*
*must double our rhythm of step*
*while Orquestra Charanzón belts a dizzying* son
*the faster the better, I say*
                    lo más pronto posible


*you echo me in Spanish all night*
*just as our bodies mirror a flawless step*
*your swivel is my "little kick"*
*something learned not through thoughtful practice*
*but mindless loyalty*
*to the* congas y timbales
*Cuban style, you say, is to rely on your hips*
*to push with the curve of a lateral* tilde.
*We become equivalence.*


*Later,* las calles de La Habana *lead me through hisses*
*and the distinct smell of 1952 carnival-blue chevrolet jams*
*or along the Malecón*
*where a stranger would call to me:*


                    Brasilera?


                    Italiana?


                    ¡Ven acá!

*I could simply respond with a silent ignorance of an outsider*
*or say no,* una mestiza, una indígena
*and slowly pronounce A-ni-sha-na-be*
en el norte de los Estados Unidos
*and it is here, as the waves power toward us from African*
*winds*
*where slave ships once carved new crowns for Spain*
*here, where I see pairs of dancers*
*swirling the most beautiful bronze into the night*
*the spray misting us*
*bringing in centuries of sugarcane money and the business of* ron
*here, in this moment, he finally says,* oh, Indian
*as he extends his finger on top of his head*
*an indication of a feather*
*and I*
*only nod my head*
*in recognition*
*of its ubiquity.*

I toss my map away and go anywhere, can follow the shorelines for days in the landscape of memory. This is where she is, washing her hair in the middle of the lake, in the middle of the night. She sends me the songs of who I am:

## Composition

*I assemble with the hands of a poet*
*who does not know the end*
*of her poem, ink is an afterthought.*
*Piecing myself together I use all the material I can gather:*
*Potter's clay and her acrylic paints, thick and thin*
*camel-hair brushes; a Chinese jump rope that noosed my ankles,*

*twine she and I used to hold the tomato plants up.*
*If I use food, it's mostly*
*what I can recall: Wild rice and fried walleye,*
*peeled oranges left for me in the morning.*
*The crescent-moon cashews she loves.*
*If I need markers, I locate northern lakes,*
*lilac bushes that guarded our back yard,*
*overgrown and drooping with fragrance:*
*The cotton-blue bed sheets she draped on the line.*
*I must sit patiently to do this, to place it all in order,*
*from memory. But will it matter*
*if I can't quite get the smell—*
*her hands as they tied red ribbon round ends of my braids?*

Answer. Seen the whooping savages running across football fields; seen the stoic Tonto figure on TV, in the movies; have been told that all those Indians are drunks (with my mom in the room and her eyes to the floor); I know these metanarratives, rip open their seams and scream: Manoomin my grandma cooks, mayagibinewag my mother prepares, ogaawag my father catches.
Stories she keeps are patterns of memory
Different every time
Over cups of coffee
This is nothing like
      what you want me to be:

**Legend**
    *My body remembers*
    *the time we rolled out dough*
    *for two days*
    *flour hands*

*salted heat*
*a kitchen like fire*
*careful not to pat it*
*too thin*
*biscuits should fill*
*empty stomachs*
*you tell me*
*how you were taught this*
*no more school*
*after fourth grade*
*what's a little girl to do*
*but listen*
*and follow the mark*
*of a hand*
*hear a history*
*punctuated by story*
*when your mother*
*would whisper hers*
*in between scaling*
*and gutting*
*the walleye*
*ashamed to admit*
*how lakes had always*
*fed her family*
*how she had married*
*a pale Frenchman*
*moved away from the water*
*and you*
*a daughter once removed*
*from the fact*
*now stands next to me*

*says history doesn't have to mean*
*coming over in a boat*
*says this is how*
*you feed a family:*
*until your hands and arms ache*
*until your body remembers*
*the blood in its lines*
*like fried fish*
*and flour biscuits.*

Simultaneously: Listener/Dancer/Woman. I defy patterns of recognition. In the bar, they tell me who I am, who I ought to be. On the bus, they tell me who I am, who I ought to be. In the university, they tell me who I am, who I ought to be. I blur their lines in motions of song, the waves I hear lapping upon shore, the color it makes when I hear in two tongues. This is who I am.

# MANITOWOC: SPIRIT PLACE IN ANISHINAABE

### Tim Hays

For Calvin & Judy in Chicago

NOTE:

The Field Museum of Natural History in Chicago houses the remains of more than forty thousand Indigenous people. This does not include other entities that have been or are still alive: Kachina dolls, flutes, drums, headwear, and ceremonial instruments from holy people. Many of theses bodies were "donations" for the 1892 Columbian Exposition and the World Parliament of Religions, marking "First Contact" in this hemisphere. Indigenous people were excluded from this event.

*To the Voices of the Ancient Ones,*
*now, long unheard . . .*

*I stand by a secure glass case,*

*a*

*DISPLAY*

An Ancient Voice, composed of wood,

eyes, a mouth,
smooth, soft in appearance

I am full of

> WONDER
> AWE
> ENCHANTMENT

at this Magic Flute

But . . .

In this great Temple to western ideology
this One Ancient Voice-
has been silenced.

As a tongue cut out,
displaced,
>       lost,
Fury in Grief,
>       Rage in despair

This Voice has been . . .

> COATED
> COVERED
> VIOLATED
> SUFFOCATED

*by scientists' POISON-*

*a resin made to "preserve" the skin of*
*this*
*One Ancient Voice / TOXINS*

*cover the wood, not allowing*

*any one / person / being*

*to Breathe LIFE into the Flute*
*as it is*

*POISONOUS*

*to Human Touch.*

*As the Western mind*
*"preserves"*

*identity*
*culture*
*mind AND*
*lack of world view-*

*This One Ancient One is*
*quiet*
*grieving*

*silenced.*

*I wonder:*
*is its thought dead because he/she cannot speak*
*by its own will or volition?*

*Would she/he live again could he/she*
*sing and tell*
*Who was serenaded . . .*
*Quiet passion, focused seduction*
*of*
*generations of ANCESTORS*

*who made Love to her / his Voice*
*and who venerated this*
*PLACE*
*rather than time*

*As*

*One Continuous Living Connection.*

● ● ●

*I <u>MARVEL</u>-*
*do the Ancient Ones*
*play*
*in voices / sounds / tones / songs*
*that are unheard to*
*deaf Western ears?*

*Do they, the ANCIENT ONES,*

*SPEAK ?*

*Will I*
*of this*

*future*

*Generation*
*be*
*ALLOWED*
*to become*
*an*
*ANCIENT ONE,*
*or, will my Being wander in <u>discomfort-</u>*

*an*
       *ENTITY*

*studied /*
*examined /*
*dissected*

*by Western minds and housed in a*
*glass case ?*
            **• • •**

    *I*
    *AM*
    *AN*
    *ANCIENT ONE . . .*
    *Ancestors walk with me*

    *Generations of*

*HEALING*
*TEACHING*
*GUIDING*

*spirit-beings*

*watch me*
*love me*
*CARRY ME*


*This one Ancient Voice*
*and Her/His/His/Her*
*Voice*
*I can Hear;*
*I am*
*not deaf*
*to the unheard*
*songs*
*that Western minds*
*do not*
*understand.*

# Pyramids, Art, Museums, and Bones: Some Brief Memories

### David Bunn Martine

I 've always been involved in the arts, my mother being a classical opera singer and artist, and Chiricahua Apache, my father a Hungarian pianist/voice teacher whose own father designed the Vatican embassy in Budapest. Grandmother, a Shinnecock Montauk Indian by whom I was raised on the reservation, loved to read European history and do beadwork taught to her by my grandfather. It was natural, therefore, for me to be interested in history, mostly American and Native American, music, and art.

I had three great-grandfathers on my mother's side who remain vividly in my mind's eye, all of whom I never met. The first one, named Chin-Chee, was a well-known Chiricahua Apache warrior who was killed two weeks before Geronimo's final surrender in Mexico in 1886, whereupon his wife, my great-grandmother, Cah-gah-Ashen, married "Old Martine," a very tough ex-warrior turned U.S. Army scout, who with a cousin helped persuade Geronimo to surrender. I grew up with stories only the family knew concerning the Apache wars and the years of Geronimo's imprisonment at Fort Sill, Oklahoma. The tales of ancestors such as Victorio, Mangas Coloradas, Nana, Chato, and Cochise have always loomed large in imagination.

My other great-grandfather was named Charles Sumner Bunn. He was a professional guide and hunter and farmer from eastern

Long Island whose Algonquian ancestors (Shinnecock and Montauk) are from an ancient stock documented to nearly ten thousand years in this area and were "off-shore" whalers from dug-out canoes before the English arrived. He was a well-respected elder, leader, and also a prolific wood-carver of duck decoys. The culture had been a product of three hundred years of coexistence with first the Dutch then the English colonial settlers. His father was a first mate on whaling ships that went around the world, finally drowning with ten other men of the tribe during a salvage operation in the Atlantic Ocean near Long Island on a ship called *Circassian*, ironically in 1876. Some of his hunting clients were interesting people such as Kermit and Quentin Roosevelt, sons of Teddy; Christian Herter, a former secretary of state, and many other wealthy businessmen and politicians who vacationed on Long Island's East End at the turn of the last century.

History such as this colored my perceptions in childhood, which was rich, varied, and flavored by both the Indian and white worlds. I was raised with the idea that Indian culture was just as dignified, important, and great as any other culture. The juxtaposition of Indian culture and European or American culture easily coexisted in our household.

Music and spirituality have always been a part of my world, a part of the understanding of living simultaneously in two worlds. My mother took voice lessons for years, gave many concerts, and was one of the few Indians in classical music at that time. I was raised in the Protestant Christian tradition though fully respected and admired the traditional Indian spirituality. Aware that we had medicine people in the Apache side of the family, I also began studying the mysticism of India and other esoteric wisdom traditions.

During the 1950s, my family appeared on several TV shows. My grandmother described the history being depicted in the then-new movie called *Apache* with Burt Lancaster and Jean Peters. This was a movie about the last days of the "Geronimo war" and was quite accurate and sympathetic toward the Indian cause for the time. Grandpa and Mother sang Apache songs with Steve Allen, Ernie Kovacs, and Dave Garroway. My grandpa had been comfortable as a lecturer and performer since his days before 1920 at the Hampton Institute in Virginia. He was a traditional Chiricahua yet was very comfortable interacting with other Indian cultures and the white man's world as well. The family also took part in powwows and operated a gift shop called Teepee in the Hills Indian Trading Post, where they made everything they sold.

I was raised with the support and freedom to pursue anything I was interested in, which were music and the arts. The culmination of this interest began with my high school training, and attending the University of Oklahoma as well as Central State University in Edmond, Oklahoma. I also attended the Institute of American Indian Arts in Santa Fe, New Mexico, where I found the combination of all my interests in the museum training program. There I studied techniques for showcasing the different Indian cultures to the best advantage. I learned what makes the "Indian museum" unique as opposed to the ordinary museum—how there are different sensibilities regarding sacred objects and about the correct presentation of said objects. But generally the emphasis was that of a positive portrayal of the cultures, using the best up-to-date methods.

There was also a strong emphasis on the intercultural relationships between North, South, and Central American Indian cultures, exemplified by a trip to Mexico City as a special effort at establishing a connection with the National Restoration Institute. I toured a "community museum" that was created largely by the

Indigenous tribal people of the country as well as the Pyramids of the Sun and Moon. This trip greatly broadened my vision of the vastness of the Indigenous cultures of the hemisphere.

All during this time I had simultaneously been continuing my own work at painting Long Island Indian, Apache, and other Indian histories, and depicting historical scenes and portraits based on research and personal knowledge. I had established a good working relationship with the local archaeological association on Long Island and had begun contributing numerous illustrations and artwork to books and mural exhibits for a museum.

During the late 1980s I became interested in archaeological site preservation, and eastern Long Island seemed to have an abundance of opportunities to become involved in this sort of activism. I even confronted the phenomenon of the "hobbyist" movement. There were others who felt the same way as I—which was that we should stand up for the dignity of our history and people and the "religious freedom" of our culture.

One site called "Sugar Loaf Hill" was an important multiple burial pit on a high hill that was about four thousand years old. It had been studied and looted twice this century, but the town council had apologized and claimed ignorance at the importance of the site when confronted by us Indians at a public meeting. We literally carried a four-by-eight foot mural into the council session and described what sort of ceremony may have taken place there, to present an idea of the sacredness of what had been destroyed. But it was to no avail. The developer who bought the site leveled twenty feet off the top and built his mansion there despite protests.

The second involvement was an interesting situation involving a small but influential Indian museum in the area. There were human skeletons on display for decades representing the old "pseudo-scientific" reasons. We had to directly confront the board members and bring negative publicity to get them to remove the remains from view. They eventually did and even invited me to join the board of the museum, which I did for a time. But we were disappointed that they did not return the remains to us for reburial.

A third and final situation had to do with staving off developers from a grave site that was ancient but continued to be in use until the 1930s. In this case the developers thought they could railroad the situation and catch the Indians sleeping. But there were two elements to our advantage. The archaeologists hired by the pro-Indian side were technologically superior in that they had access to satellite technology and they had worked with the Iroquois Confederacy. Accusations of incompetence on the part of the developers' archaeologists blew the developers' case out of the water. Also, we launched a massive protest and great quantities of negative publicity, which turned the tide in our favor.

Needless to say, my experiences in the cultural preservation area were now becoming mixed. These negative experiences helped crystallize my thoughts concerning Indian cultural presentation and perceptions—which were that the unique, special nature of the culture, importance, and validity of Indian cultural preservation is not viewed as positive by everyone. One could see that the anti-Indian forces were either superintelligent or ignorant rednecks, or something in between. Seldom were they led by intimations from the heart.

My time working at the National Museum of the American Indian during the 1990s put a capstone on some of my experiences. When I was hired at NMAI, I thought the opportunity was a dream come true. I would be paid the best I ever had, and continue in the field I had studied so many years before. At this point I was the director of our tribal museum. Now I was being recognized for the ability to assist in a large project, that of dismantling the old Museum of the American Indian in New York City after the Smithsonian took over. I was being hired as part of a select few called the "move team." We actually packed up and handled forty-five thousand objects in the most massive collection of Indian materials in the world. However, I began to understand the detailed history of George Heye, the founder of the museum, and the methods he used to divest the Indian people of their property those many years ago. It was a challenge working in an atmosphere in which there were forced culture shifts, such as adding a large influx of Indian staff to the museum, then the museum being forced to deal with having to return objects to the tribes from which they came. This concept was, of course, completely foreign to the concepts established by the anthropological and ethnographic fields. This was also sometimes difficult for the older museum staff and the non-Indian scholars who backed the museum.

We were intimately involved with repatriation issues and all of the objects, many of which had no business being outside of the communities in which they had been created. Those of us on the Indian staff, with the support of our supervisor, tried to institute "traditional care procedures" regarding the handling, transport, and storage of the various objects. Personally, it was an honor to be present at the repatriation of medicine bundles and other sensitive items when the visiting delegations came to the museum. Being allowed to be present during the receipt of the objects and to see the elders with tears in their eyes was indeed an honor. Our supervisor was a strong supporter and advocate for the rights of the traditional ways of dealing with the collection, and through her guidance we sponsored medicine people to come and care for the objects. We dealt with objects from all over the hemisphere, and there were memorable circumstances involving people from Central and South America in this regard. It was also a privilege to work with objects belonging to some of our greatest Indian leaders such as Geronimo, Chief Joseph, and Joseph Brandt, as well as a five-thousand-year-old Nazca ceramic trumpet, the tremendous Mayan figurine collection, and the jade and gold material.

I learned how difficult it was finding a resting place for remains when the culture from which they came did not want them returned because of their beliefs, or because identification had not been made as to the culture of origin. There did seem to be a lack of any kind of spirituality connected with the handling of the material or any spiritual feelings shown by most members of the non-Indian staff, though they tried to be as respectful as they could. The prevailing attitude was usually the superior position of science and the scientific imperative. Sometimes one could detect a patronizing attitude with regard to our beliefs. I don't think it was conscious behavior. But I personally feel that society at large has lost the feeling of the sacred in whatever belief system they might subscribe to; therefore, I was not really surprised but disheartened at the lack of such appreciation of the sacred when dealing with the Indian materials in this institutional setting. This did manifest as occasional strain in staff relationships between Native and non-Native staff. It also presented difficulties among the Indian staff as well.

All in all, working in Indian museums can be a wonderful experience if done with respect and awareness of the unique characteristics of the collections and cultures represented. Currently I am involved in management decisions as well as the creative aspects of exhibits and design, leaving political activism mostly behind. But I am grateful for all experiences and looking forward to a future, by the grace of the Creator, to be of service in the days ahead.

## Shinnecock Whalers

Behemoths they were to ride the waves
Into the breakers and currents they came
Since time immemorial from dawn to dusk
The whales swam by unstoppable thrust.

When to the shore he floundered and sank
They came close by, sacred body to thank
Great gift of God, Creator Spirit, were they
The behemoths and great fish of the bay.

Into canoes of tulip and oak
Shinnecock men navigated the stroke.
Through wave and shoals, they pulled the trees
Finely carved vessels of wood and dreams.

Fins and tails they said long ago
Were considered holy, from nature on loan
Fearless and reverent Shinnecock men they were
Who venerated nature, the spirit to stir.

Then manning the crews aboard whaling ships
They sailed seven seas at a furious clip
Among three years time, sailing the great vessels
To process and harvest the whales they wrestled.

Until at last it no longer paid
For whalers to sail amidst storm and hail
Whales they did kill in great numbers long
Before oil and blubber disappointed the throng.

*Oil it was which took their place*
*Black gold was used to fuel the race.*
*All whaling ceased, by the ancient ways*
*Of years sailing, toiling, oceans and bays.*

## Apache Mountain Spirits

*The Chiricahuas have a dance; but it is more than a dance:*

*it is four men painted in soot and ash whose*
*base is for celestial pattern in white—*
*of moons, and stars; of rainbows and mountains,*
*of slicing lightning, cracking through the deep*
*darkness of the evening sky*

*it is the bon-fire, tall as a white pine, roaring*
*to life with the substance of gold, and orange*
*crackle and hot with the heat of a*
*hundred blast furnaces*

*it is the round clearing, symbol of the*
*cycles of cosmos, around which the people dance*
*side to side, or one behind each—*
*offering the life within all*

*it is the mystical move of the deer and horns;*
*the headpieces and masks and swords of the*
*protectors, the avengers who avenge the affront*
*of the light by foe of darkness*

*it is the slash and spin of their movements, the*

*jagged, posturing grace of other-worldly souls*
*sent as guardians to the people*

*it is the songs of the singers and their drums,*
*drumming the chant of the soil and the flowers,*
*the spirits of yesterday and the spirits of a thousand years ago,*

*it is the powerful songs,*
*it is the ancient songs, which underscore all*
*creation as the heartbeat of earth and sky*
*and the "Giver of Life."*

## The Sacred Hill

*The prayers went forth—*
*five thousand years ago*
*five hundred years ago*
*yesterday.*

*It makes no difference; the sound resounds in*
*the earth—for the preservation of this world,*
*for safe passage to the next;*
*charnal houses and sacrifice, almost Egyptian-like*
*to preserve to the journey beyond, fire, air, water and*
*earth—they were familiar with these. And*
*they came and went chanting their sacred*
*sounds of the earth:*

*giving thanks to the sun*
*giving thanks to the eagles and the clouds*
*giving thanks to the plants and the fire and the seas,*
*but there was power here too—sacred power,*

*power to transcend time and space, to ride*
*the trails of spirit and matter;*

*the grave was multi-sized, containing pottery and*
*stone, wood and bone, ash and ochre, mysteries*
*all were these. On the east they buried them,*
*facing the sun and its pathway to the creator,*
*to absorb the golden substance of life above and*
*below with portals, high frequency portals to other*
*worlds they say—worlds above or worlds below?*

*Shades of Egypt again and shades of Cahokia*
*and the moundbuilders, shades of Palenque or*
*is it ancient Peru—this sacred hill of the Sugar Loaf?*

# IDENTIFICATION PLEAS

### Eric Gansworth

S o it's the summer of 2002, late spring actually, May, in the town of Del Rio, Texas, perhaps one of the last places on earth I thought I would be engaged in an identity crisis. For the sake of accuracy, though, the crisis occurs externally, not internally, but truly, I should have been more careful. I am here with a friend, Donnie, who has a piece of land in this small border town. He is showing me around the state to facilitate some research. He asks me if I want to cross the border into Acuña, as it is right there. Though the temperature is over a hundred degrees, we walk across the bridge above the Rio Grande into Mexico. On the exact border, large metal pegs mar the full surface of the pavement, gleam in the heat, and announce the change of country in full-size versions of that dotted line one sees on maps.

Here, trucks pull up, from the United States' end of the bridge, and stop, right on the dotted line. Other trucks meet them on the Mexican side. The drivers descend from their cabs and carry large boxes from the cargo areas of the United States trucks to those of the Mexican trucks. The border guards sit disinterested, watch this transaction under the bright sun, so I take a cue from them that this activity is nothing worth noting, and move on.

Acuña's commercial districts evidently consist almost exclusively of three things: souvenir shops, severely economical dentists, and pharmacies, where the picture windows are full of containers housing large quantities of discount prescription drugs, in the same manner candy is displayed in the windows of chocolatiers. Cipro is, by far, the most popular drug. It is mere months after the anthrax scare of 2001, and the national obsession with this antibiotic as the cure-all for its fears of biological terrorism has not yet waned. Donnie has obtained prescription drugs here before as, for most, a prescription is not needed at these places, and a man standing in one of the shop doorways invites me to buy a prescription, which I can then take into the building to make my purchase. Donnie explains this is for controlled-substance prescriptions, which the border guards would need to see with official documentation. The man shows me his prescription pad.

This offer seems more than slightly illegal, but Donnie assures me the border guards have no interest in examining these sorts of drugs all that closely—this is routine. I have no need for controlled substances at the moment, so I decline and we move on, past more competitive dentists, stores displaying, among other things, taxidermy armadillos and alligators, and lastly, we pass buses advertising reasonable rates to cross the span to the United States. While it was an unpleasantly hot walk across, I see little justification for a bus to make the trip, and again Donnie clarifies that sometimes it is less of a hassle for Mexicans to cross the border if they use the bus instead of walking the bridge.

We leave Mexico a few minutes later, on the bridge's northbound sidewalk, again stepping on the hot metal pegs, delineating one place from another. Below us, the Rio Grande seems more like the Rio Average, a muddy stream surrounded by dense growth of cane, and above the sidewalk overlooking the river, heavy-gauge steel mesh curves inward on sturdy beams nearly encircling us overhead. This architectural feature is designed to dissuade jumpers from making the five-story leap into the river or thick brush below. Donnie mentions that people have made the attempt and that random surveillance cameras are mounted in the cane— all of this to keep people from entering the United States in inappropriate fashion. As we continue, young men all around us are engaged in last-ditch efforts to catch a ride into the country, attempting to avoid interrogation, holding their thumbs out to all vehicles, even within sight of the immigration office.

Walking past them, I make eye contact with one of the young men and nod, but I hold no interest for him in my current state of carlessness. We arrive at the office and are both relieved that it is air-conditioned. Donnie shows his license to the officer, who waves him on, and I reach into my pocket, pull out my wallet, and wonder how many minutes it will take for Donnie's truck cab to cool down.

Opening the fold, I am momentarily confused by the version of my face staring back at me from the plastic card in the easiest access slot. I am almost ten years younger, wearing enormous late-eighties glasses, my hair is long, wavy, and pulled back, and behind me the lush foliage of a reservation road fills the rest of the image. It is my tribal identification card, documenting my name, birth date, clan, tribe, reservation address, blood quantum, and the signature of the man on the reservation who officiates on such matters, next to my own signature. Mine is a little more complicated than some, but not unfathomably so. I am a member of the Onondaga Nation, although the Tuscarora Nation, which involves its own little hierarchical messes, issued the card, but those generally concern intertribal animosities and have nothing to do with issues anyone from beyond tribal borders would even understand, much less engage in. The back of the card lists several agreements with the United States, asserting the sovereignty of the

Haudenosaunee, the league of six nations to which both the Onondaga and Tuscarora nations belong, known in the United States as "the Iroquois."

The card itself is not confusing to me, of course, but it usually rests in my wallet behind a document I tend to need much more frequently: my driver's license. My license is nowhere to be found within the wallet, and then I suddenly can see the card in my mind, can picture its exact location, and thus can confirm it is not on my body. I had flown into Lubbock the day before, and though I hate flying, I realize it is a necessary annoyance of what I do professionally, so I accept it and try to make the situation as uneventful as possible.

Since September 2001, flying has changed, and while I most definitely do not mind greater security, I have had to remove my shoes several times in airports, and have my bags rifled through as well, but the most consistent change has been nearly relentless requests for my identification from airport personnel. To make things easier on myself and on those asking, I have gotten a "flight wallet" the size of an airline ticket, and in this I keep my boarding pass, frequent flyer card, and, yes, while I am traveling, my driver's license. The flight wallet, at the moment I approach the immigration officer, sits approximately a hundred yards away, in Donnie's truck, across the road, but more important, across the border.

"Identification?" the officer asks, and I hand him my Native American Identification Card. He looks at it, tosses it down, and looks at me, smirking. "Now," he says, and before he can go on, he notices Donnie paying attention to this interaction, standing on the far side of the turnstile and asks what he wants.

"Just waiting," is Donnie's reply—perhaps not the most useful one for me at the moment, but we go with what we have.

"You can wait outside," the officer says, and Donnie looks at me. Being in no position to convey much information, I shrug my shoulders and watch him leave the air-conditioned building. The officer turns back to me, lifts the card again, and apparently engages the scenario he had foreseen a couple of minutes before. "Now," he repeats, snapping the card on his desk this time, perhaps for emphasis, as if he had gotten an ace in a game of solitaire, "do you have any real ID?"

I am what you might call ethnically ambiguous in appearance. Over the years the odd looks, vague frowns, and unasked questions have become the routine. It has been kind of interesting, existing as a walking, breathing Rorschach test for others' perceptions and stereotype templates.

I have been mistaken for Italian, Armenian, Middle Eastern, Hawaiian, Russian, Polish, German, Portuguese, and Jewish, but I am most often wrongly assumed to be Latino. The first time it happened was in a men's room at a concert, when a drunken patron at the next urinal insisted I was a member of Los Lobos, the band whose set had finished about a half hour before. I insisted I was not, as you can imagine, but he was convinced, and told me not to worry, that he was cool, that my secret was safe with him. That confusion was amusing the first time, under those circumstances, as I have only infrequently been mistaken for a urinating rock star. The less glamorous mistake with my ethnicity happens nearly every time I am in the Southwest. This stands to reason, as Mexicans are Indians across the border, in essence, and we are the same in that we had very different, unique cultures before colonialism came along and divided us up with those stainless steel rivets in the bridge.

I was born and raised on a reservation in western New York State, a small place, home to fewer than two thousand people. Many of those people claim full-blood status, though some are blond, some have blue eyes, and some have complexions more fair than those babies have, you know the ones, those babies who star in detergent commercials. My complexion is slightly dark, and deepens easily in the summer, so that by the end of June, even with minimal exposure, I usually sport what used to be called "a savage tan." My eyes are dark brown as well, and my hair appears to be black most of the year, but by late summer dark red highlights have burned into it. My body also reveals other telltale signs that prevent me from claiming full-blood status. I have genetic qualities that allow me to grow a beard and a mustache, and I have chosen to cultivate those traits.

This was not always the case. My hair was long a fair amount of my childhood and through adolescence—though not the long, straight Lakota hair all Indians are *supposed* to have. It seems many eastern Indians have a rougher textured hair, and mine falls into this category. No matter how much I might brush my hair out every morning, invariably I looked less like any Indians in Edward Curtis photographs and more like Jerry Garcia from the Grateful Dead, or Gilda Radner playing Roseanne Rosannadanna, on early *Saturday Night Live* episodes (yes, they do look like one another, and yes, I looked like their child). My brothers, being brothers, insisted on reminding me of this resemblance every single day, in efforts to encourage a trip to the barber for me. They even offered to drive me there and pay for the haircut. You can imagine, it was not pretty.

I resisted, for years, though. On the reservation, as in many other places, hair is a political statement. I learned this reality early. One of my brothers, Lee, the only one, incidentally, who did not encourage me to go to the barber, began growing his hair long in the late 1960s, before he burned his draft card but after our oldest brother had been shipped out to Vietnam. Lee was suspended from high school a number of times for having his hair too long, until one time my mother grew tired of his forced removals, took him to school herself, grabbed an idle white kid in the hallway whose hair was longer than my brother's, and dragged them both into the office to confront the principal with this discrepancy. My brother was reinstated, but one of his instructors insisted he had missed too much time in his suspensions to graduate, so he went to summer school, but he did it in long hair and graduated in August.

He is not the first member of my family to have an educational institution concern itself with his hair. In the early part of the twentieth century, the Dawes Act was in full swing, and my grandfather's parents were persuaded by government agents to allow their son the great privilege of attending one of the Indian boarding schools. They claimed that he would have a much better chance of surviving in the world if he could learn a trade in the broader culture. He learned to play a western instrument, the piccolo, I believe, and eventually remembered nothing about water drums but was well versed in snare and bass. Before his musical transformation, however, the school administrators had introduced other changes to him.

A few years after I had begun teaching in a college, I received in an interoffice mailer one day a few pages that had been photocopied from a book on the industrial school at Carlisle, Pennsylvania, and a note from the acquisitions librarian, wondering if the young man in the photo on one of the pages had any connection to me. I flipped through the sheets quickly, and there, on the third page, my grandfather looked out onto the future, a twelve-year-old in some sort of military uniform, his hair short, clipped, blunt. The only other photo I had seen of his childhood had been taken when he was five or so, and his hair streamed wavy and thick from his head, past his shoulders—seven years before the industrial school asserted itself into his life. My own hair at the time I examined these pages was growing out of its "job interview cut."

Through college I had kept my hair in various stages of long, but it always looked wild, like some cross-pollination between Howard Stern and Paul Stanley, from the rock group Kiss. In graduate school I got rid of it all and kept a reasonably short style through that period, until I graduated and got past my first set of job interviews. As I began teaching at the college a few miles from the reservation where I grew up, my hair was still fairly short, appropriate for the era, the early 1990s, but as soon as I signed the contract I let it grow back out, and in 1998 my braid was about a foot and a half long, when I decided to get rid of it.

I had been involved in the Indian academic community for a number of years by that point. The more I looked around, the politics of hair seemed to have grown into some absurd hierarchy, people trying to out-Indian one another with all sorts of visual landmarks, secretly eyeing the braids of others, comparing, calculating whose was longer, thicker, more impressive, who had more ribbon shirts, more turquoise, accumulating identity in acquisition. There seemed to be some unspoken club, and the membership card—our approximate resemblance to those Edward Curtis photographs, as if that somehow defined our experience as indigenous people.

At a group, Native American Poetry Reading (a great selling label that), sometime in 1999, I read with three other Indian writers, and at the conclusion, one of them leaned over and whispered to me that I was the only one who looked like I should be up on the stage. Though I was the only one that night who had grown up on a reservation, that was certainly not represented in my appearance. In response to my puzzled look, she clarified, "Well, you know, that braid and all. Look at me, I'm blond, for Christ's sake."

"I have a goatee," I pointed out.

"So," she said, which was not really a reply per se. She seemed to want so badly to not be blond that night. In some unclear part of her thoughts on herself, blond hair apparently negated her identity for her, but my goatee was all right as long as I had a dark braid.

Other, strangely resonant events occurred in the few months following that, and I finally decided that while I could not stop the perpetuation of this stereotype, I did not have to be a contributing member. Tying off both ends of my braid, I cut it off in 1999, reduced my hair to a flattop, and grew my mustache to join the goatee at the same time. The braid is in my top-right desk drawer, where I keep it to remind me of where I have been.

My brother has kept his long hair forever, was married in a ribbon shirt, and his wardrobe contains more AIM shirts than anything else except perhaps for Grateful Dead shirts, and for him this is a way of life. He does not care if you're aware of Leonard Peltier; he is, and continues to be, and that is what is important to him. He has never attended one conference, but he has read volumes on our roles in history and in the current world when he is not working twelve-hour shifts at a radiator factory.

Here, at the border, I am suddenly in Los Lobos land again, and my tribal identification is not good enough. National identification papers, it seems, are good enough documentation for the United States from every other nation except those housed within its borders. Haudenosaunee law stipulates we are not citizens of the United States, regardless of any federal laws on Indian citizenship. I am still not sure what the full dynamics are here. Perhaps it is not that our ID cards are not legitimate enough, but instead that braidless and hairy, I am not legitimate enough for my ID. This officer, I see, stares at me, is certain my name is Pedro, Hector, Jesús, and as a result of this perception he wears his illegal alien Polaroid sunglasses. Regardless of what might or might not be in my pocket, he has decided it is all right to treat me with disdain because I have been forward enough to attempt crossing borders without swimming my way in, and am merely getting what I deserve.

The accumulated artifacts stowed in my wallet are as follows: laundry carbons for shirts being cleaned while I am away, a frequent shopper card for the local music store, credit cards, a half-used phone card, phone numbers of people from home, even my prom picture, where I am sixty pounds lighter, clean shaven, and my hair is cropped short.

My faculty ID card looks promising. It is contemporary and formal, professionally laminated, and even has a bar code on it, and you know, all bar-coded ID cards are, at their least, impressive. They indicate that I am catalogued somewhere. I hand this over and the officer looks at it. He rapid-fires questions at me. Suddenly I am taking a pop quiz on the academic calendar where I teach—when were finals, when was graduation, when does the school year begin, how many courses do I teach, and then it comes: What in Acuña, Mexico could possibly interest a college professor from New York? This question is so odd, so full of his emptiness, that no answer I can give short of "cheap dentistry," "stuffed armadillos," or "controlled substances" would be satisfactory. Back to the wallet.

My driving license convictions card surfaces next. This has my New York State license number on it, and a spotless driving record, I might add, the entire convictions section blank. The officer rejects this offer as well, observing it has no photograph. I suggest he can match the names from this to my other documents, and he merely raises his right eyebrow in a knowing way. It is apparently a slow day at immigration, so there is no pressure of a line behind me encouraging him to be more accommodating.

Finally I remember that the attendants at the gym where I work out insist on picture ID, in addition to their own issued member-ship card, every time I enter. Presumably this regulation has been etablished to prevent other, less-committed fitness enthusiasts from sneaking in to use the facilities pseudonymously. We solved the dual ID show by photocopying my license and taping it to the gym card. I rifle back through the less-convincing documents in my wallet and find the card, my shoddily photocopied license taped to it, and I am in luck; the numbers are visible, and more important, they match the numbers on my convictions record. I feel like a lotto winner as we compare numbers, the officer and I, and he is satisfied enough to run them through his international-criminal-driver's-license database and see, indeed, that I do live in western New York, or at least that someone who looks remarkably like me does. He gathers my variety pack of ID cards, hands them to me, and tells me, reluctantly, that I am free to go.

My braid is seventeen hundred miles from where I am as I leave the air-conditioned building and head out into the West Texas sun, and the fact that I can now slide my license back into my wallet and become someone I am not—a citizen of New York State, and thus a citizen of the United States of America as well—is no great comfort.

# RAISING THE AMERICAN INDIAN COMMUNITY HOUSE

### Mifaunwy Shunatona Hines

n the summer of 1994 New York City's Indian Center at 404 East Lafayette Street celebrated its twenty-fifth anniversary to the delighted surprise of its earliest organizers. Time, in its stealthy way, had passed. How can it go so quickly? One day the people who will have brought the American Indian Community House, Inc., through its latest years will be wondering the same thing as they dodder to their various fiftieth-anniversary celebrations. They may enjoy reading about the AICH origins.

In a sense there has always been an Indian center here, because Indians have always lived here, and died here. Those early Algonquian tribes have made this a hallowed ground since long before there was a World Trade Center. On the occasion of the 9/11/01 disaster, the American Indian Community House held services in memory of that day's victims, and in memory of our victims of long-ago atrocities. We prayed for other people as well as for our own.

Since its beginnings AICH and its programs have grown beyond expectations, and it continues to do so. My role as innovative founder was finished after the start-up year (1975), when a federal grant was over. I had been at work on this without realizing it since the 1960s.

I learned one day in the spring of 1963 that the Indian group that had tried to produce an American Indian exhibit in the

1964–65 New York World's Fair was unable to find the funds for the effort. This meant there would be no official recognition of independent American Indian participation. I took this very personally, particularly as this was practically in my own backyard. I didn't need an elaborate, costly exhibit; all I needed were Indian craftspeople from whom to purchase fair wares, and the money to purchase these. I had many resources at my fingertips in both the white and Indian worlds, and I could use them. This was the communications center of the world, and I would start communicating. I took out a loan, leased a booth for the duration, and became an owner-exhibitor duly noted in New York World's Fair 1964–65 official papers as Shunatona's American Indian Store.

The many Indians who came to the fair frequently asked if there was an Indian center here, and from conversations it seemed it would be a good thing socially and politically if there were. The entire experience had stirred me to a wider yearning in this matter of Indian pride. I pondered how everything we did seemed to be under white authority with no real respect for the Indian person. Tribal representatives came to New York for funding but rarely knew whom to approach. Indian organizations or clubs had existed all along, certainly since the 1920s, but were easily lost in this city. Obviously the United States government had never considered this as a feasible Indian melting pot. I had rarely thought of these situations, never brooded over them. I realized my two worlds were doing strange things. They were trying to come together. Why do we need an Indian center? Why not? How would I find the answer?

Shortly I was on the path to a beginning. Our oldest organization, the Indian League of the Americas (ILOTA), elected me secretary, and this gave me frequent opportunities to question community members. Since ILOTA had associate members, there were white as well as Indian opinions. Everyone wanted an Indian center where we could learn from each other. No one had feasible ideas on how to begin.

It made sense to me to put myself at the center of things as best I could, and one day the way to do this presented itself. I was looking for a phone number and realized that none of the "American Indian" listings were actually run by Indians. I called the telephone company and gave my home number as a volunteer service to be known as the American Indian Information Center. On May 7, 1967, the service was initiated, and now an Indian would be at the business end of the line. Any questions I couldn't answer would be referred to someone who could. My one-woman network grew, and soon it was clear that our local Indian activities were being stimulated without the "guidance" of non-Indian organizations. We were making strides of our own.

Concurrent with my ILOTA stint as secretary and the initiation of my information center, I mailed questionnaires to community members in both organizations and to nonmembers of either, asking for suggestions and/or assistance. Everyone was supportive, but only Mary Helen Deer (Kiowa-Creek) and Chy Pells (Wampanoag) volunteered to work when possible. We discussed what approaches to take to locate the as-yet-unknown larger Indian community and decided it would be as a women's group. We welcomed the offers of two ILOTA members, Doris Diabo Melliades (Mohawk) and associate member Margaret Meixner, plus an information center caller named Doris Travis. They were all businesswomen. Margaret initiated the excellent AIWL newsletter. Concurrently I contacted the major figures I knew on the national Indian scene and arranged a monthly lecture series (pro bono) with dates coinciding with their trips to New York. Speakers such as John Belindo (Kiowa-Navajo), executive director of the National

Congress of American Indians, Robert Bennett, (Oneida), commissioner of Indian Affairs, Oren Lyons (Onondaga), chiefs' council, Hank Adams (Assiniboin Sioux), Survival of American Indians Association, Alice Shenandoah Papineau (Onondaga), Clan mother of Eel Clan, Henry and Leonard Crow Dog (Sioux), medicine men, and dozens more brought the national Indian community into our lives. Our community was experiencing a new sense of inclusion, awareness, and involvement. Our ever-present underlying thought was our push to establish an Indian center.

I gained self-confidence to the extent that one day on reading a *New York Times* story about black women organizing, I was inspired to call Charlotte Curtis, the *Times* special sections editor. She created history for us by appointing reporter Judy Klemesrud to do a story complete with head shots, which became the first *New York Times* story about New York City American Indian women. It was September 18, 1968, and this article was the springboard we needed. The overall story was about our efforts to promote the new "Indianness" to combat the emerging "Indian is in" fashion madness. It ended with this reminder: Their main goal, however, is establishing an American Indian center in Manhattan.

We became instant local celebrities and were provided countless opportunities to publicize our Indian center drive. At the same time, we were also inevitably drawn to the ever-increasing national Indian drumbeat. Scattered Indian groups had created "Indian power," demanding reform of their local Bureau of Indian Affairs offices. In November 1969 this culminated in the taking of Alcatraz by some eighty young Indians, under an 1868 treaty allowing Indians squatter rights on unused federal land. This became a nationally sensational story. In March 1970 a group of young New York City Indians came together as an eastern element to the takeover. They contacted two San Francisco Indians, found funding to bring them here for guidance, and planned a takeover of Ellis Island. The attempt was made predawn on March 16. Unhappily a leaky gas tank on their eighteen-foot launch foiled their efforts. But it was a heroic start at bringing our local community into national efforts.

Early in 1969 AIWL undertook a sample head-count with the help of Dr. June Nash at New York University; her students volunteered to send out our two hundred questionnaires. We received over one hundred replies, providing us some background for future funding efforts. It was time to start investigating the legalities of Indian center organizing: alas, in those days we had no Indian lawyers in our neighborhood. But we were fortunate to acquire lawyer Nathaniel Rock, whose sister Lillian was a renowned lawyer. She had been impressed by our AIWL group when we spoke before a women's law group. She persuaded her brother to take over our cause for acquiring an Indian center, which he did, and remained to more or less donate his services until illness overtook him.

My information center volunteer service took me into many levels of activity, each of which I considered to be one step closer to our Indian center. Contacts were developed with job offers, including modeling, acting, office workers, etc. I decided I was better able to work toward the center through the AIIC with its proven results, so I faded out of the Women's League to concentrate on legal necessities and meetings. Attorney Rock had advised us to have nine people to serve as official charter signatories, including one non-Indian. Since my husband's Choctaw blood quantum is meager, and since he had been my major help since the World's Fair, he was our unanimous choice. The signatories of the Statement of Purpose are Chy Pells (Wampanoag), Mary Helen Deer (Kiowa-Creek), Olive Ward (Onondaga), Louis Bayhylle (Pawnee), Louis

Mofsie (Hopi-Winnebago), Oren Lyons (Onondaga), Charmaine Lyons (Cherokee), Mifaunwy Shunatona Hines (Otoe-Pawnee-Wyandotte), and Willard C. Hines.

At the end of August my father died and was buried in the Otoe Cemetery in Oklahoma. I stayed with my mother until November. He was well known to many New York–community people, and from the moment of his death my Indian center work was dedicated to his memory.

On January 22, 1970, we elected officers for our now officially named American Indian Community House, Inc. These were President Louis Bayhylle (Pawnee), vice president Louis Mofsie (Winnebago), treasurer Chy Pells (Wampanoag), and secretary Mifaunwy Shunatona Hines (Otoe-Pawnee-Wyandotte). Not long thereafter we became tax exempt, allowing us certain advantages, including mail privileges and fund-raising. Our first outreach was over NBC's Channel 4 with Roger Horn (Mohawk) making spot announcements for the American Indian Community House. Other radio and TV spots would follow. We received some donations from these, but the best results were the calls from new Indians. Our first mailing address was at the Center for Urban Education with my own little office, in exchange for my input on Indian affairs. A few months later the community church provided us at no cost with a two-room space in a building separate from the church. Now we had our own address and telephone, which would soon be listed in the Manhattan directory. The free rent was possible through our tax-exempt status. We started AICH office residency in January 1971. In our smoking ceremony we included thanks for the return of Blue Lake to the Taos Pueblo in December. Some of us had early ties to the people, and we hoped their strength during their long struggle would reach us. City and reservation Indians are often the same people.

In the freedom of our own digs, we finally felt like an independent organization. I was a one-woman staff, but volunteers came and here I give appreciation to a pair of strangers, young white women, who volunteered their time for weeks before they gave up on ever seeing real service. They had read the headlines through recent years, and were hoping for action, not office work. But they did put files in order and compiled Rolodexes with Indian reservations, agencies, and individuals' names and locations, and they faithfully manned the office when I had to run my many errands. They appreciated my efforts to attain an Indian center, but they wanted to be real activists, where the real action was. They never realized how important their office work was toward getting what the action groups really needed—funding. That will never change unless we find an Indian who can develop an honest Enron for Indians.

Meantime, the headlines continued, only now the inclusion of New York City Indian presence became almost routine. In 1971 *New York Times* stories covered the Puyallup fish-ins in Washington, the New York State Senate's bill to return wampum belts to the Iroquois, and similar, including this headline: "Six young New York City Indians smear paint over the statue of Theodore Roosevelt" (outside the Museum of Natural History). These were some of the aforementioned Young American Indian Council who attempted to take over Ellis Island in 1968.

Militancy was growing stronger nationwide, but on October 20, 1972, the American Indian Movement (AIM) made its first worldwide attention-getter under this headline: Five hundred Indians seize U.S. building after scuffle with capital police. This was the takeover of the Bureau of Indian Affairs, which continued for nine days, and with which AICH became involved through aid to stranded Indians (tax exemption allowed for funding) and through active participation by various members. A middle-aged woman from AICH who camped in the building during the takeover had carefully rescued and wrapped thirty-one paintings, which we managed to sneak out and return to safety via the nearby YMCA, which was providing shelter for off-premises Indians. In this takeover no one had been harmed physically, but damage was done to BIA property.

It was a different story a few months later. On March 1, 1973, the headline was: "Armed Indians Seize Wounded Knee, Hold Hostages." On May 9, a disarmament agreement ended the occupation, during which two Indians had been killed. This siege was doubtless the most wearying time in Indian Country as a whole than any other recent period. New York City Indians became involved, including AICH members who went to Wounded Knee to remain to the end. Medical supplies were the major need, which several carloads of local people drove out with on different occasions. Our AICH members who stayed there were professional people who could help in various ways. Meantime, we also had local daily lives to carry on.

In July 1974 AICH received a $110,000 start-up HEW grant, and a few months later a one-million-dollar Manpower grant. Now we could enlarge our present headquarters and pay rent. I was appointed executive director which I accepted with a letter stating I would seek a replacement at the end of the year: It wasn't a job I wanted. I could enjoy the innovative ideas I anticipated putting into effect, but I was not looking forward to government white tape tying my hands, and I was not expecting a smooth ride with the community who would now be seeing us only in terms of money. I was caught totally off guard with what proved to be the real danger. Our federal representative, who had been quite charming, soon revealed her other self at our first board meeting.

At the conclusion of her introductory words, she finished her presentation with these unforgettable words: "Remember, I am your federal government."

It was difficult to ignore her, try as we might. She wanted no part of opinionated independent Indians. She wanted to handle our grant her way. It soon became an "anti-Miffie undercover movement." This is the pattern of all such melees. I had too many supporters for the anti thing to succeed, but I still had too much work to do to allow myself to be caught up in the "movement." We carried out our first year by locating our Indian community primarily with the two sample headcounts AIWL and AICH had conducted earlier. I composed spot announcements with an illustration by Lloyd Oxendine, Lumbee, and our name American Indian Community House with address, and voice-over by president Louis Bayhylle: "Are you an American Indian? If so, call us. We need you." We also pasted posters with the same message all over the most Indian-populated neighborhoods. Admittedly we attracted numerous individuals who had no provable Indian backgrounds. We wanted tribal-connection backgrounds, whether federally recognized or not, but we did not want dreamed-up Indian heritages. When these are acceptable, as it seems now to be the case, then our true heritage is lost.

The end of the first federally funded year of AICH found my closest allies in other parts of the country all doing well. My only original AICH cosignatory left was and is Louis Mofsie, who has attained world fame as director of the Thunderbird American Indian Dancers and Singers. My original staff members went on to upgraded positions in various Indian centers or careers in the Indian world. And I remain in New York City, where I have now lived most of my life, with the same husband, daughter, son-in-law, and now fourteen-year-old twin grandsons. I remain in touch with Rosemary Richmond (Mohawk) the executive director of AICH, but rarely visit their offices, because they are on the eighth floor, which requires an elevator ride, and I have become a raving claustrophobic.

# THE SECRET OF BREATHING

### Steve Elm

I was in the theater with my friend Vicki in the uppermost reaches of the balconies, and I was having trouble catching my breath. I tried to convince myself that I was simply laughing too hard at the slapstick English comedy playing on the Broadway stage far below. Vicki, a proud and defiant Tuscarora woman from over the Canadian border, looked into my eyes and whispered, "Steve, are you all right?" Flushed and unsure, I said, "Of course. I'll live."

The next evening I was on a commuter flight to Rhode Island, where I was to present a workshop on theater and storytelling the following morning. I was feverish but convinced myself that I was simply exhausted from the past busy week. As I tried to manage and disguise my hacking cough, I heard a voice coming from the plane's intercom system. Immediately I recognized the warm tones and familiar vowels of the woman's accent. Looking up to see if I was right, there in the front of the plane, giving oxygen mask instructions, stood an American Indian stewardess.

The flight was only an hour long, so there was no meal or drink service. I gulped my bottle of water to deafen my cough. The stewardess walked up and down the aisle, giving candy and Cokes to the few children on board. "So typical of an Indian woman," I thought, "making sure the kids are okay, giving treats and giggles."

I made myself small in my seat, feeling that perhaps she would offer me some candy if she saw I was poorly, or if she saw I was, like her, an Indian. But her job was to ensure the passengers stayed safe and seated, and the children sweet and sated for the duration of the short flight. I stayed small, and in reverence to her professionalism decided to become invisible so as not to interrupt her duties.

She was beautiful, with the dark hair and fair skin so often like that of the Menominee, those neighbors of my father's people, the Wisconsin Oneidas. As I remained hidden, not wanting to reveal myself as the sick passenger in 12F (and thereby hiding the impending severity of my illness), I thought of the fine Menominee women I have known: the gifted and wonderful actor Sheila Tousey and the heroic Flying Eagle Woman Ingrid Washinawatok El Issa. Both women are messengers of the talent, strength, spirit, and sheer humanity of Native women. Sheila through her determination and success in giving Indian voice to film and theater, and Ingrid through her legacy as being one of our greatest humanitarian warriors. I decided this woman, safeguarding her passengers in the skies so soon after September 11, was surely Menominee.

I gathered my bags and what breath I still had as the plane emptied of fliers. Waiting to be among the last, I debated whether or not to greet her in Oneida. My knowledge of my father's language is purely anecdotal, but I thought it might be appropriate in light of her being Indian and my being Indian, and Wisconsin and Sheila and Ingrid, and my feeling unwell and poor of spirit.

She was saying good-bye to the last few passengers as I stepped up. At the last moment I changed my mind and voice to English and looked at her beautiful Menominee face. "Hello," I said. "I'm

Oneida. You wouldn't be Menominee wouldja?" She flinched, turned her head away, and in the same instant said, "Nope."

Stunned, immediately uncomfortable, and embarrassed, I said, "Well, you are an Indian, aren't you?" She kept her head turned away and tightly said again, "Nope." I think I said, "Sorry," and awkwardly descended the folding stairs down to the runway. Maybe she wasn't Menominee and I should be contrite for being so presumptuous and assuming. Maybe she was a lighter-skinned Apache or a Cree or Ho-Chunk and was annoyed with my wanton familiarity. Still, I wanted to turn around and call out, "Yes, you are! Yes, you are!" I pictured myself running back up the stairs, pointing at her, and shouting, "J'accuse! I accuse you of being an Indian!" Instead, I swallowed what air I could, picked up my pride, wiped my brow, and wondered why she was keeping herself secret.

On the bus to the hotel, through what was becoming a ride into delirium, I found reasons to both explain and excuse her. It was only a month after the tragedy of September 11. Perhaps security prevented her from personal disclosure to dark-skinned passengers. After all, I've been told I look more Arab than Oneida. Or she was not interested in what she may have thought was a red-faced, feverish stranger chatting her up.

In the hotel room I turned off the lights and sat by the open window, hoping the sea air would cool my burning skin. I gazed out at the dark, dark sky and wondered if there were any Spirits watching with whom I could bargain. "Make me well so I can be in the light again. I'll pay. I'll be better. Please don't tell anyone." Then I thought of the stewardess. Was she sitting, like me, in her own darkness, and if so, with whom was she bargaining? And if she was, what was the cost?

Later I awoke on the hotel bed drenched in sweat and freezing, dreaming the face of my mother. I saw her hands, the nails painted red, gently laying a cool washcloth on my brow. I saw her in shadow, the blond of her hair and the blue of her eyes barely visible. I saw her at the kitchen table the day I told her my secret.

It happened gradually, as these things do . . . becoming Indian. In all the photo albums there is the beautiful blond woman cradling the brown baby. There is the photo of the brown boy running in dirty sneakers, looking for a place to hide. There is the photo of the brown boy next to his white cousin, all clean and pretty. He wanted to be clean and pretty too, and the beautiful blond woman told him he was the best, but he didn't believe her. Then, one day, a sleeping bear woke up and told my siblings and me who we were. Then there are pictures of me in a bustle awkwardly holding a rattle, standing next to my beautiful brown cousins. Then I have long hair and an AIM patch on my denim jacket. Then there are us kids at the Longest Walk, looking to the bear, our father.

After that photo was taken I came home and at the kitchen table I told my mother my secret—I wasn't white anymore. She asked me how long I had felt like this. My sixteen-year-old face burned with purpose and a hint of shame as I explained the facts. We lived here. We, us kids, were the product of a mixed marriage. We were half-breeds on the outside but all Indian on the inside. She sat quietly as I denied her European blood, her confusion only a blush we shared as we ate the dinner she had prepared so many years ago.

I got up from the bed and filled the sink with steaming water. Leaning over it, trying to inhale the fumes, I thought of my parents and the secret they kept from us kids for so long, the secret of survival when the past is too full of death. The way they both flew from the lost grounds of their respective births to land together, in love, on a new earth. The way they gave breath to their children, and the secrets they kept from them so they would grow up free and painless as Americans, believing in this with all the innocence only the truly violated are gifted with. This is my heritage, and this I came to understand, and this found hidden in the secret of my breathing. Before the dawn broke, I made peace with the stewardess and her secret.

The next morning I told stories, using my lack of breath as dramatic pause. I took a coach to the Pequot's casino that afternoon and won ninety-dollars at roulette. On the way back to my room, my fever mirrored the twilight of the early evening sky. Outside the hotel, I hugged a tree to stop from shivering. I had to get back to New York.

My friend Vicki came to sit by my bed in the hospital a few weeks later. She brought candy and Cokes. With worry and love in her face, she adjusted my oxygen and asked how I was feeling. "I'll live," I told her. I took as deep a breath as I could and said, "I'll live."

I often think of the stewardess and her secret. The more I breathe, the more I understand we should be allowed the secrets that serve us well. I am learning to breathe with mine, and to forgive others the breadth to breathe with theirs.

# The Indians Are Alive

## Virginia Driving Hawk Sneve

When the Indians were alive," a blond male third-grader asks, "why did they always scalp the whites?"

His question is the first after I had spent thirty minutes telling about the American Indians I write of in my books. I patiently explain that Indians did not *always* scalp, and white people also perpetrated this vicious act. The boy gives a smirking glance, but other hands are in the air.

"Are you an Indian?"

"Yes," I respond. "I am a member of the Rosebud Sioux tribe."

Several hands shoot up and I hear, "Do you live in a teepee?"

After I say "No, I live in a house just like yours," the youngster says, "Well, you're not an Indian, then. Indians always live in teepees."

Now a little girl shyly raises her hand and quietly says, "I'm Indian, and I don't live in a teepee."

The boy who had asked the question about when the Indians were alive was incredulous. "No, you're not!"

"Yes, I am," the girl replied. "My mom says so. And my grandma lives on the Rosebud Reservation."

"You're making that up."

"I'm not either!" The Indian girl is close to tears.

The boy turned to his friends. "Hey, if she's an Indian, let's put her in a cupboard."

"Nooo." Now the little girl is weeping.

The teacher intervenes, comforts the little girl, then admonishes the boys. "That was just a story. Real people aren't put in cupboards."

This episode is, unfortunately, not an isolated incident in urban schools throughout the United States. Eastern Abenaki author Joseph Bruchac has reported that many times he has gone into schools and children have asked him, "Are Indians still alive? I thought they all died a long time ago."

Gayle Ross, Cherokee writer, also visits schools and has stated that she had a five-year-old in Kansas City tell her that she couldn't be Indian, that the Indians were extinct, just like the dinosaurs.

And when my mother, who lives in California visited a Sunday-school class to talk about the Medicine Wheel, she was asked, "Are there still Indians around?"

As a retired teacher who still visits classes in urban schools, and as a writer of children's books, I'm well aware that the myth of the vanishing American Indians lives on in urban schools because it is perpetrated in children's literature. Well-meaning non-Indian writers who publish children's books retell legends or relate historic action-packed fiction in which an Indian boy is always brave and a girl is a noble princess. This kind of writing informs children about traditional American Indian heritage and culture, but it also implies that American Indians are no more.

Apache/Hopi Tewa artist, storyteller, and author Michael Lacapa is quoted in Aine J. Norris's, *The Unheard Voices on Turtle Island:* "There was a time in my life when I thought I wasn't Indian because I didn't wear a headdress like the Indians in my schoolbooks wore."

Those textbooks and stories children read have locked American Indians into that fabled era of hunting buffalo and living in teepees. But there is more distortion when the Indian characters in children's stories are often only minimally developed because they are stereotypes. A non-Indian author can ignorantly and unintentionally present a racist view of Indians, or, at the least, show the reader a bland nonperson.

The late Native author Michael Dorris had concern about the images his children were getting of American Indians in the stories they read. In the book *Through Indian Eyes*, which reveals how Native peoples react to stereotypical writings about Indians, he argued: " 'I' isn't for Indian; it is often for Ignorance. Native Americans appear not as human beings but as whooping, silly one-dimensional cartoons."

This is most apparent at Thanksgiving, when paper products are illustrated with cute, happy Indians and smiling turkeys on disposable plates, napkins, and cups. Is this a comment on American Indians as also being disposable?

When I visit schools, I explain that modern Indians dress like everybody else and speak English. That our tribal regalia, the buckskin and feathers, are not everyday garb but are reserved for special events. I say that we are proud of our beautiful, colorful clothing, which is important in our traditions, but it is only a part of being Indian. The part that they can't see, our beliefs, our values, make us Indian even though we no longer wear buckskins, beads, and feathers and don't live in teepees.

As an adult I can handle the stereotypes, and as an author I try to correct the misconceptions and tell the truth about American Indians. Unfortunately, Indian children can have negative feelings about themselves because they don't fit this false image. Educators have found that the way children view themselves is important to their success in school and how they relate to others. But an unrealistic idea of what and who Indians are supposed to be confuses a child when he or she compares those images to his or her parents and other relatives.

Some children in urban schools may be the third or later generation living away from reservations. They do not really know their cultural history or background. When they are asked about feathers and dancing, they're embarrassed. By the time they face the intense pressure of peer approval in high school, more confusion develops when an adolescent wonders "Who am I, where have I come from?" Sometimes teenagers are so ashamed of being Indian that they will even deny their heritage.

When I began writing for children, I did so with the specific purpose of informing my own children about their heritage. My daughter began reading Laura Ingalls Wilder's Little House books and asked questions about their locale, which was not too far from where her father grew up in South Dakota. "Was this the way the Sneve homesteaders lived?"

In order to answer her, I read the books. Always interested in history, I enjoyed them. Then I read *Little House on the Prairie* and found the only reference to Indians in the whole series described them as "naked wild men" with "bold and fierce faces," from whom there was "a horrible smell."

What did my daughter think about Indians after what she had read? I already knew that she wasn't learning much about them in school; I had taught from the same texts, which either ignored our place in American history or briefly mentioned the wars and how "savages" hindered western movement. I began to read children's literature and found that Indians were a popular theme but always Indians of the past—brave warriors and cute princesses, or brutal savages. I found no stories of modern Indian children.

How did my children view their Indian relatives from where we lived in Cedar Rapids, Iowa? Our visits to South Dakota were only a few days in the summer—usually during the Rosebud Fair or Sun Dance time. We'd make a stop to see Grandma, then go to Uncle's in Pine Ridge. My son was fascinated with Uncle, who worked in the maintenance department in the Pine Ridge School, where his wife taught fourth grade. On one visit Uncle had given the boy a picture of himself wearing a wig with braids hanging over a breastplate. My son hung the picture in his room and proudly displayed it to his four-year-old-friends. Unbeknownst to me, he told his pals that Uncle hunted buffalo from a horse and was a warrior.

Uncle and Aunt were coming to visit us, and my son eagerly anticipated their arrival. He and several of his buddies camped on the edge of our driveway to welcome Uncle, who came riding up in an air-conditioned automobile wearing a sport shirt, slacks, and shoes.

Later a mother of one of the boys told me that they had been furious with my son. Uncle wasn't an Indian; he looked just like any other guy.

So, my son and daughter were in my mind when I began writing for children. I tried to correct misconceptions and write truthfully about American Indians. I never dreamed that almost thirty years later I would still have the same mission; this inaccurate image of American Indians has not changed for my grandchildren.

This image has nothing to do with reality. Society keeps re-creating us in the form non-Indians want us to be. And why does there seem to be such a virulent resentment of us when we actively move to change this image? Several American Indian leaders, including Michael Haney, Seminole, and Clyde Bellecourt, Ojibwe, carried placards outside a stadium where the Atlanta Braves were playing. They were protesting the use of Indians as mascots. They were spit upon, cursed with racial epithets by Braves fans who brandished plastic tomahawks, and one fan yelled, "Go back to where you came from, you filthy redskin!"

In an off-reservation school in South Dakota, a seventh-grade Indian girl suggested that the middle school's mascot "Warrior" was offensive because it was of a fiercely scowling cartoon Indian in a flowing headdress—a totally inaccurate image of a warrior. She was called "dirty squaw" and told to go back to the reservation, where Indians belonged.

American Indian artists who illustrate children's books haven't been able to move beyond what is considered traditional Indian art: horses, feathers, teepees, maidens, and warriors. The difficulty for writers and illustrators is that publishers have their own idea of what an "authentic" Indian is, and this idea is far removed from reality. Publishers want "saleable" stories. Too often the result is that the "saleable" stories are not truly authentic.

I have taught and mentored aspiring American Indian writers who are often puzzled as to why they can't publish stories with modern settings. However, even established American Indian writers have difficulty publishing contemporary fiction and poetry both for children and adults. In the book *Winged Words: American Indian Writers Speak*, Simon Ortiz, Acoma Pueblo, said of the acceptance of his poetry: "Their [non-Indians] understanding of my poetry is based on their acceptance and judgment of what a Native American should write about. He should write about Native American settings; he should use images that are Native American, and should use the language and values of that, otherwise the poetry is unacceptable. It is very stereotypical as well as racist."

Linda Hogan, a Chickasaw poet and novelist, commented in a 1994 interview in *Native Peoples* magazine: "It's easier for non-Indian people to write a book about Indian people and get it published than it is for us. Our own experiences and our own lives don't fit the stereotypes."

Children who have little access to contemporary American Indian literature come to believe distorted images as the real thing. Non-Indian children don't recognize or relate to their Indian classmates. Indian children can't understand their own lives within a contemporary context when their experiences of being an American Indian do not fit with what they read. Children need literature that is truly representative of the culture in which they live, and this literature must be free of stereotypes and bias.

All children can benefit from reading about American Indians; after all, we are what make this continent different from Europe. It's necessary that we all understand that we live in a multiethnic society, that no one group's beliefs and customs are better than those of any other. Our richly diverse cultural backgrounds are part of our unique individuality but should not separate us.

American Indian children who read accurate literature of their ancestors, where and how they lived, will be proud of their past. But they and children of all races should read contemporary stories of American Indians so that they know Indians are a viable presence even though we no longer hunt buffalo or live in teepees.

If American Indian children can have positive contemporary images with which to identify, they will know that they have value in the present and can realize they are just as important as the Indians of the past. They will learn to apply the wisdom of the past to contemporary life.

It is important to preserve American Indian cultures in the writing of traditional stories, legends, songs, poems, and historic fiction without stereotypes. But more urgent is the need for balance with the writing of contemporary literature so that one is not being addressed at the expense of the other.

This is a real challenge for writers of children's books, to show that Indians value their heritage and history, but that Indians are still very much alive today.

# "Indians," Solipsisms, and Archetypal Holocausts

## Paula Gunn Allen

The basic paradigms that underlie Native American and "other" American thought differ in a number of particulars, and these paradigmatic differences lead to endless misunderstandings of the Native world by outsiders. Native people are neither like non-Natives nor like American popular conceptions of us, be those conceptions generated by New Age materials, films, histories, or other media. Nor can we be seen or understood in the terms by which African Americans or other "minority" racial groups define and describe themselves. Our situation in the United States, as well as throughout the western hemisphere, is unique, for we are First Nations people, indigenous; we aren't so much a political minority as we are displaced persons. Further, there are federal and state laws that specifically address the legal relations between our Nations and the United States or the separate states. According to a Cherokee friend, *The Wall Street Journal* recently reported that stockbrokers carry or wear animal icons signifying their "totem." Another Native American/Chicano graduate student tells me that one of his English professors said he didn't consider the bright, articulate young man a minority person. The remark certainly gave my friend—small, curly-haired, and dark-skinned—pause. Not content with pontificating on the student's identity, the professor mentioned another student in the class, a gifted Native American poet who comes from the reservation and speaks English with a tribal accent. "I love having her in class. It gives me a chance to see how real Indians think." Not surprisingly, my friend barely restrained himself from decking the man upon whom his grade depended. I have been in therapy (with a number of different people) for nearly thirty years off and on, and only one of those therapists (an extremely aware white woman) has had the wit to help me explore the degree of difference between me and white people; her most significant aid consisted in her describing to me how she, as "a privileged white woman" (her words) saw the world, "reality," and herself in relation to nonwhites.

The problem would not be so urgent for mental health issues in the Native community were we not engulfed by white culture: It is the basis of our educational systems; its media surround us on every hand, as do its political, cultural, popular, economic, aesthetic, architectural, legal, childrearing, and population patterns, its familial structure and bonding, and its religious norms. We are hard put to find ourselves—as communities and as individuals—in this mind-destroying, endless barrage.

All but overwhelmed by ubiquitous redefinitions of ourselves and our sense of reality, one tries to write. To think. To get some kind of clarity about almost anything. One tries to function. To stay sober, to stay connected with the deeper stratum of being that is one's identity, one's tradition, one's very perception and consciousness. All too often, one gives up. Drops out of school. Flunks too many courses. Quits too many jobs. Gives in to all-pervading despair, to the murderous thoughts the white world projects daily, hourly, year after year. One gives up and lies down and dies.

Meanwhile, there seems little to do but to keep on keepin' on, as the saying goes. One writes, thinks, works, talks, hopes against hope that the horror of white-think will somehow be turned around, that white madness can be cured. (White is used here to denote a mind-set or system of mental processes rather than a racial or genetic term. There are many Caucasian people and communities who in the past and at present are as distant from "white-think" as any traditional Native American.)

White culture employs the mechanism it identifies as projection to avoid facing itself around the fact, history, and current situation of Native people and communities. Though in this instance it functions on a global scale, projection is all too clearly operative in the white world's version of Native America. In breathtakingly classic fashion, split-off fragments of the Anglo-European psyche take on an energetic life of their own, appearing to non-Indians as actual people, ideas, systems, attitudes, and values the Western collective mind dubs "Indian."

As many a therapist knows, little is more frightening than being perceived as a fragment of the other's mind; interaction with someone who is fixated upon his or her disowned and misnamed fragments is devastating because it entails a loss of self at the deepest levels of the psyche. Like all projection, white-think is almost entirely unconscious; nameless, formless, unacknowledged, it exists as a powerful barrier to authentic communication across cultures. While it works for the survival and expansion of white culture, it also results in the spiritual and psychic murder of those who exist outside its protection.

One example of this process in writing will have to suffice here. The following excerpt from David Rockwell's book *Giving Voice to Bear: American Indian Rituals, Myths, and Images of the Bear* is almost a caricature of itself, so full is it of objectification, projection, attribution, and redefinition. Rockwell employs the past tense throughout this excerpt, whether the practice being discussed is still in use by living Native people or not. "The Lakota considered the bear to be a curing animal. They associated their medicinal herbs with bears . . . and they *believed* . . . doctors *acquired* powers . . . they *were* not . . . Most of the tribes in North America associated bears with curing . . . and called upon [bears] . . . when they performed. . . ." One is unsure whether the practices, the bears, the beliefs, or the Lakota, et al., are extinct. The subtext, of course, lets us understand that all of the above are long gone; this makes white people feel safer. If we are all dead, their genocide, terrorism, pain, and the fear stemming from their history vis-à-vis Indian America can be safely banished.

Rockwell is relentless in his recontextualization of our traditions and heritage: "The American Indian's perception of the bear as a healer proceeds from a knowledge of bear behavior." He is of the opinion that the eating patterns of the bear people, which, he says, are mostly vegetarian, are what held our attention. (Never mind that many a bear likes a bit of good fresh fish now and then, and an occasional fat larvae is something of a treat.) Rockwell didn't come to his misunderstanding on his own: He is simply replicating the analytic babble that characterizes white-think. The truth of a people's past and present—whether those people are Native Americans, Muslims, Africans, or Bosnians—provides most of the scholarly material published in the past several centuries in the West. "Indians probably saw bears not as hunters or grass eaters but as the plant gatherers of the animal world. It was a natural step from observing this behavior to associating bears with healing, especially herbal healing. As an animal gatherer of herbs and roots, the bear served as guardian of the first medicines and communicator of the knowledge of healing." Indeed.

The subtext of Rockwell's carefully crafted personal fantasy invites readers to draw some unwarranted conclusions: Native people are fashionably vegetarian (false Aryans of the Hindu

Brahmin class and Adolf Hitler are/were vegetarian); "Indians" are observant (a group noun that lumps all members of the race under a common rubric, eradicating our personhood); "Indians" take "natural steps" that rely on associative thinking (a projective construct characteristic of Western but not of Native thinking).

By way of white observations culled from (white) literature on animal behavior, Rockwell informs us that the herbivorous bear liked (likes?) to munch on herbs, many of them possessing medicinal properties. Relying on these white "scientific" observations, Rockwell attributes their methodology to our ancestors, defining us as white (but we "associate," implying that white researchers do a "higher" kind of analysis). His construct enables him to simultaneously use the Native world to validate white "science" and make it "environmentally friendly."

This latter ploy is reinforced when we are told (via the subtext) that Bear is spiritual and wise: for is not bear defined as guardian—a New Age buzz word that signifies "Indians" and "shamanic" "spirituality"—of the first medicines? (Bear as guardian of the first medicines has a subtext: It tells us, among other things, that Bear is even better than Indian, being before us and the true guardian of human health.) The net effect is eradication of Native thought and peoples: For could not any observant person, associating naturally, derive the medicines from bear behavior? Assuming, of course, that there were still herb-gathering bears around to observe!

For a wildly different view of the matter of bears, I suggest the following titles: Leslie Marmon Silko's novel *Ceremony* and poem "Story from Bear Country" (in *Storyteller*), N. Scott Momaday's novels *House Made of Dawn* and *The Ancient Child*, and Gerald Vizenor's novel *Darkness in Saint Louis Bearheart*. As each of these works makes clear, logical positivism is quite opposite the situation of bears, healing and human relations with bears in the Native world. Mr. Rockwell's piece—which I have excoriated somewhat mercilessly (though it deserves an even deeper deconstructing)—has served merely to exemplify a common mental process, one that enjoys very high status in the modern world. It substitutes white-think for Native philosophical/spiritual thought, attributing white assumptions and thought processes to us and our ancestors—without a hint that white cultural assumptions are neither universal nor necessarily shared. Thus continues the horrifying process of colonization, only now it's New Age shamanic thought masquerading as Native American in order to annihilate the Native mind. Small wonder that far too many Native people, especially children, are suicidal. It is not that we possess a death wish but that the huge culture around us projects its homicidal wish onto us.

One more example of white-think to demonstrate its all-pervasiveness: This one is an example of New Age cooptation and recontextualization of Native thought. In Ariel Spilsbury and Michael Bryner's book *The Mayan Oracle: Return Path to the Stars,* a New Age "deck," there is a passage about lucid dreaming as the technique is (purportedly) practiced in Tibetan dream yoga. Ignoring for a moment the obvious fact that Tibet is pretty far from Mayaland, I'll cut to the chase. The authors tell us "[Lucid dreaming] is the practice of focusing conscious awareness on the illusory nature of reality, becoming lucid in life. It can be experienced in either the waking or the dream state—primarily through realizing that life is *all* a dream."

On the face of it, given the level of American misapprehension of the actual bases of various spiritual systems, this sentence may sound perfectly lucid. However, it is exactly wrong when placed within the context of Native thought. No Native who has given much thought to tribal spiritual systems—in all their aspects and multiplicity—would agree that life is all a dream. We think that life is all real—*all* of it. The personal, the spiritual, the supernatural, the "cosmic," the political, the economic, the sacred, the profane, the tragic, the comic, the ordinary, the boring, the annoying, the infuriating. Our traditions tell us that when someone meets a supernatural on the road (or in the kitchen), that is real. And when someone meets a BIA official at a meeting, that is real. We are neither dreaming it nor making it up. Nor is the numinous (or the Great Mystery) a psychic territory peopled by split-off fragments of our unconscious, a split occasioned by repression, failure to mature in a timely fashion, or massive trauma. (Now, "trauma" *does* mean dream!)

To Native thinkers, the mythic is not a trick of the human mind but a pulsating fact of existence as real as a village, a trailer court, a horse, a spouse, or a tradition is real. Native people of the Americas are aware, as were pre-Renaissance peoples of the British Isles and on the Continent (and as are many of their modern descendants) that the numinous may be different from the "mundane," separated from it by a kind of penetrable psychic barrier, but it is no less real for all that.

Perhaps Leslie Marmon Silko is accurate in describing the white world as illusory (*Ceremony*). Perhaps that is why its writers and thinkers are so convinced that reality is, at base, an illusion. But we must remember that while white reality may indeed be a very powerful illusion (on the order of a horrible bad dream), Native reality is fact. In his novel *The Courts of Chaos*, the late Roger Zelazny (who is not Native American but seemed pretty sane anyway) quotes writer Isak Dinesen: " 'Few people can say of themselves that they are free of the belief that this world which they see around them is in reality the work of their own imagination. . . . ' " Then he pursues the thought:

Do we make the Shadow worlds? Or are they there, independent of us, awaiting our footfalls? Or is there an unfairly excluded middle? Is it a matter of more or less, rather than either-or? . . . Yet . . . there is a place . . . where there comes an end to Self, a place where solipsism is no longer the plausible answer to the locales we visit, the things that we find . . . here, at least, there is a difference, and if here, perhaps it runs back through our shadows, too, informing them with the not-self, moving our egos back to a smaller stage.

It would be well for mental health practitioners and others interested in the system wide development of a balanced, centered, transformational worldview to seek that place. Perhaps if such people could move their egos back to a smaller stage, find footing in a place where solipsism is no longer the plausible answer to the locales they visit, the entire country would be a healthier place. Certainly, Native people could sleep a bit easier knowing that it is not they alone who must represent all the denied, split-off longings and unowned rages that far too many influential white writers and thinkers call "myth," "shamanism," "shadow," "archetype," and "spirituality."

For as matters stand presently, Native people are uneasy knowing that if we fail to live in accordance with the false identity foisted off on us to the satisfaction of the powerful white world, we will again be consigned to the outer darkness of poverty, disease, and hopelessness. The threat is very real, and the mindlessness, the culturewide delusion that occasions it, is very dangerous to those of us who live in accordance with another view of the nature of reality and of the role of human consciousness within it.

Perhaps there is some consolation in being the archetypes for an entire nation, particularly since that nation is still in the process of locating its own sense of self. But the cost of trading humanity and one's own languages, customs, and worldview for that dubious privilege is very high. For the most part, Native American peoples would rather be viewed from their own perspective, a matter of respect certainly, but not easily done when that worldview is so entirely alien to one's own as the Native worldview is to white-think culture.

Which takes us to the other word in the title of this piece, "solipsism." The second edition of *The Random House Unabridged Dictionary* defines the term as "1. *philos.* the theory that only the self exists, or can be proved to exist, and 2. extreme preoccupation with and indulgence of one's feelings, desires, etc., egotistic self-absorption." The word derives from *sōlus,* which is Latin for "sole"—meaning "only" or "alone." It is allied with terms such as "solitary." The root of the compound term is "soli," which is defined as "a combining form meaning 'alone', 'solitary', and is used in the formation of compound words." An intriguing side note that sparks all sorts of possibilities for exploration is that the next entry after "soli" is "soli 2," which is defined as "a combining form meaning 'sun' used in the formation of compound words" such as "soliform." As you can guess, it's allied to compounds such as "solarium." The solar deity has functioned as the central archetype for all of Western pre-Christian and post-Christian civilization. Indeed, historians note that until his death, Constantine, Roman emperor from 324 to 337 C.E., was a devout follower of Mithras, the ancient Persian god of light and the primary deity of the solar religion that dominated Rome and its outposts during that epoch. It was he who determined that Christianity would be the state religion, and he ordered the great center of culture, Byzantia, to be renamed Constantinople, signifying the shift. Some are of the opinion that he did not convert to Christianity on his deathbed as Christian legend has it but merely ordered the change in the official status of both Mithraism and Christianity in the empire. It was thus a brilliant political decision, as subsequent events over the ensuing sixteen centuries attest.

As for the first word in my title, "Indian," it speaks to the fact that the indigenous peoples of this continent are not perceived as human beings or national communities by the dominating worldview. We like to joke that we're glad Columbus wasn't looking for Turkey! He thought he was in India; consequently the people he met on that Caribbean Island had to be Indians. But he wasn't, and they weren't, and we aren't "Indians" except in Anglo-European discourse that ranges from history, psychology, literature, to every kind of popular culture.

A careful examination of the process by which the indigenous inhabitants of this hemisphere were dehumanized and made into Disneyesque characters, villainous or noble, will demonstrate how destructive of rational thought and consciousness stereotyping is. It is not only the target group that is distorted and dehumanized. The users of the stereotype are greatly harmed psychically as well, and they haven't any means of noticing or assessing the psychic damage done to themselves because they lack any outside reference.

It is difficult to decide which comes first: "Indians," "solipsisms," or archetypes in the discourse of dehumanization that surrounds and engulfs American Indian nations and their people, but it is very clear that in combination the three lead indeed to holocausts of the mind and spirit of all who engage in or are discounted, disappeared, by them.

One day soon, Native peoples and our religions, national identities, and sovereignty can emerge from the shadows into which we have been cast by the immigrants. In the full light of day—the light we cast on ourselves, that is—we can live long and prosper. Until that time, the terrible consequences of consignation to the outer darkness of American consciousness will continue unabated. The dreadful suicide rates for both our youths and the professionals among us (the latter said to be the highest suicide rate in the nation), the high rates of early death and infant mortality, endemic poverty, and the low self-esteem that must accompany a life as a stranger's shadow, might then come closer to the national norms.

# Buffalo Medicine: An Essay and a Play

### David Seals

eople aren't going to do it. The buffalo are a wistful curiosity
to them at best, a romantic photo-op when they come upon
a lone bull out in the Black Hills chewing some dry brown
grass by the side of the road, massive, supernaturally beautiful as if
his dark shoulders and horns are higher off the ground than many
of the sleek comfortable machines stopping for a quick minute or
two to enrich their Western vacations on the way to Mount Rush-
more, on the way home from Yellowstone and the Little Bighorn
River. A quick, easy illusion of some American nonsense about a
mythical time in the "Good Old West" when myths weren't always
the lies they were taught in school and church but a cleaner, finer,
richer thing these magnificent beasts symbolized, ritualized, psy-
choanalyzed as a sacred national legend far too mysterious to
understand; like the thunder lances of a Lakota Sioux Indian, or
the Mahuts Four Arrows of a Cheyenne. The happy tourists in their
Rams and expensive Explorers stop for only a minute for these per-
functory reflections of their lost dreams and then head on down the
road, forgetting them in an hour or two, wandering again into
their empty moral vacuum of television commercials and Custer
State Park, South Dakota, USA. They're not going to do anything
about the real animals out there enclosed in a tightly governmen-
tally controlled wildlife loop that makes millions a year charging

317

admission to the show that also includes plenty of cute prairie dog towns and frontier villages in the nearby metropolis of Custer City, where the deer and the antelope play, and the bear country with real white wolves in cages sitting next to Flintstone Village, and, oh yeah, Crazy Horse Memorial Mountain, where dynamite is blasting the hell out of an undeveloped hill to show how proudly we've hailed our fellow Native Americans. Eleven dollars a carload. "C'mon down, free coffee!"

Americans aren't going to do anything about all those geldings of the species who didn't make it to the lonely roadsides with Grampa Bull, rounded up every Fall (from Paradise Lost) in a big cultural event everybody learned from Hollywood, California, about how to be Cowboys and Indians in Custer State Park. Calamity Jane Fondle and Kevin Custer showing us how a "hunt" is really done if you're really a man, herding the poor stupid things into big expensive metal gates and chutes to be sold to the highest bidder, to be shot with a 30.06 to the brain, to be eaten by those good hungry families going on down the road to Disneyland, their bellies full with the ever more profitable Bison Logos making the country strong again (like it never was). Not that their fat-free healthiness is any kind of serious option or competition for the $150-billion-a-year cattle and hog industries; not to mention the additional trillions to the McDonalds and Safeways and packing plant/railroad empires that would be wiped out tomorrow by one Mad Cow or a dirty Mo Terrorist infecting us all with a hoof-and-mouth disease. No, the buffalo source would be impervious to those strange modern ailments. No, the Marlboro Men around Yellowstone's tightly governmentally controlled/ protected misfits have to shoot them too if they take one step out of the Old Faithful excuse of brucellosis onto their ranches, private property. Buffalo Bills keeping down the unprofitable threat of a natural food supply: about one-trillionth as dangerous to us as King Burger, John Wayne's cholesterol, the celluloid residuals of Manifest Destiny. You can only go as far with all this unfenced land of the free and wide open range business. History pricks. ABM Treaties. Yeah, you can have a permit to have an Annual Buffalo Roundup and Arts Festival and Chili Cookoff because that's kind of cute, and it's harmless to the public school curriculum; it's good wholesome church PR.

These good ol' folks around here are culling out the herd, strengthening it by thinning out the sick and old and weak, honoring their healthy down-to-earth outdoor lifestyle and burgeoning recreation industry with some good family fun on the weekends attracting thousands and thousands of new customers from the wealthy disillusioned suburbs moving out into the cheap real estate opportunities with low interest rates for your diversified stock portfolios; investment analysts separating mothers from children, er, cows from calves and butchering them. "We have to make a living, what's wrong with that?" All over the lowly populated rural states the inevitable failure of the last century's demographics of controlled, fenced, subsidized, drought-ridden, polluting agriculture is giving way to more and more bison ranching as if that commercialization is honoring the same pathetic creatures, the same pathetic criminals slaughtered in the last economic cycle, just like the dynamite and huge asphalt parking lots and curio shops selling every cheap aberration of plastic buffalo key chains, peace pipes, Howdy Doody war bonnets and Chief Wahoo baseball caps are honoring the sublime Wicasa Wakan who hated all this unholy stuff so completely he never even allowed his photograph to be taken, not once, saying it would "steal his Spirit." That's how un-progressive a real Conservative was.

No, the Indians aren't going to do anything to liberate the land either, liberate the buffalo, powwowing routinely up into the sacred Black Hills, a ceremonial Sepulchral Isle where only the gods lived from time immemorial, to get their own photo-ops at the Columbus Day Cattle-Call Powwow and Chili Cookoff, Sun Dance and Rodeo and Carnival, honoring 510 years of genocide and counting. "Reconciliation" in casinos, and plenty of their Inter-tribal Bison Cooperatives sucking up to plenty of the Ted Turners CNNing all around with their own TNTeed-off baronial estates throughout the savannahs and steppes of Montana, Californicated Colorado and Nebraska, and acting up in their movies too. Red Cloud and these same BIA Boys conspired to assassinate Crazy Horse all the way back in 1877, as the Pte and Tatanka were dis-appearing inexplicably (from the history textbooks) at the same time, not un-coincidentally, in the same heap big dead piles that are still snuck away from our national consciousness, in our psy-chosis, in the night, inside loaded semi-trucks on their way to the ConAgra and Archer Daniels Midland stock-and-bondyards and beef "processing" factories, so the federally controlled Tribal Councils on the nearby chronic (slow and silent genocide that is, as opposed to Auschwitz and Ram Allah) Concentration Camps, er, Indian Reservations, er, Sovereign Indigenous Nations, aren't going to do a damn thing to alleviate their *80% unemployment* unless it is to help in the roundup and kill the shaggy products for a cut—and of course a blessing for a fee, of course: "Jesus, we have to make a living," from every other wino-hustler calling himself a Medicine Man. It ain't no "New Age" at all from the liberal starva-tion in Cree villages in northern Alberta to the fetal alcohol syn-dromes on Papago slums in Mexico, across the whole Buffalo Commons. But you wouldn't know that when every politician in South Dakota respectfully takes off his hat and bows his head to pray before the slaughter, God-guys and God-girls yapping in every forked tongue from Navajo to Latin about how holy they are, as babies with black eyes wait in panic to be drawn and quartered.

That's where the buffalo are, while all this is not happening. The calves are separated from their families and are getting fattened up at nice stockyards like American children, with clean hay and fresh water troughs. Their branded mothers and castrated big brothers and confused sisters are out in the high fenced pastures by the hundreds around the baby corrals, probably wondering what happened to their dads and their uncles. Yearlings, genetically preserved handsome young men artificially trucked off in the night like Army draftees protecting the economy by being their own (involuntary) suiciders, families torn apart by cold, brutal, two-legged apes staring at incomprehensible illusions in account books, in pickup trucks, with guns, cell phones, laptops, bulldozers, and tractors digging and barbed-wiring huge bull-proof fences taller than a guerrilla around every square inch of dirt on earth, every logarithm or algorithm the Market will bear, bare, naked, murder, Genocide, the deepest ecology.

We walked out there, my children and I, rehearsing a new Tragicomedy, a few weeks after the awful September Roundup, on a nice Sunday morning Service before the snows flew and after most of the vultures had gone back to their vaguely empty perches in Texas and Rapid City: buzzards gone after picking the carrion clean. And the kids looked at the huge fence posts, strung tightly with high wire, and asked, "Can't they knock those down?"

"No, the people will just catch them and kill them."

"Can't they dig under here and get out?"

"Yeah, but they know they'll get in trouble if they do."

"They know that?"

"Yes."

"How do the buffalo know that?"

They were good questions and it made me rethink my observation, all my life, like Sitting Bull out there who once said, "Everything I know I learned from the buffalo," knowing that it's going to take a Taoist strategy to renew our world, to clean it of the impossible obstacles of America and Agriculture by sitting quietly and patiently out there like a bull in the solitude and somehow that will stop the shit: Not-doing. But then if all this is a true mythological paradigm like Frodo's One Ring is The Machine that cannot be stopped—all those billions of automobiles destroying everything, World War for oil to keep them moving, the Economy—then the old bulls aren't any wiser than the Traditional Elders because they're not stopping the traffic. This is a new kind of mutant Devil-Orc we're up against. They know it's pointless to tear down the fences.

I replied, "They need us to help them. To stop the Americans."

My kids understood that.

"So we have to be warriors, huh?"

"Always."

"Girls too?"

"Yes."

We look at the Pte cows and Tatanka bulls and every single one of them, every man, woman, and child, is a revolutionary, an anarchist, and a free spirit. They're reading all the best books—"Bury my AIM at Wounded Knee," "Wally Black Elk Speaks," and "Dances with Hyenas." Their hearts are not broken, amazingly enough, after a thousand Auschwitzes, and an oral literature that surely rivals Aeschylus for the tragedies of the buffalo gods bound to mountains in prehistoric chthonian memories; white goddesses like pure cows in a pre-spectral world of negative imagery where their black awareness of illusions is so heightened we can't even see them—the invisible world, the Spirit World, where there are no illusions (of money, patriotism, death)—for I see in their calm brown eyes and relaxed shoulders and indomitable wisdom, I really do. I know somehow if we sit out there with them long enough, like Sitting Bull did, we'll figure out how to stop the machine. We'll make it safely to Mount Doom. I don't know how, but every time I'm with them, silently, totally silently, I feel certain there is a medicine in this ceremony of incomprehensible words that will save us from the Unreal Estate chiselers. We won't be so homeless on the range. Only a semi-nomadness will challenge our survival.

I think of an Algonquian Ceremony that hasn't been performed in at least one hundred years, probably more like one hundred and fifty, before the methodical national Policy of Slaughter got into full swing and tens of millions went to the ovens. "Massaum" is the Zezestas word that's come down to us describing the vast two-month-long ceremony of ceremonies, but nobody's quite sure anymore what it means or where it came from; probably from the same proto-tongue that has given us other incoherent names like Wyoming and Mitakuye Oyasin. As a superstitious malcontent, I like to think it means "I'm a Cheyenne myself." We all are re-imagining a Crazy Animal Dance, an archetypal Dionysian Rock'n' Roll Festival in which sun dances become moon dances and Fall means a Hunt for Grace instead of an original sin. Where pow wow becomes a healing ceremony again, a shaman, and our quests are just little fragments of greater Canunpa pipe-bowls, buffalo bones, numinosities of Jung and Shakespeare, bits and pieces of prayers in the Greater Solemn High Mass of the Mysteries and MASSAUM is an epic sung by the first buffalo Bard, a regular coyote wanna-be Breed the old folks at home called a trickster. A breed apart. A Muse thyself. We call him a liar these days, a wise ass, or a clown at best, a muse-poet

given to irreverent reverence, contrary criminality, jackass delu-
sions, scrawling sandstone petroglyphs of comic relief. Naturally
I unnaturally identified with him, hallucinating out there on the
great plains in a vision quest for the golden fleece—"Hey, you
been gettin' fleeced, Boy?"—The Mythic Times, my one daily
newspaper, remembering the dragons and woolly mammoths the
old bullshitters began to tell me about after about the tenth such
quest in my Western lifetime, out there, with the birds and the
bees. So? I updated the drama and called it "Buffalo Medicine,"
writing it on speculation, never expecting to find a livestock
Producer for it.

It has everything Vine Deloria, Jr. once said every culture has to
have if it's gonna be real, and which the USA does not (have)—a
creation myth, a sacred mountain, and a prophet. The Buffalo
Nation has all three, and so does their drama; and so do the Massaum Nation(s). The buffalo and wolves are the actors, the coyotes
and kit foxes are doing the costumes, Thunder is directing it, and
the whole Wildlife Loop will be the stage and set, with plenty of
crows and eagles as extras. [For references and footnotes, see the
bibliography, which includes the "The Buffalo Hunters" by Mari
Sandoz, "The Wolves of Heaven" by Karl Schlesier, the 1851 Ft.
Laramie Treaty, etc.] People just ain't gonna do it. I may be allowed
to watch rehearsals, and double as a donkey extra, as the playwright in residence, but of course I won't be paid anything. So
what else is new?

(Free Admission)
Overture. 7 drum groups, dancers . . . (no pay)
ACT 1—
We discover Wisdom nailed to a rock, the Needles in the Black
Hills, a Bull-like man like a god out of Homer or Saint Mark, the

Divine Nobility, and he says in a deep voice like thunder coming out of the ground, in the pitch-black darkness:

**"Wisdom"**

> *A long time ago the buffalo*
> *came out of the ground,*
> *tricked by the gods*
> *into becoming mortal."*

# POSTCOLONIAL HYPERBAGGAGE:
# A FEW POEMS OF RESISTANCE AND SURVIVAL

Carter Revard

I have tried to jam into these poems some of the more horrible and hopeful fruits of political, semi-scientific, and other actualities gathered in the United States of America over the years 1931 to 2000.

## Postcolonial Hyperbaggage

*If only Vuitton would make a suitcase*
*with modem and hypertext—or at least windows*
*to let us put new folders in, where*
*jackets won't wrinkle and all*
*the smelly socks can be hung with care in*
*the hyperspace herb-drawer—and with*
*still cooler files whose chocolate*
*truffles would never melt*
*into a cashmere sweater. We need these*
*neat reversible black holes for crossing Borders,*
*things we could pack and close*
*at a single touch and never pop a seam*
*or rip a zipper. They'd make the Eurodollar*
*        zoom up in value—*
*and hey, just think,*
*Stealth Bombers could be replaced*

by diplomatic pouches full
of virtual assassins,
used terrorists could be dumped
>    out of the Trash Can, leaving
>        a Virtuous Reality.
All Indian Reservations could be desaparecidos
into Death Valley, yet accessible through
their golden icon, the Sacajawea Dollar.
Such a Pandora's Apple, I think,
even the seediest Satan could have sold
to the smartest Adam and Eve, just by saying
one taste of this, my dears,
and you're back in Eden.

## The Secret Verbs

They're hidden right in plain sight.
Take Unassigned Lands for instance: what's the verb?
To Unassign.
A powerful verb, in 1889 it grabbed
almost two million acres of Indian lands
where Oklahoma City squats with all
those other towns, wheat farms and ranches
oil wells and politicians.
(Yes, I know how SQUAT infects its many subjects.)
Why call them Unassigned?
Well, after the CIVIL War, the Creeks
and Seminoles were forced to concede
this land for settlement by freed slaves.
Quite understandably, no one ever
assigned the land to slaves.
So what that past participle means is this:

*We UNASSIGN these lands to Blacks or Indians.*
*We now ASSIGN them to Americans,*
*so long as they are WHITE.*
*That's all the grammar lesson for today,*
*but for tomorrow, why not look around*
*at other participles and adjectives*
*which have deleted agents and unspoken objects,*
*and which are negative?*
*You see how powerful they are—*
*and how they hide their power? And how*
*like redstriped sheets they cover both*
*the SUBJECT and the OBJECTS of their actions?*
*Just for instance,*
*the words DIScover and COVER,*
*or DISinform, or UNAmerican,*
*or UNused land.*
*How we UNuse our language*
*is maybe worth a thought, in a*
*CENTENNIAL year—and every year's*
*centennial of something, isn't it?*

## Firewater

*Sometimes I think how alcohol's*
*a marvelous solvent, can remove*
*red people from a continent,*
*turn bronze to guilt. What was DuPont's*
*old motto—Better things*
*for better living*
*through chemistry? You take*
*potatoes from Peru,*
*barley from Palestine, maize*

*from Mexico, sugar cane*
*from Indo-China—*
*put in some wild yeast from the air,*
*ferment it and voilà! you've now*
*got Vodka for the Volga, beer*
*for the Brits, Bourbon for*
*Balboa's kids, Joy-juice for*
*the Kickapoos.*
*Pour this into an Inner City and create*
*your Designated Criminal Class purely*
*to blame for everything,*
*or rub it on the Reservations and you'll see*
*each fetus wizen up inside*
*its fertile womb.*
*Yet drip it into the veins*
*of Congress or a Corporation, just watch*
*those Mountain Men outwrestle steers,*
*gulping their liquid god go wildly*
*enthusiastic so they can*
*write laws in stone with one hand while*
*joysticking lovers with the other,*
*sacking Montana and out-dunking Jordan,*
*out-leveraging—who was it,*
*Archimedes, popped the world's blue eyeball*
*into a Swiss snowbank? See, ghettoites,*
*how sociable our masters are,*
*these Bacchanalians, never alcoholic,*
*immune in suburbs where bad sex has died*
*and gone to heaven, no AIDS, no illegitimate*
*children, all the schools*
*have classic curricula and every personal fetus*

*will be delivered right on time,*
*uncorked like Chateauneuf du Pape, unscrewed*
*like Southern Comfort to gurgle on*
*its snowy tablecloth, caress with rosy fingers*
*its parents' egos and become*
*a tax loophole. Classic,*
*ah Classic these Metamorphoses of Alcohol—*
*but please, be careful how you tell of them,*
*remember Ovid shivering on*
*the Black Sea shores, wondering how to get back in*
*to one of the Roman villas once again.*

## November in Washington, D.C.

*The guards are friendly when you walk*
*at night up toward the Capitol,*
*standing floodlit,*
*white and shining above*
*its Roman pillars—*
*"Good evening, where*
*are you folks from?"*
*"Ah, St. Louis—we live there."*
*"Faan-TAS-tic!"—*
*but there's an interruption,*
*as siren and a flashing cop-car swirling up*
*through the parking lot behind two lost*
*cars filled with tourist families*
*—or maybe terrorists?*
*But then the cars stop, the cop's*
*lights stop flashing, there's a friendly*
*palaver and they swing around and drive*
*out down the street,*

*and the young friendly guard, mustached,*
*in black gloves and overcoat who has*
*been watching us and them, pounds*
*his gloved hands and says again "FanTASTic!" in a way*
*that means he's checked us out, so we*
*walk on, around the Capitol*
*and down dark steps and sidewalk to the*
*Reflecting Pool—it must be*
*several acres of still and*
*shimmering dark alive*
*with streetlights, brilliant green*
*and red of traffic signals, tail-lights' Red Glare—*
*and then, from its other side, we see*
*the white unreal dome of the Capitol in it,*
*pointing down, down, at a star glittering deep*
*in the pool below it, a large bright*
*star—Venus, we think. At the moment,*
*this most powerful building in the world's*
*asleep in Xanadu*
*(a little water cleans it of its deeds),*
*a Pleasure Dome where people*
*—Chinese? Japanese? are setting up their cameras now*
*to capture Pool and Capitol in one silver shot.*
*We could walk further, down the Mall,*
*and past the National Gallery where*
*they've captured Veronese's paintings for a time—*
*or by the Space Museum, where Astronauts*
*are dummies in their capsules, and*
*sleek missile-launchers stand like Michaels waiting*
*to stop Time for us*
*(they also served)—*

*or past the Smithsonian, where (I'm told)*
*the symbols of our Osage people wait, that let*
*us come down from the stars to form*
*a nation, here.*

*Instead, the night being damp, we turn*
*and walk on back along East Capitol, past*
*some trash receptacles on whose dull orange, painted*
*in yellow profile, is a Redskin—*
*RE-located from the Buffalo Nickel—*
*and now PRESIDENT over*
*the old news of this 1988 election, as we*
*walk eastward, into the full*
*and orange moon.*

## Parading with the Veterans of Foreign Wars

*Apache, Omaha, Osage, Comanche, Kiowa, Choctaw,*
*Micmac, Cherokee, Oglala—*
*our place was ninety-fifth,*
*and when we got there in our ribbon shirts,*
*with drum and singers on the flatbed truck,*
*women in shawls and traditional dresses,*
*we looked into the muzzle of*
*an Army howitzer in front of us.*
*"Hey Cliff," I said, "haven't seen guns that big*
*since we were in Wounded Knee."*
*Cliff carried the new American Flag,*
*donated by another Post; Cliff prays*
*in Omaha for us, being chairman*
*of our Pow-wow Committee, and his prayers*
*keep us together, helped*

*by hard work from the rest of course.*
*"They'll move that 105 ahead," Cliff said.*
*—They did, but then the Cavalry arrived.*
*No kidding—here came this troop outfitted*
*with Civil War-style uniforms and carbines*
*on horseback, metal-clopping on*
*the asphalt streets, and there*
*on jackets were the insignia:*
*the Seventh Cavalry, George Custer's bunch.*
*"Cliff," Walt said, "they think you're Sitting Bull."*
*"Just watch out where you're stepping, Walt,"*
*Cliff said. "Those pooper-scoopers*
*will not be working, once the parade begins."*
*"Us women walking behind our trailer*
*will have to step around it all so much,*
*they'll think we're dancing,"*
*was all that Sherry said.*
          *—We followed*
*the yellow line, and here and there*
*some fake war-whoops came out to us*
*from sidewalk faces, but applause*
*moved with us when the singers started,*
*and we did get our banners seen, announcing*
*this year's Pow-wow coming up in June,*
*Free To The Public in Jefferson Barracks Park—*
*where the Dragoons were quartered for the Indian Wars.*
*When we had passed the Judging Stand*
*and pulled off to the little park, all*
*green and daffodilly under the misting rain,*
*we put the shawls and clothing in the car*
*and went back to the Indian center, while*

*Cliff and George Coon went out and got*
*some chicken from the Colonel—*
*it tasted great, given the temporary*
*absence of buffalo here in this*
*Gateway To The West, St. Louis.*

## A Brief Guide to American History Teachers

**Q:** *Name several American Holocausts, the nations involved,*
*and the places where these were accomplished.*
**A:** *Missouri, Illinois, Miami, New England, Virginia, and*
*most place names in the United States. For more advanced*
*students, the answer can extend to North and South America.*
**Q:** *What kind of un-American creep would give that answer?*
**A:** *A Native American. Of course, a truly patriotic American*
*might have known better than to ask the question. In such*
*cases, silence is the only way to avoid acknowledging guilt.*
*There have been no American Holocausts, and we all should*
*realize this truth. It is self-evident, since we believe all men*
*are created equal, that we would not do what those nasty*
*Europeans did. They are racist bigots, we are the people who*
*got rid of the old prejudices and refused to do terrible things,*
*unless the Lord commanded it. We have pure hearts, pure*
*motives, and pure history.*
**Q:** *What advantages are there to the true Americans if they*
*deny that there has been any American Holocaust?*
**A:** *It allows them to be outraged at Other Monsters. Also, it*
*lets them focus on the terrible things done overseas—in*
*Ruanda, Bosnia, the Caucasus, Iraq—so that no one will*
*notice what is still going on here. Since there was only the one*
*Holocaust, we can be wonderfully virtuous in supporting its*
*victims, and we know that we do not have to worry about*

*being on the right side. So this justifies our putting up a monument in Washington D.C. to that one Holocaust, and not putting anything there which might hint that there was anything like it in this country.*

**Q:** *Is this matter relevant to the origins, makeup, and functions of the*
*United Nations?*

**A:** *Yes. I do not dare, however, to answer in more detail. No true American can afford to consider the question of whether Native American nations are truly sovereign. De facto, De Deo must be their mighty fortress. When Franklin Roosevelt, about 1942, discussed the postwar realignments with Winston Churchill, he reminded Churchill of what the English were doing in their colonies. Churchill then reminded Roosevelt of two cases: blacks in Mississippi, and Navajos in Arizona. Roosevelt shut up. It is the only safe answer.*

**Q:** *You conclude that American History should not be taught.*

**A:** *Of course not: it never has been, and this is no time to begin doing so.*

# ABOUT AMERICAN INDIAN ARTISTS, INC.

## Diane Fraher

Native American culture has been exiled between nineteenth-century vanishing-race theories, which supported the inevitable disappearance of indigenous cultures in the western hemisphere through assimilation, and entertainment-industry-generated images that made claim to authenticate the one true noble Indian. As a result, Native peoples' genuine voice has been silenced and their mere existence erased from the national consciousness since the close of the American frontier in 1890.

But Indians refused to accept their cultural banishment and there is now a spirit of empowerment that is ever growing in Native communities throughout the Americas. The prophecies of the elders are unfolding as Indian peoples reaffirm their sovereignty and turn inward to listen to their own voices for revitalization and renewal. Cultural sovereignty is at the heart of identity. What it means to be an Indian must now be portable as contemporary Indian people move seamlessly between the two worlds of reservation and urban communities.

Indian people are emerging from the invisibility of a romanticized past and a mythological tipi and cowboy-killer culture confined to roaming the short grass prairie and uttering ecological and religious prophecies only. The voice that is emerging is a rich cultural mosaic that invites the listener in and shares a profoundly interesting and surprisingly universal story. Could it be that what it means to be an Indian in contemporary society could be so much richer and interesting than all the fantasies non-Natives hoped, even guaranteed, it would be? That the audience would actually prefer stories about real people with whom we can all identify in their quest for meaning in this life? I am reminded of a time when, after a reading of a screenplay I had written, a non-Native who had never even met an Indian person before me jumped up and gave an impassioned speech about how an elder character would never say a line like "Let us come together and be of one mind." This single phrase is the recognized basis for the formulation of the Iroquois' Great Law of Peace and the resulting foundation of the Iroquois Confederacy, the acknowledged partial blueprint for the United States Constitution. Silence is not golden.

In this climate of increased interest in the history and culture of the Native Americans there is a Native organization that is solely dedicated to empowering Native peoples to interpret their own history and create a contemporary artistic presence and vision in the heart of western culture.

Established in 1987, American Indian Artists, Inc.— AMERINDA—is a community-based nonprofit organization whose purpose it is to make the indigenous perspective in the arts available to a wider audience through the creation of new work by emerging and established Native artists. AMERINDA works to empower Native people, break down barriers, and foster intercultural understanding and appreciation for Native culture. The organization is governed by an all-Indian board of directors and supported by a traditional Circle of Elders and an advisory council of Native and non-Natives. AMERINDA is unique in that it is one of only two Native arts service organizations in existence.

With the publication of *Genocide of the Mind*, AMERINDA is

emerging as a community-based Native American arts organization with national outreach and stature. In these times of economic difficulty and extreme politics, AMERINDA is committed not only to supporting the appreciation of the beauty derived from cultural diversity but also to working in partnership with others. On behalf of the community we serve, we would like to extend our heartfelt thanks to the following: our Native American elders; MariJo Moore (Cherokee), editor; Victor Navasky, publisher and editorial director of *The Nation*; the staff at Nation Books; and the Literature Program of the New York State Council on the Arts, for working in partnership with us to achieve our goals. We hope you will join us in continuing to advocate an inborn sanctity of all human creative spirit regardless of race, creed, or heritage.

Visit the AMERINDA Web site at www.amerinda.org.

# CONTRIBUTORS

**Paula Gunn Allen,** Laguna/Metis, Ph.D. Professor Emerita, UCLA, has written numerous anthologies of critical studies and American Indian fiction which include *Studies in American Indian Literature* (1983); *Spider Woman's Granddaughters: Traditional Tales and Contemporary Writing by American Indian Women* (1989); and *Voice of the Turtle: American Indian Literature;* two collections of her essays, *The Sacred Hoop: Recovering the Feminine in American Indian Traditions* (1986) and *Off the Reservation: Reflections on Boundary-Busting, Border-Crossing, Loose Canons* (1998); several poetry books, including *Skins and Bones* (1990) and most recently *Life Is a Fatal Disease* (1998), and a novel, *The Woman Who Owned the Shadows* (1982).

**Carol Snow Moon Bachofner,** Mississquoi Abenaki, is originally from Maine and a poet and freelancer. Her poems have appeared in over a dozen journals and anthologies in the United States and Canada. Currently Carol is a graduate student working on an MFA in writing at Vermont College. A major focus for Carol is to help ensure that Indian writers and storytellers have an equal voice in the literary and academic worlds.

**Mary Black Bonnet,** twenty-eight, is an enrolled member of the Rosebud Sioux tribe of South Dakota, currently attending the University of South Dakota in Vermillion, studying creative writing. Her writings have appeared in *Nagi-Ho Journal* and *Tribal College*

*Journal,* and her essay "In Search of Mother Turtle" was published in *Frontiers: A Journal of Women's Studies.* Mary's future plans include presenting seminars and workshops to women and teenagers on the empowerment of writing. She feels that writing can be a powerful way to deal with all the horrible things that happen to a person and states, "You can either sit down and mope or you can pick up your pen and take back your power."

**Joseph Dandurand,** Kwantlen, is from the Kwantlen First Nation in British Columbia. He is a poet, playwright, fisherman, researcher, archaeologist, and most important, the proud father of a beautiful girl: Danessa Renee Wa yothe. His produced plays include *Crackers and Soup* (1994), *No Totem for My Story* (1995), *Where Two Rivers Meet* (1995), and *Please Don't Touch the Indians* (1998) for the Red Path Theatre in Chicago. His poems have appeared in numerous journals and anthologies and are collected in *Upside Down Raven, I Touched the Coyote's Tongue,* and *burning for the dead and scratching for the poor, looking into the eyes of my forgotten dreams.*

**Vine Deloria, Jr.,** Standing Rock Sioux, is a leading Native American scholar and author of numerous nationally acclaimed books such as *God Is Red, Custer Died for Your Sins, Red Earth, White Lies,* and *Evolution, Creationism, and Other Modern Myths.* Named by *Time* magazine as one of the eleven greatest religious thinkers of the twentieth century, his dedication to historical accuracy as well as to Native rights is unequivocal. He resides in Golden, Colorado.

**Steve Elm,** Oneida, is an actor, writer, director, and is editor of

*Talking Stick: Native Arts Quarterly.* He was a founding member of the Chuka Lokoli Native Theatre Ensemble and director of American Indian Community House Youth Theater Project. He is currently a Master Artist with the Wolf Trap Foundation for the Performing Arts and the Creative Arts Team at NYU, as well as a creator of theater for young people for various companies in New York City. He resides in Brooklyn.

**Sean Lee Fahrlander** was born in Minneapolis, Minnesota, and raised on the White Earth and Leech Lake reservations in northern Minnesota. He joined the United States Navy during his freshman year in college and served through the Gulf War. He returned home and finished school at Leech Lake Tribal College, where he graduated with honors. He has worked as a cultural coordinator for Northwestern Minnesota Juvenile Center, a public relations coordinator for Mille Lacs Band of Ojibwe, and has held many civic positions throughout the state. He now lives in Duluth, Minnesota, where to his daughter also resides.

**Diane Fraher,** Osage, is the writer and director of *The Reawakening,* a contemporary dramatic feature film about a Native man's struggle to identify with traditional values. She also wrote and directed *You're Looking at the First Draft of the Constitution,* the award-winning public service advertising campaign for print and broadcast on television. Ms. Fraher is a contributing author to *Creation's Journey—Native American Identity and Belief* (NMAI), and she wrote the afterward to *Mean Spirit,* Linda Hogan's novel of the Osage Oil murders. In 1987 she founded American Indian Artists, Inc. (AMERINDA), a nonprofit corporation governed by an all-Indian board of directors, dedicated to promoting the indigenous perspective in the arts through a variety of programs and services for Native artists, and is its artistic director.

**Lee Francis,** Laguna Pueblo, is national director of Wordcraft Circle of Native Writers and Storytellers (www.wordcraftcircle.org). A published poet: *On the Good Red Interstate: Truck Stop Tellings and Other Poems* and author: *Native Time: A Historical Time Line of Native America,* Lee has had his essays published in a wide variety of anthologies and journals. He resides in Albuquerque, New Mexico.

**Eric Gansworth,** Onondaga, was born and raised in the Tuscarora Nation in western New York and is an associate professor of English at Canisius College, in Buffalo, New York. He has published two books: *Indian Summers,* a novel, and *Nickel Eclipse: Iroquois Moon,* poems and paintings. His work has appeared in many anthologies and periodicals. A second novel, *Smoke Dancing,* will be published in 2004.

**Ben Geboe** is an enrolled member of the Yankton Sioux tribe of South Dakota and grew up on the Rosebud Sioux Reservation. His collective life experiences on and off the reservation have given him a unique perspective on American Indian culture and identity, which he shares in lectures and teachings. He also specializes in teaching Plains/Sioux–style beadwork. Currently he is a full-time social worker, providing services to homeless mentally ill people in New York City.

**Tim Hays,** Ho Chunk, is the first American Indian pianist to play solo recitals at both the Institute of American Indian Arts in Santa Fe, New Mexico, and the American Indian Community House in New York. Born and raised in Nebraska, he began piano studies at thirteen, and at seventeen played the Ravel G major Concerto with the Omaha Symphony. He has played various concerts in the New York metropolitan area, including for the American Landmark Festival Series and at the Cathedral of St. John the Divine, and worked with the Zurich Opera in Switzerland and Opera du Rhin in France. Active as both a Native cultural worker and chamber musician, he resides in Brooklyn, New York.

**Barbara-Helen Hill** is a writer and visual artist from Six Nations of the Grand River Territory in Southern Ontario, Canada. She is a Cayuga/Mohawk, mother of three, and grandmother of two beautiful granddaughters. After graduating from college with an MA in American studies, Helen had to change careers due to ill health and started to focus more on her art than on her teaching and counseling career. She is the author of *Shaking the Rattle: Healing the Trauma of Colonization,* now in its second edition, and has stories and poems published in various anthologies. She is the owner/operator of Shadyhat Books, Publishing and Art Company, and has just started venturing into fiber and textile art as a new medium.

**Mifaunwy Shunatona Hines** was born in 1920 in Pawnee, Oklahoma, to an Irish-Wyandotte mother and Otoe-Pawnee father. She has volunteered her services as resource, public relations, and liaison person benefiting tribes, organizations, and individuals from 1963 to 2003, though infrequently since the 1990s. For the past ten years her work has concentrated on her full-blood Otoe grandfather's biography, including research into the tribe's history. She resides in Briarwood, New York.

**Gabriel Horn** (White Deer of Autumn) is a nationally recognized lecturer on writing and Native American philosophy and its intricate connection to the rights of indigenous people, animals, and the welfare of the natural environment. He has a BA in language arts and an MA in writing and Native American studies. His written works include *Ceremony—In the Circle of Life, The Great Change,* and the Native People/Native Ways series. His two critically acclaimed books *Native Heart—An American Indian Odyssey* and *Contemplations of a Primal Mind* are now used across the country in secondary school and university curricula. He lives with his wife, Amy, in St. Petersburg, Florida.

**H. Lee Karalis** is a mixed-blood Choctaw/Irish adopted Greek who lives in northern Virginia. Originally from southern California, she received her MA in creative writing from San Diego State University. She has taught composition at Howard University and American University in Washington, D.C., and now teaches literature and creative writing at Northern Virginia Community College. Her work has been published in the *South Dakota Review;* she is currently working on her novel *Bone Picker.*

**Maurice Kenny,** Mohawk, was born in Watertown, New York, and has been a poet, editor, publisher, and professor at North Community College and the University of Oklahoma. He earned a BA in English literature in 1956 from Butler University. Author of numerous books, Kenny's writing and editorial work have led many Native Americans to appreciate the values and political insight of their cultures. Kenny has been a leading figure in the renaissance of Native American poetry since the 1970s. He now resides in Potsdam, New York, where he teaches at the State University of New York.

**Kathryn Lucci-Cooper** is a Cherokee/Sicilian author and bead-weaving artist. A member of the Native American Journalist Association and Word Craft Circle of Native Writers, she was selected as one of ten new North Carolina Writers in 2001 when her short story "Luther's Storm" was featured in the *Raleigh News and Observer/Sunday Journal*. Her reviews, poems, and articles have appeared in various publications, including *Frontiers: A Journal of Women's Studies/Special Indigenous Women's Issue* and *News from Indian Country*. A member of the Speakers Forum for the North Carolina Humanities Council, she has received recognition for her work with indigenous women in North Carolina's Correctional Facilities and an award from Building Community from Diversity Program, Lenior-Rhyne College, Hickory, North Carolina. She resides in Raleigh, North Carolina, with her husband of thirty years and her four sons.

**David Bunn Martine**, Shinnecock/Montauk (Algonquian), Nednai-Chiricahua Apache, and of Hungarian descent, is from the Shinnecock Indian Reservation near Southampton, Long Island. David has worked in tribal government, education, and the museum profession during the past twenty years. He is a professional painter, wood-carver, illustrator, and a current board member of Amerinda.

**Molly McGlennen** is of mixed heritage (Anishinaabe, French, and Irish) and was raised in Minneapolis, Minnesota. She received her MFA in creative writing from Mills College and presently is pursuing her PhD in Native American studies at the University of California, Davis. Her dissertation is on four contemporary female Native poets.

**Neil McKay** is from the Sacred Lake Dweller Nation of Dakota and an enrollee of the Spirit Lake Reservation in North Dakota. He is the first in his family to attend college and graduated with a degree in American Indian studies with a focus on the Dakota language from the University of Minnesota at Minneapolis in 1997, where he is now the Dakota language instructor. Neil's lifelong goal is to ensure that the Dakota language continues to live on within the people.

**MariJo Moore**, Cherokee/Irish/Dutch, is a poet/author/essayist/ artist/publisher. Her books include *Spirit Voices of Bones, Red Woman with Backward Eyes and Other Stories, The Cherokee Little People, The Ice Man, The First Fire, Crow Quotes, Desert Quotes, Tree Quotes*, the bilingual (Dutch/English) *Woestijnwoorden (Desert Words)*, and the novel *The Diamond Doorknob*. The owner of rENE-GADE pLANETS pUBLISHING, she is the recipient of numerous literary and publishing awards. She has a son, Lance and a granddaughter, Zoey Makayla, and resides in western North Carolina.

**Simon J. Ortiz,** poet/fiction writer/essayist/storyteller is a native of Acoma Pueblo in New Mexico. His published works include *Men on the Moon, Woven Stone, The People Shall Continue, Speaking for the Generations,* and *Out There Somewhere.* Ortiz has been involved with Native educational endeavors from elementary school to college levels on a number of Indian reservations and urban Native communities. He is the father of one son and two daughters and is also a grandfather. Currently he resides in Toronto, Canada, where he teaches creative writing, contemporary Native North American literature, and Aboriginal studies at the University of Toronto.

**Carter Revard** was born in Pawhuska, Oklahoma, in 1931: Osage on his father's side, he was given his Osage name 1952. He grew up on the Osage Reservation and graduated from a one-room country school in Buck Creek, Bartlesville College High, the University of Tulsa, Oxford University and received his PhD from Yale University. He has worked in hay- and wheat- and cornfields and as a greyhound trainer. He has taught English (medieval, linguistics, and American Indian Literature) at Amherst College and Washington University at St. Louis and is now retired and is Professor Emeritus of English. He has written *Ponca War Dancers, Cowboys and Indians, Christmas Shopping, An Eagle Nation, Family Matters, Tribal Affairs,* and *Winning the Dust Bowl.* He resides in St. Louis, Missouri.

**Kimberly Roppolo,** Cherokee/Choctaw/Creek, received her Ph.D. specializing in Native American Literature from Baylor University in May, 2002. She is a full-time instructor at McLennan Community College, and the Associate National Director of Wordcraft

Circle of Native Writers and Storytellers. She has published reviews, poems, and articles in various publications including *Children of the Dragonfly*. Her works–in–progress include a book–length work of tribal–based critical theory, *Collating Divergent Discourses: Positing the Critic as Culture-Broker in Reading Native American Texts*. She resides in Hewitt, TX, with her husband and three children.

**Steve Russell** is a citizen of the Cherokee Nation, a high school dropout, a retired Texas trial court judge, and currently associate professor of criminal justice, Indiana University, Bloomington. He is a member of the Wordcraft Circle of Native Writers and Storytellers and Native Writers Circle of the Americas.

**David Seals** is the author of many books, plays, and essays, including the novel *Powwow Highway* and the film *Sweet Medicine*. His latest novels are *The Libyad*, about North Africa, where he lived for three years, *The Rheia Excerpts*, and *The Hymnody*. His mother was Huron from the Lorette Reserve at Quebec Ville, related to the Siouis—going back to Michel Sioui—a seventeenth-century chief of the Bear Clan. He lives with his family in the Black Hills near Rapid City, South Dakota, and works with AIM, Earth First!, and Animal Liberation Front to free the buffalo.

**Leslie Marmon Silko,** of Laguna Pueblo, Cherokee, Mexican, and white ancestry, is a novelist, poet, short-story writer, film writer, artist, and essayist. She grew up at old Laguna village on the reservation west of Albuquerque, where she was born in 1948. She's lived in the Tucson mountains since 1978 because she likes the rattlesnakes that live under the kitchen floor of her old ranch house there. She has a novel in progress, *Blue Sevens*.

**Virginia Driving Hawk Sneve** was born and raised on the Rosebud Reservation in South Dakota and is an enrolled member of the Rosebud Sioux tribe. For twenty-five years she was a teacher/counselor in the public schools in White, Pierre, and Rapid City, as well as the Flandreau Indian School near Sioux Falls, and was an adjunct instructor at Oglala Lakota College, Rapid City Extension. She retired in 1995. The recipient of numerous prestigious awards, she is the author of over twenty books, numerous short stories, articles, and poems. She resides in Rapid City.

**Dave Stephenson** is a Tlingit/Eagle (Tlingit and Haida tribes) from southeast Alaska. His Tlingit name is Gunéi _ik. He has a bachelor's degree in communications from Fort Lewis College in Colorado, where he graduated magna cum laude.

**James Aronhiotas Stevens** is a member of the Akwesasne Mohawk tribe in upstate New York. He attended the Institute of American Indian Arts, the Jack Kerouac School of Disembodied Poetics at Naropa, and Brown University. Stevens is the author of *Tokinish* and *Combing the Snakes from His Hair*. He is a 2000 Whiting Writer's Award winner and currently is assistant professor of English and American Indian studies at the State University of New York at Fredonia.

**Wiley Steve Thornton** is Osage and Cherokee. He is from the Deer Clan and a member of the Native American Church of Oklahoma,

Osage Chapter. A graduate of the University of Oklahoma, he works for the National Park Service. A contributing author to *Talking Stick: Native Arts Quarterly*, he is currently working on a Native American children's story. He resides in New York City.

**Alfred Young Man,** PhD, (Eagle Chief) is Cree and full professor and chair of Native American studies at the University of Lethbridge, Alberta, Canada. His published works are *Networking*, (ed.), *Visions of Power: Contemporary Art by First Nations, Inuit and Japanese Canadians*, "The Metaphysics of North American Indian Art" in *Indigena: Contemporary Native Perspectives, Kiskayetum: Allen Sapp, a Retrospective*, "Native Arts in Canada: the State, Academia, and the Cultural Establishment" in *Beyond Quebec: Taking Stock of Canada, North American Indian Art: It's a Question of Integrity*, and *Indian Reality Today: Contemporary Indian Art of North America*.

**Joel Waters,** Oglala Sioux, is twenty-four years old. He is currently attending the University of South Dakota in Vermillion, majoring in English. His writings have appeared in *Red Ink* magazine and the *Vermillion Literary Project*.